Queer Angels in Post-1945 American Literature and Culture

Queer Angels in Post-1945 American Literature and Culture

Bad Beatitudes

David Deutsch

BLOOMSBURY ACADEMIC
LONDON • NEW YORK • OXFORD • NEW DELHI • SYDNEY

BLOOMSBURY ACADEMIC
Bloomsbury Publishing Plc
50 Bedford Square, London, WC1B 3DP, UK
1385 Broadway, New York, NY 10018, USA
29 Earlsfort Terrace, Dublin 2, Ireland

BLOOMSBURY, BLOOMSBURY ACADEMIC and the Diana logo are trademarks of
Bloomsbury Publishing Plc

First published in Great Britain 2021
This paperback edition published 2023

Copyright © David Deutsch, 2021

David Deutsch has asserted his right under the Copyright, Designs and
Patents Act, 1988, to be identified as Author of this work.

For legal purposes the Acknowledgments on pp. viii–ix constitute an
extension of this copyright page.

Cover design by Eleanor Rose
Cover photograph © Getty Images

All rights reserved. No part of this publication may be reproduced or
transmitted in any form or by any means, electronic or mechanical,
including photocopying, recording, or any information storage or retrieval system,
without prior permission in writing from the publishers.

Bloomsbury Publishing Plc does not have any control over, or responsibility for,
any third-party websites referred to or in this book. All internet addresses given
in this book were correct at the time of going to press. The author and publisher
regret any inconvenience caused if addresses have changed or sites have ceased
to exist, but can accept no responsibility for any such changes.

A catalogue record for this book is available from the British Library.

A catalog record for this book is available from the Library of Congress.

ISBN: HB: 978-1-3501-9895-1
PB: 978-1-3501-9899-9
ePDF: 978-1-3501-9896-8
eBook: 978-1-3501-9897-5

Typeset by Integra Software Services Pvt. Ltd.

To find out more about our authors and books visit www.bloomsbury.com
and sign up for our newsletters.

To Bella

Contents

Acknowledgments	viii
Uncovering the Queer Angels in Our Midst	1
1 John Rechy's Angelic Outlaws: Surviving the Desire for Salvation	27
2 Richard Bruce Nugent's Angelic Erotics: Rebellious Spirits in Multiracial Same-Sex Romances	65
3 Allen Ginsberg's Angelic Economies: Sex, Spirituality, and a Queer Anti-Imperialism	105
4 Angels amid Affliction: Angelic Immigrants and an Expansive Americanism in the Era of HIV/AIDS	143
Conclusion: Angelic Anxieties and Outlaw Expectations	179
Notes	184
References	194
Index	204

Acknowledgments

Writing this book came at a tough time for a variety of personal and professional reasons. I'm grateful to have parents and siblings that I enjoy spending time with out of work hours, as well as a patient and encouraging husband. This topic too continued to spark my interest, influence my teaching, and it made me want to return to the library, to books, and to my computer. In addition, I was fortunate to have students and colleagues that made working in academics seem worthwhile. David Ainsworth provided a valuable sounding board more than once. Merinda Simmons, Nathan Loewen, and Andy Crank all provided valuable feedback in thinking through angelic outlaws, while Cassie Smith, Albert Pionke, and Trudier Harris have spurred my thinking in new directions by allowing for good literary side discussions to distract from committee meetings. Seth Stewart pointed me to useful literary letters and is an inspiring colleague. Sara Whitver graciously and quickly helped with access to electronic books, for which I was grateful, especially toward the end of this project when the physical libraries at University of Alabama shut down due to the Covid-19 pandemic in 2020.

During an all too short visit to the ONE Archives in LA, Bud Thomas and Michael Oliveira helped to find materials and pointed me toward the art of Deni Ponty. Vishnu Dass who manages the Steven Arnold Archive offered valuable technical insight into Arnold's work and somewhat uniquely responded to permission requests in an efficient and kind fashion, for which I am extremely grateful. This makes Arnold's work, I'd say, even more appealing to me. L. Lamar Wilson suggested years ago that I read Richard Bruce Nugent, a suggestion I am glad I took to heart, and I remain grateful to Thomas Wirth, Nugent's late literary executor, who placed Nugent's work in the public domain.

I've enjoyed working with Ben Doyle, Lucy Brown, and the Bloomsbury Academic Staff. Last but not least, I'm grateful to two really good peer reviewers who took the time to help me to refine my work.

Part of Chapter 1 was initially published as "John Rechy's Bad Beatitudes: Surviving the Desire for Salvation" by David Deutsch from *Texas Studies in Literature and Language*, Volume 61, Issue 3, pp. 244–69. Copyright © 2019 by the University of Texas Press. All rights reserved. Part of Chapter 2 will also appear as the essay "Expanding Queer Archives: Richard Bruce Nugent's Unpublished

Modernism" in the volume *Historizing Modernism*, edited by Matthew Feldman, Erik Tonning, and Anna Svendsen.

"Love Letter," "Two Sonnets," "Psalm II," "Hymn," "The Terms in Which I Think of Reality," "The Green Automobile," "Howl," "A Supermarket in California," "America," "Violence," and "Thoughts Sitting Breathing," currently collected in COLLECTED POEMS 1947–97 by Allen Ginsberg. Copyright © 2006 by Allen Ginsberg, are used by permission of the Wylie Agency LLC and by permission of HarperCollins Publishers.

The third-party copyrighted material displayed in the pages of this book is done so on the basis of "fair dealing for the purposes of criticism and review" or "fair use for the purposes of teaching, criticism, scholarship or research" only in accordance with international copyright laws and is not intended to infringe upon the ownership rights of the original owners.

"Heal-a-zation Swathe a la Gob Ba" quintuple exposure photograph, 1985. Courtesy of the Steven Arnold Museum and Archives.

Uncovering the Queer Angels in Our Midst

For the past few years, I have enjoyed lingering, often in the evenings, often with a drink, over Steven Arnold's esoteric angels. I find them comforting and confusing, exciting and sedating, sensual and chastely ascetic. The winged man in his photograph "Heal-a-zation," for instance, I find particularly moving. Ascendant yet chained, twisted yet frozen, venerated yet abjected, accompanied yet alienated, a man so effeminately fey yet so masculinely or perhaps just so marmoreally muscled lies simultaneously exposed and concealed in an erotic chiaroscuro. Referencing the stylistics of Italian renaissance martyrdom paintings and of American beefcake magazines or pulp fiction covers from the mid-twentieth century, Arnold evokes a tense buttressing of the sacred within the profane and the profane within the sacred. To do so, he foregrounds one angel surrounded by four additional male images, actually the same man in different positions fashioned through repeated exposures, which viewed together evoke an uncertain psychomachia or a community bolstered, perhaps, by lesser angels. To structure the uncertain tension, two of these latter reach out toward the central figure with one touching his chain, indicating how the chains that imprison are also the chains that assure connection to one's self and to one's companions. Here the muscles that strain and struggle simultaneously achieve a beautiful refortification, intimating how the same touch, depending upon context and interpretation, can seem freeing or restraining, can provide pain or pleasure. Indeed, the placing of these images in the picture indicates how as queer oppression offers agony, it just as often offers an ambiguous realization of healing, of self-awareness, of new communities, and of painfully pleasurably strategies for resistances within a larger society or nation. The uncertainty here is intoxicating and maddening, and it lends to a beautiful ambiguity in time and in place, evoking the possibility for almost endless potentials.

Here and in companion photographs, Arnold's fraught yet ecstatic aesthetic crystallizes in an ethereal otherworldly surrealism as he portrays queer bodies and queer desires ascending through and against the religious, psychological, medical, legal, and social pathologies so consistently attributed to queer men. Gentle yet powerful his figures both embrace and reject indictments that queer men must be damned, mentally and physically weak, and socially alienated criminals, equally monstrous and infirm because of their queerness. In effect and in all their glory, Arnold's angels draw from and invert the spiritual and secular constraints, cruelties, and shames that excited, however unintentionally, rebelliously pleasure-seeking same-sex outlaws. Reappropriating the rich symbols of repressive regimes, his angelic queer men reexamine how ostensible degradations paradoxically offered parallel elevations. Melancholic muscular queer angels, for instance, educe both intrinsic alienations and exaltations, just as queer sex once so often sparked shame as well as a noble, transcendent pleasure achievable for a queer man only with another queer man. Just as an ostensibly dirty, too often dangerous darkened gay bar through its very marginalization could provide fertile ground for cultural fruits that would elsewhere get crushed by static conventions, so queer angels call to mind the painful freedoms of angelic rebellions that leave them in celestial margins, mourning the calm security of heaven's rejected hierarchies. Arnold's angels then, especially when considered in these contexts, exude unconventional spiritual and aesthetic graces that manifest by their very embrace of the conventionally degrading or profane desires and identities. In doing so, they help to crystallize the aesthetic trope of queer bad beatitudes that I explore in this book.

By "bad beatitudes" I mean, to be clear, states-of-being that embody an unconventional grace obtained through reconceptualizing and even exalting, if frequently uncertainly or ambivalently so, conventionally degrading behaviors or identities, such as same-sex sex or nonconformist genders. These behaviors or identities often create a hybrid state-of-being in which the conventionally profane signals the unconventionally sacred and the conventionally sacred signals the unconventionally profane, with both inverted concepts held in tension in the minds of the participants and of their subculture. The excitement of forbidden sex, the ecstasy of repressed love finally released, the opportunities presented for cross-dressing and identity expression in dank, dirty spaces that authorities generally leave alone, all merged uncomfortably to form such bad beatitudes, the sacred in ostensibly profane and the profane in ostensibly sacred practices and environments. The very intensities of religious language, moreover, evoke epic forces of good and evil, salvation versus damnation, peace and calm versus pain and torment, which raise the spiritual stakes for the queer desires and identities to which bad beatitudes become attached. Unfortunately yet inspirationally, part of the uncomfortable pleasures in bad beatitudes comes from uncertainty and contradictory desires and identifications. As I suggest above, any longing for the calm, stable dogmatic certainty of a tyrannical heaven, for instance, can concurrently evoke a writhing desire for the relatively unstable painful pleasures of a more chaotic hell, as in Arnold's "Heal-a-zation" the angelic man appears to want to remain frozen while also wanting to escape his bounds. One might, moreover, justly interpret the floating men around the foregrounded image as other selves taking other paths or as other angels in an angry god's employ, challenging this angel's rebellion, or as fellow angelic outlaws working to unchain him, or even as representatives facilitating the rejuvenation of an erotic pagan sensibility, thereby emphasizing Arnold's references to Botticelli's *Birth of Venus* (*c*. 1485) and to any number of renaissance depictions of a sensual yet tortured St. Sebastian. Such competing, confused, and often ambivalent desires and identifications represent, as I will show, a hallmark of bad beatitudes in queer American writing.

Angelic Inspirations

Twentieth-century American writers, in particular, frequently represented such complex queer bad beatitudes through angelic outlaws, most often men who exhibit varying degrees of masculinity and effeminacy and who rebel willfully and nobly against the dictates of religious, medical, legal, and social regulations. Angelic imagery, this is to say, is a trope that applies equally to butch and to femme men, and those in between, who rebel against an exalted and tyrannical status quo. Foreman Brown's *Better Angel* (1933) offers an early example of this trope but angelic outlaws appear with increasing frequency in the second half of the century, in works such as Alex Federoff's novel *The Side of the Angels* (1960), poetry anthologies such as Winston Leyland's *Angels of the Lyre* (1975), and in a variety of complex pulp or pornographic contexts, such as Carl Corley's *Black Angel* (1968), Gordon Daniels's *Black Angel* (1972), and Perry Brass's more recent *Angel Lust* (2000) and his more literary *King of Angels* (2012). From the 1980s onward, angelic imagery took on particular importance in HIV/AIDS-centered work such as Tony Kushner's *Angels in American* (1991–2), James Pickett's *Queen of Angels* (1992), and Bill Russell and Janet Hood's *Elegies for Angels, Punks, and Screaming Queens* (1996), as well as in novels such as Rabih Alameddine's fairly contemporary *Angel of History* (2016). This constellation of queer literary bad beatitudes expands exponentially if one considers, as I do in the following chapters, works that rely on angelic outlaw tropes without signaling them in the title.

While I will focus on literature in the following chapters, I began with Arnold's photography for several strategic reasons. I reference Arnold in part because I enjoy his work, in part because it evidences how angelic bad beatitudes permeate queer art beyond just literature and thus provide a broadly influential cultural trope, and in part because his aesthetic artifices demonstrate so beautifully and so quickly how angelic imagery consciously and strategically characterizes queer outlaws as attractive rebels who fight diversely repressive regulatory bodies.[1] Much as for Arnold, moreover, the angelic inspiration for the writers I discuss stemmed not so much from dogmatic approaches to cosmological essences but from how angelic figures could work to reconceptualize queer men for many twentieth-century audiences. One central facet for such inspired reconceptualizations is that, as with Arnold, a sociocultural aesthetic far superseded any dogmatic theology. None of the writers I discuss were professional theologians and while they used religious rhetoric and images, they were only loosely interested in doctrines or theological systems. They willfully used Catholic, Protestant, Jewish, and sometimes Islamic images and concepts, but they did so for primarily cultural and for profoundly humanistic reasons, emphasizing the humanity as well as the spirituality of angelic figures. Most significantly, their presentations of queer men or gender nonconforming individuals as angelic provided an aesthetic means to reinforce the innately spiritual, psychological, and even physical value of allegedly damnable portions of humanity and human behavior. Such conceptual reinforcements, for instance, could refigure the often degraded winged "fairy" into a being of splendor, power, and at times danger when evoking the concept of a "fallen" angel, especially one who tempts others into rebellion. These angelic outlaws fashion bad "beatitudes" because they reimagine a spirituality or a blessedness not condoned by institutional religious definitions but by the grace, or the benevolence, defined perhaps by a higher spiritual power but most certainly by the artistic, physical, sensual, intellectual, psychological, and emotional beauties and pleasures to be created within and often through horrible human circumstances. As such, writers' interest in queer angels remained primarily aesthetic and cultural rather than pedantically theological in nature.

The aesthetic focus of bad beatitudes then complements and adds to recent scholarship that links queer concerns to diverse spiritual engagements in both literary studies and in queer studies. Recent work in queer African American culture, for instance, has been particularly productive in these arenas. Marlon

Rachquel Moore, for instance, while noting the persistent need for an "anti-homophobic resistance" in black queer literature, has also demonstrated how "African American artists commonly create queer-affirming texts that depict a pro-sex, pro-erotic approach to notions of sacredness, religious rituals, and/or spiritual endeavors" (2014: xv). Moore illustrates how diverse black writers use "spiritual encounters and ecstatic experiences" as a means "to critique homophobic religious exclusion and to redefine the role of sexuality within the spiritual experience," often leaving "the reader with the notion that sacredness, if not God, is in the details of everyday life" (111). From a more institutional religious angle, Kevin Mumford offers valuable biographical critiques of how James Tinney "pioneered the study of the African American origins of Pentecostalism" and "agitated for the recognition of gays and lesbians in the church" and of the "relatively unknown black gay activist Brother Grant-Michael Fitzgerald," who had taken vows with the Catholic Salvatorians (2016: 147, 100). My study keeps in mind the importance of various religious traditions for diverse queer communities, and how these communities often pushed or broke through the boundaries of heteronormative religious exclusions, though I emphasize much less theological and much more aesthetic uses of spirituality, uses that engage bad beatitudes, those tensions that trouble lines between profanity and sanctity.

This aesthetic perspective thus also works in concert with studies by literary scholars who emphasize how inventive spiritualities, rather than secular rationalities, effect social forms of intimacy and communal organizations. I work in a similar vein, for instance, to John McClure who in *Partial Faiths* explores how a range of post–Second World War American writers "tell stories about new forms of religiously inflected seeing and being" that are "dramatically partial and open-ended" and "do not promise anything like full redemption" (2010: ix). McClure begins his study with references to Tony Kushner's *Angels in America* but neither queerness nor angels remain a focus of his analysis. McClure shares though with subsequent queer studies critics a willingness to suspend dogmatic belief for a partial spiritual understanding of the material everyday world. Elizabeth Freeman, for example, uses what she calls a *"sacra/mentality"* to explore a "queer hypersociability," a "sociability" not specifically concerned with "identity or even queer sex practices," in a study that links queerness to spiritual ways of thinking about "temporal control and response to that control" in bodies shaped by biopolitical forces (2019: 25, 18, 8). While Freeman focuses on groups such as the Shakers and forms of Catholicism, Peter Coviello uses similarly theoretical queer approaches to demonstrate how "early Mormons were the purveyors of what was all but universally recognized as a deviant carnality," one centered around a patriarchal polygamy, and he argues that "this is so much the case that we profit greatly, both historically and conceptually, by considering them through the terms offered by queer theory, queer historiography, and queer critique" (2019: 217). Indeed, he adventurously uses queer theory and queer religious historiography to consider how "deviants" in sexual pleasure or "*zealots*" of a religion that admitted the power of earthly pleasure might help to rethink spiritual intimacies and the constraints of nationalism (2). Coviello shows, for instance, how spiritual intimacies might justify breaking free from unjust positive national laws or more secularized moralities grounded in primarily Protestant faiths, even as he likewise argues that the bounds of statehood and citizenship often provide a motivation to curb erotic spiritual deviancies. In many ways, my investigation of bad beatitudes combines the explicit focus on spiritual same-sex eroticism inherent in Moore's and Mumford's twentieth-century focused studies and the spiritual queer studies less determined by same-sex sex practices found in Freeman's and Coviello's, which are grounded in the nineteenth century.

Angelic outlaws, I think, nicely encapsulate such various strands of queer thinking because while they rely on images drawn from long-standing institutional religions, they frequently diverge into new forms of sociability that break free or at the very least intensely challenge the constraints of religious, moral, and secular citizenship. Because literary angels, generally speaking, are the epitome of an embodied celestial existence, they insist on a variety of subversively non-secular, non-state sanctioned intimacies that justify their existence—not always but quite frequently—through a specifically same-sex eroticism that combines elements of sanctity, profanity, high art, and plain old vulgar crudity all at once. Angels then allow for a more readily erotic, extended spiritually embodied experience than most other religious images or iconographic figures, such as for instance mortal saints or prophets who are so frequently associated with asceticism, chastity, and overwhelming regret for any rebellion against God. Angels, too, both fallen and not and those somewhere in between, strike a variety of registers all at once, while also emphasizing a fluidity of time, space, spirituality, embodiment, and morality, as I will outline more clearly below.

This critically celebratory, yet rarely scholarly, refiguring of non-secular imagery likely explains the complex uses of "angel" in everyday post–Second World War slang, upon which authors frequently drew even as they generally avoided pinpointed theological scholarship. As Charles Ford and Parker Tyler once asked, "[w]hat is divine besides slang?" (1989: 134). Indeed, for slang so often uses artifice to spotlight an overlooked quotidian truth or state-of-being and, in so doing, it appropriates the divine power of creation to fashion new perspectives. Thus, if in the 1940s the slang term "angel" may have originally stood for both "a person easily victimized" and "an effeminate man who has womanish traits or qualities; a male homosexual," by the 1970s "angel" as queer slang had inverted any sense of victimization as gender queerness and same-sex desire also signaled strength and a rebellion against tyrannical norms. In his slang dictionary *The Queens' Vernacular* (1972), Bruce Rodgers notes, for example, that "angel" could mean "any homosexual male. Angel, to some, mends the crumpled wings and pride of the denigrated fairy" (21). Beauty and effeminacy come to signify a divine strength, including sometimes even physical strength or bravery, as indicated by terms such as "iron angel" evoking "a muscle man" or "angel food" evoking men in the "air force" or even a brave "fallen angel," which Rodgers notes signifies a "male homosexual," a "reminder of Judeo-Christianity's moral condemnation," which the out queer male challenges and, at least in part, powerfully rejects (23, 140, 79).[2] In a society where American religious leaders often considered queer individuals as damned, legal officials indicted them as criminals, and medical authorities diagnosed them as physically and psychologically sick, imagery that characterized such men as spiritually valuable, as representing a form of extra-judicial morality, and as physically beautiful specimens with often psychological vitality would be undeniably welcome.

    Angelic imagery was, though, more than a way of challenging conventional religious, legal, and medical condemnations of queer men. It also inspired a connective aesthetic. The association of gay men with angels, for instance, hints at the ability of both angels and queer men to bridge multiple worlds. By referencing quasi-divine figures who manifest in often beautiful human shapes, angelic characterizations of queer men serve to emphasize an earthly spirituality that exists within a human materiality, as an intrinsic part of it. More importantly still, references to queer men as "fallen" angels recall coercive, even frightening forms of subversion and collaboration within only seemingly discrete, even discreet realms. As angels can bridge heavenly, earthly, and infernal realms, traveling one through the other, so queer men would often have to navigate the straight world, the queer underworld, and the often blurring boundaries of their public and private, professional and personal lives. Both conformist and more non-conformist same-sex desiring individuals, for instance, could carry their queer identities into allegedly "straight" arenas, such as the military or government agencies, or could find friends and lovers in the workplace, queering, however tangentially and unsatisfactorily, the supposedly straight world.

As one might imagine, as exciting as any such bridgings could be, they were often fairly fraught and risky endeavors. Most of the writers I consider in this study draw tangentially, yet consciously, on Miltonic and Blakean conceptions of Lucifer's Fall, again emphasizing aesthetic issues over theological ones. In part, this aesthetic emphasis gives authors the freedom to reimagine the homoerotic elements that critics have long acknowledged exist in both Milton's and Blake's religious poetry and in Blake's engravings.[3] By reimagining these homoerotic elements, these more contemporary queer authors engage what I call neo-Miltonic or neo-Blakean tropes to give greater emphasis to how liberal, individualistic angelic rebellions can work seditiously or undercover (in all covert and erotic senses of that word) to challenge profanely sanctified ideologies even as other queer angelic men collaborate with their tyrannical oppressors. John Rechy, Allen Ginsberg, Countée Cullen, and Langston Hughes, for instance, recall how Satan managed to recruit a number of powerful fellow angels to his cause before God mobilized his naive and subservient host to banish their fellow angels from Heaven to Hell. These writers also reimagine Satan's fall in ways that legitimize a psychological relativity that could resist tyrannical hierarchical norms, a strategy that once so dismayed Milton. They celebrate, in other words, the contingencies of Satan's declaration that it is "better to reign in Hell, than serve in Heaven" and that the "mind is its own place, and in itself / can make a Heav'n of Hell, a Hell of Heav'n" (2005: 1.263, 1.254–5). If Milton considers such claims to be false, queer bad beatitudes tease out and insist on the relative truths in them. Rechy, Nugent, Ginsberg, and Alameddine do not naively celebrate turning a Hell into a Heaven without any qualifications, but they do portray how certain heavenly elements, such as a qualified safety, love, creative excitement, and aesthetic beauty, can exist within and even because of Hellish circumstances. In doing so, they likewise reimagine Blake's imputation in *The Marriage of Heaven and Hell* of the positive active energies of Satanic or Luciferian forces as a counterbalance to the staid tyranny of a hierarchical Heaven. They also expand the homoerotic elements found in Blake's engravings for *Milton* and *Jerusalem*.[4]

Already part of a long-standing English-language literary tradition, these aesthetic and social portrays of angelic outlaws and collaborators took on new resonances as writers wove them into post–Second World War American cultural contexts, ones in which boundary bridging queer men were often scapegoats for national anxieties surrounding public moralities and only ostensibly stable masculinities. Queer individuals and queer writing became nationally important lightning rods for vicious attempts to stabilize discrete moral, gendered, and criminal boundaries. The *Howl* trial and other battles over censoring so-called obscene literature, such as the Mattachine Society's *One* journal or lesbian pulp fiction or Manual Enterprises physique magazines, publicly debated what sorts of queer literature and imagery existed in the realms of the morally obscene or of art or even as permissible public discourse (Eskridge 1999: 95-6). Did sending such material through US customs or the US Postal Service, with physique magazines flying out like little rebel seraphim, subversively or rebelliously blur boundaries of public and private morality? Did such actions subvert the use of the federal government and of public tax dollars to promote seditious queer agendas? The answer, of course, is a qualified yes, depending upon one's precise definition of rebellion, sedition, and an agenda. The point is, though, that any discrete American moral or cultural boundaries were blurry and permeable. Long before Stonewall, for instance, the attractions of queerness presented state authorities with difficulties in policing norms of sexuality and masculinity. Indeed, sources as diverse as a military trial over same-sex entrapments in 1919-20, John Rechy's *City of Night* (1963), Daniels's *Black Angel* (1972), and the controversial film *Cruising* (1980), all indicate the dangers of sending ostensibly straight men into queer spaces where they might be tempted into erotic and gender deviancies, much as Satan tempted weaker angels and a still weaker humanity to betray a tyrannical God.[5] Writers who develop angelic bad beatitudes draw on and reimagine such specifically American contexts of porous boundaries and the inextricability of covert queer desires from the United States and its official representatives.

Particularly porous in the post-Second World War period were the boundaries between queerness and political radicalism as officials anxious to sustain exploitative versions of capitalism in America frequently conjoined both the so-called Lavender and Red Scares. Beginning in the late 1940s and reaching a zenith in the 1950s, hysterical congressman, senators, and influential establishment figures feared that queer individuals could permeate straight spaces unnoticed and would then wreak havoc analogous to or as themselves fifth-column communist spies. Knowing that a malicious government and society had forced queer individuals to become familiar with living covert lives, existences filled with secret relationships and habits, government officials at all levels feared betrayal from within by people who seemed to be loyal Americans but who had stronger loyalties to diversely oppressed groups. "Although indistinguishable from mainstream society," David Johnson notes, both communists and queers "were thought to be able to identify one another" and "[m]embers of such subcultures were feared to have a loyalty to one another transcending that toward their class, race, or nation" (2004: 33, 34). Such associations of the Lavender and Red Scares by government officials were later echoed by the Ku Klux Klan and other reactionary conservative groups in the South, which, as John Howard has discussed, "explicitly linked civil rights activism and communism to male homosexuality" (1999: 149). As Howard has shown, such reactionary rhetorical strategies were likewise deployed by southern government officials at the state level, who "conjoined anticommunism and homophobia with white supremacy" (155). Much like Satan's initially unnoticed rebellion in Heaven and his subsequent success at slipping past Uriel, in Milton's *Paradise Lost*, to destroy Adam and Eve's existence in Eden, queer individuals, officials insisted, could stealthily disrupt the government officials' zealous pursuit of a capitalist, patriarchal, and often white, Christian nationalism. Such nationalist fears persisted, as Johnson points out, prompting "congressional hearings, presidential executive orders, and executive agency security briefings" even though it appears that "no gay American was ever [proven to be] blackmailed into revealing state secrets" (2004: 9–10). Aside then from actual espionage or from simply needing a scapegoat for national anxieties, a broad unconscious social guilt over the mistreatment of same-sex desiring and gender nonconforming individuals and a perhaps slightly less unconscious desire for individuals in power to distance themselves from such ostracized communities both reinforced vitriolic and reactionary stances that portrayed gay men and women as anti-American.

Of course rather than pursue sedition or even liberal critiques of reactionary US policies, many queer individuals actively collaborated, sometimes reluctantly and sometimes all too eagerly, with conservative forces. Roy Cohn, perhaps most famously, represented a virulent proponent of anticommunism and public homophobia combined, despite his own covert same-sex relationships.[6] Rumors of queerness also swirled, fairly consistently, around the homophobic J. Edgar Hoover, who whatever his actual erotic or emotional investment in men or in cross-dressing nonetheless lived an extraordinarily unconventional intimate life with his close companion Clyde Tolson.[7] Authors, of course, emphasized and critiqued such collaborators through their references to economically, socially, and politically conservative queer men, men who collaborated with oppressive institutions, if to varying degrees. Ginsberg's critiques of the "fairies of advertising" in *Howl* (1955) work in conservative economic counterpoint to his "angelheaded hipsters," while Federoff's biting depictions of affluent, closeted, exceptionally conservative government workers and media consultants in *The*

Side of the Angels (1960) and Kushner's acidic characterization of Roy Cohn and his protégé, the Republican lawyer Joe Pitt, in *Angels in America* (1991–2) present intensely reactionary angelic collaborators, men who pursue power, prestige, and influence by remaining loyal to homophobic causes even as they covertly pursue same-sex sex. While loosely analogous to the angels who fight to banish an ambitiously individualistic Satan from Heaven to remain in God's favor, these contemporary fictional characters act much more hypocritically, for they proclaim public allegiances that actively hurt those rebels fighting for the sexual freedoms in which the reactionaries themselves indulge, albeit in private. Such reactionary angelic collaborators in America evoke the often tortured and unhappy decisions queer men had to make as they navigated their allegiances to diverse facets of society, to their internalized homophobia, and to their physical and psychological desires. In actuality, many individuals seem to have found an uneasy middle ground, collaborating with oppressive regimes so that they could have a career, make money, and generally live their lives, while subtly yet powerfully subverting officials' attempts to destroy the lives of those with similar erotic interests.[8] As such, unlike Milton's angels, who eventually fall into one of two camps, angelic figures in queer fiction often reflect these bridging of multiple worlds, cultures, and loyalties all at once.

While angelic bad beatitudes challenged then, at times forcefully and at times more obliquely, national conversations regarding the toxicity of queer individuals within society, they also engaged debates more internal to queer communities. Individuals who were more "out" or even just assertive in terms of their sexual and/or gender nonconformity were understandably angry at or frustrated with those individuals who seemed to prostrate themselves to social norms regarding behavior and dress, while more conservative lesbian and gay activists were reluctant to rebel too stridently against any political, gendered, economic, or even racial status quo.[9] Gender nonconformists such as Leslie Feinberg and Audre Lorde, for instance, recall feeling isolated in the late 1960s from a variety of feminist groups who preferred their members to be both conventionally feminine and predominantly white or even to fall into a clear butch/femme dichotomy.[10] As Lorde notes in *Zami*, "[n]on-conventional people can be dangerous, even in the gay community" (1982: 224). Notably, while the authors I consider here depict characters who are socially, politically, and economically radical queer or trans individuals as angelic outlaws, they also depict more homonormative yet still proudly out gay men and even the occasional closeted gay man in angelic terms, as either lesser outlaws or collaborationists. As there are hierarchies of angels in Milton's and Blake's cosmologies, so there are stratifications of angelic outlaws in post–Second World War American literature, although these stratifications follow no clear dogmatic taxonomy from author to author and in more metaphorical or slangy uses of angel images they occasionally get elided. When they do appear, though, such queer angelic categorizations tend to engage debates within the US queer community regarding the values and pitfalls of diverse degrees of socioeconomic, political, sexual, and gender radicalisms and conformities. Some angelic outlaws inevitably rebel more than others, but across the board authors use angelic characterizations to highlight conventionally profane sanctities within same-sex desires and gender nonconformities even if certain characters' more conservative values, such as a social intolerance or a Christian-sanctioned exploitative capitalism, get portrayed as horrifically pious profanities.

Queer authors likewise used bad beatitudes to consider a similarly internal debate regarding whether or not queer culture might be superior to or even just innately separate from any larger predominantly straight culture. Beginning systematically in the Anglo-American modern era, Edward Carpenter, Havelock Ellis, and Henry Gerber cautiously wondered whether queer men and women had unique capacities for the arts, counseling, and human relationships, perhaps through innate physiological and psychological traits or perhaps through skills acquired due to their socially marginalized position.[11] By 1944, the American poet and essayist Robert Duncan could complain that "[a]lmost co-incident with the first declarations for homosexual rights was the growth of a cult of homosexual superiority to the human race" (1944: 210). In opposition to this separatist stance, Duncan argued for a more assimilationist sense of queer culture, for a broadly general "devotion to human freedom, toward the liberation of human love, human conflicts, human aspirations," according to which "one must disown all the special groups (nations, religions, sexes, races) that would claim allegiance" (211). A more middle-ground perspective set aside the question of superiority and focused simply on differences in queer culture, art, references, and language, such as slang or metaphors, and variations in a diversely "normal" America. Douglas Mount observed in 1972, for instance, that though there are many in the queer community who "would prefer to forget that there are any differences between gays and straights," there are also "more militant gays who insist that they be accepted without necessarily being assimilated" (9–10). Many times, nonetheless, even fairly middle-ground queer advocates or artists, such as the AIDS activist and singer Mike Callen, argued that "gay people are clued in at an early age to the duplicity in all things … [and] have a unique perspective that make us particularly adept at art" (qtd. in Duberman 2014: 45). Martin

Duberman notes that Callen "wasn't merely defending his gayness as normal, he was suggesting that it might well be superior—politically, intuitively, and aesthetically. Overstatement," Duberman observes, "was a common ingredient in the early rhetoric of gay liberation, a trope Mike indulged in with glee, viewing it as necessary compensation for the disparagement of gay lives that had long been common currency. After the extended reign and deep internalization of homophobic self-hatred, affirmation for Mike and others surfaced in the form of strenuous counterclaims" (45). In Duberman's astute analysis, queer hyperbole comfortably claims a form of learned superiority, although it also reveals the self-doubt, loss, and pain that produced many queer individuals' sense of their heightened states-of-being.

Depictions of queer angelic outlaws in American fiction, particularly those that rely on neo-Miltonic and neo-Blakean tropes for fallen angels, generally desire to present queer individuals as grander, as more righteously rebellious, or occasionally as achieving a sort of spiritually physical martyrdom through being unfairly abused by unjust normative authorities. Even if not actually believing in supernatural beings, writers use such bad beatitudes, the sacred in the profane and the profane in the ostensibly sacred, to celebrate the ecstasies within the agonies of queer life and to condemn, while still at times sympathizing with, those queer men who conservatively collaborate with their oppressors. The primarily metaphorical and at times slangy nature of queer angelic imagery resists any essentialized or clearly defined programmatic endorsement of queer superiority, but the imagery's general aesthetic epic-ness emphasizes how queer interactions with religious, medical, legal, and sociocultural institutions and environments often had uniquely high stakes, with forces opposing tolerance often being equally as larger than life as any angelic outlaw heroics. Writers' diverse depictions of angelic queer men, moreover, from outlaws to queerly conservative collaborationists, prevent any clear-cut claim to spiritual, moral, much less physical superiority. But these bad beatitudes do indicate an important sense of difference if never a clear sense of separatism, particularly as so many literary queer angels exhibit some temporary or contingent interest in women. Queer angelic outlaws' brief cross-sex encounters, even if culturally or religiously forced forms of heterosexuality, clearly resist any firm or too intransigent vision of a totalizing queer separatism.

Indeed, a sense of angelic queer outlaws as bridge characters tends to connect communities rather than to separate them. The connective nature of this theme exists, moreover, I venture, as a particularly American literary trope. David Bergman has argued that "to be American is to be queer," pointedly reversing arguments, particularly from the religious, medical, and legal fields, that worked to limit queer American citizenship, separating those with deviant desires from American culture (1991: 10). Almost ipso-facto outlaws or curtailed citizens, marginalized from full American citizenship through, among other means, ostracism, hospitalization, and imprisonment, queer Americans had to fight for their freedoms to speak, to congregate, to work, to fight for their country, and to keep their military privileges, not to mention their freedoms regarding privacy, all of which were and are intimately bound to conceptions of legal and cultural American citizenships.[12] Members of the Mattachine Society of Washington DC, as David Johnson observes, "were exceedingly careful to highlight not only that they were homosexuals but that they enjoyed rights as American citizens" and "adopted the strategy of referring to themselves as 'homosexual citizens'" (2004: 200–1). Even a 1967 drag contest in New York, with its racially and regionally diverse contestants, recorded in Frank Simon's documentary *The Queen* (1968), emphasized its adherence to a modern Americana, if a subversive one, in a flag-waving ensemble dance routine performed to "You're a Grand Old Flag."[13] Literary angelic outlaws often exhibit similarly wide-ranging degrees of their pointedly American identities, from Rechy's anonymous angelic narrator in *City of Night* and Nugent's Angel in "Uranus in Cancer" who served in the US military to Alameddine's narrator Jacob who emigrates from Yemen to San Francisco and who engages the city's literary and legal communities. These angelic outlaws serve to bridge, if with varying degrees of success, disparate communities within the United States, including gay and straight as well as homonormative and queer, native and immigrant communities that presented as intentionally American. Occasionally, authors even present such social and spatial convergences as new or emerging frontiers within America, if at times aggressively erotic ones.[14]

In addition then to serving as bridge figures linking heaven, hell, and earth, linking physicality and spirituality, and linking the human and the divine, literary angels also work to imagine ways of being in America that bridge normative and queer conceptions of time and space. Rechy's narrator, Nugent's Angel, Ginsberg's angel-headed hipsters in *Howl*, and Alameddine's Jacob all use queer chronologies and time schemes to benchmark their lives as they exist in multiple spaces and sanctify conventionally profane environments. Often, these multifaceted chronologies manifesting within rural and urban American sites reflect what Jack Halberstam has described as "queer time[s] and place[s]." Halberstam theorizes a "queer time" that involves "compression and annihilation," an intense in the moment being with little past or future, as well as queer chronologies that manifest only "once one leaves the temporal frames of bourgeois reproduction and family, longevity, risk/safety, and inheritance." These conceptions of queer time, of course, inevitably influence interpretations of "queer space," "the place-making practices within postmodernism in which queer people engage and … the new understandings of space enabled by the production of queer counterpublics" (2005: 2, 6). Literary angelic outlaws often evoke such conceptions of queer time and space, whether from a blowjob received in a cinema restroom that compresses time to one profanely sacred moment of heavenly calm and excitement all at once, or from new perceptions of time and space that arise from rebels leaving the calm but tyrannical safety of religious homes to explore multiple same-sex encounters and heavenly partnerships in what for straight individuals would be hellish circumstances. Importantly, as Elizabeth Freeman observes, although "straight and queer temporalities" often work alongside each other, sometimes "[q]ueer time overtakes both secular and millennial time" and demands its own predominance (2010: x–xi). Following Freeman's lead, we can see how queer encounters or unions marked outside of standardized ritualized events, such as dating or church marriages, or evolutions of gender presentation in bars, parks, and private apartments, which allow for these to exist, can create tenuously safe queer counterpublics that provide the touchstones for characters' lives. Authorities may initiate raids that disrupt such queer practices, but the psychological, emotional, and spiritual effects of these encounters or identities can last far longer than any religious or state apparatus might have wished for and they can re-manifest in new more protected environments.

Along these lines, analogous literary time frames and spaces develop and come to the fore as American writers merge neo-Miltonic and neo-Blakean epochal moral struggles with American queer chronological rhythms and spaces. These queer mergers insist on making literary space in the canonical tradition of great rebellious narratives to account for shifting identities, the morality of multiple sexual encounters, sex and gender transitions, and restructurings of romantic expectations within post–Second World War as well as AIDS-era American societies. In this study, for instance, Rechy's *City of Night*, Nugent's "Uranus in Cancer," Ginsberg's *Howl*, and Alameddine's *Angel of History* engage and yet take a queer predominance over the chronologies, spaces, and canonical status of long-venerated works such as Milton's *Paradise Lost* and Blake's *The Marriage of Heaven and Hell*.

To heighten this sense of such uniquely American bad beatitudes, I also want to point out that queer literary angelic outlaws frequently cross racial, ethnic, and socioeconomic boundaries that have remained shamefully all too firm in the United States. Roderick Ferguson has recently reemphasized how the "multidimensional and interactional interests" of early queer movements were subsequently "overtaken by single-issue formulations of queer politics, formulations that would promote liberal capitalist ideologies" (2019: 3). As artists, historians, and critics such as Ferguson have pointed out, often times in queer movements, middle-class gay white men unjustly dominated such single-issue neo-liberal politics, which reinforced the marginalization that queer Americans of color faced within a broader national queer culture and that echoed their marginalization in American culture more generally. Angelic outlaws, however, represent at least one American *cultural* theme that manifests, albeit in unique ways, across diverse racial, religious, spiritual, socioeconomic, and national backgrounds. As such, this study of bad beatitudes follows Robert Reid-Pharr's interest in "a clear understanding not only that the black subject might be recognized as the universal subject but also that her universalism is itself always channeled through the reality of her particularity" and in linking this understanding to queer American contexts in ways that undo a false "idea of whiteness as universal" (2001: 44, 97). The difficulty here is to balance a just appreciation for the particularity of, say, diverse Hispanic-US literary traditions and African American literary traditions, keeping in mind Hiram Pérez's warning regarding the difficulties inherent in the "symbolic origins for all racial [and cultural] differences signified by color," as well as Catholic and Jewish and Muslim literary traditions, as symbolism inherently extends, dilutes, and distorts particularity (2015: 14). Inevitably, this study will fail to achieve the right balance, for which one can blame variously my own intellectual limitations, my desire to attend to diverse authors from different backgrounds in one book, and people who talk loudly in libraries. Rather than focus on one cultural background, however, I will try to demonstrate how diverse American writers have drawn on queer angelic outlaws as a trope to help them to reimagine and to explore the sacred within the ostensibly profane and the profane within the ostensibly sacred elements of American culture. I hope that my emphasizing a similarly if diversely applied literary theme will partially compensate for my failure to focus too intently on any one cultural background.

The European traces behind these American bad beatitudes should also, I think, be acknowledged upfront as a potentially yet I hope not overwhelmingly problematic issue. The writers I consider in subsequent chapters, from John Rechy to Countée Cullen, Richard Bruce Nugent, Allen Ginsberg, and Rabih Alameddine, to name just a few, all refer back to primarily Judeo-Christian cosmologies, and much more rarely to Muslim ones, and they quite frequently refer to John Milton and to William Blake, canonical white male European poets. These authors, however, treat Milton and Blake as authors "promiscuously read," to reimagine willfully Milton's famous phrase from "Areopagitica," as they reinvigorate older angelic tropes for more modern American purposes. While the crossing of white queer men into, say, African American spaces for sex, homoerotic entertainment, and a temporary community (as described by Blair Niles in her 1931 novel *Strange Brother* and Wallace Thurman in his 1932 novel *Infants of the Spring*, as well as by historians George Chauncey and Kevin Mumford) risked being more rather than less predatory, a more democratically shared, queered, and reversed literary colonization of Milton and Blake seems less exploitative if still problematic. In other words, if a focus on Miltonic and Blakean tropes seems to privilege Europe, I do emphasize how post–Second World War American authors borrow from these tropes to critique and to celebrate more contemporary angelic outlaws rather than use these English authors to reaffirm or to promote European visions, much less any rigid theological system. It is also worth remembering that Milton and Blake cribbed their tropes, in large part if not entirely, from Middle Eastern biblical and Mediterranean pagan narrative traditions.

My sense of these prismatic narrative mergers, never homogenized but always interconnected, of reinvented or reimagined and now expansively American literary tropes, works alongside recent advances in queer American literary studies. Angelic outlaws, for instance, clearly take part in what Natasha Hurley has theorized as queer circuits and queer circulations of themes, ideas, and tropes. "Circulation," as Hurley conceptualizes it, "is at once generative and regressive, forward-oriented and backward-looking, progressive and conservative" (2018: 10). "Attending to literary circulation," she elaborates, "also allows us to measure accumulations and condensations of language, whether detailed descriptions or abstract types, over time" (19). In their circulation through American literature, queer angels certainly look backward and forward and accumulate new resonances as they move across a diverse body of American literature. Through their engagement with bad beatitudes, for instance, angelic outlaws circulate around queer scholars' and particularly queer American studies scholars' interest in teasing out the implications of both self-denigration and self-exaltation. Eve Kosofsky Sedgwick, Darieck Scott, Hiram Pérez, and Heather Love, for instance, have focused on the various, often productive significances of queer shame or abjection.[15] Love in particular makes an angelic connection in her exploration of "the queer historical experience of failed or impossible love," noting that while "Lucifer is an apt emblem of high modernism," for "his stand against God is both courageous and doomed from the start," Benjamin's "angel of history," that "preeminently backward figure," looms as a much larger figure for any study of or politics engaging "nostalgia, regret, shame, despair, *ressentiment*, passivity, escapism, self-hatred, withdrawal, bitterness, defeatism, and loneliness" (2007: 30, 55, 147, 4). While bad beatitudes certainly encompass this productive pessimism, accounting for the despair of queer angelic outlaws, I also try to attend to what Michael Snediker has called a "queer optimism." "Queer optimism doesn't aspire towards happiness," Snediker notes, but it does function as "a form of meta-optimism: it wants to *think* about feeling good, to make disparate aspects of feeling good thinkable" (2009: 3). While queer angelic outlaws do, as we will see, aspire to happiness, they also provide a unique way to think through versions of queer pessimism and queer optimism simultaneously, as they insist on the almost indissoluble tension between the shame and ecstasy in profane sanctities and sanctified profanities, ones that look backward and forward in angelic depictions of queer outlaws of different races who draw on diverse socioeconomic classes, masculinities, cultural backgrounds, and literary traditions.

True, too, is that following this circulating trope into post–Second World War literature offers opportunities for examining how queer shame and queer optimism play out to new extremes and with greater nuances in a wider variety of spaces, environments, and discourses that due to censorship and social constraints most writers looking to publish in the late nineteenth and early twentieth centuries would not have been willing to explore. Following angelic outlaws, with increasingly more explicitly gay and queer consciousnesses, through queer bathhouses, gay bars, pornography theaters, parks, and private apartments and homes where men lived not as friends but as lovers who have sex, explicitly so and not by implication, and through two world wars and the advent of the civil rights movement and gay liberation and their aftermaths, including the HIV/AIDS crisis, allows for increasingly articulated, idealized, critically imperfect, and realistically multifaceted reassessments of queer spiritual, social, and political engagements in American culture.

My particular emphasis on holding in tension the profane and the sacred, pessimism and optimism, idealism and imperfections in these late-twentieth- and early twentieth-first-century narratives, also puts bad beatitudes and angelic outlaws into conversation with intriguing strands of queer thinking that investigate how destruction, pain, and the repudiation of current social symbolic systems might lead to an often secular version of transcending one's personality, ego, and even the claims of the state. Leo Bersani, most famously, has explored how "self-shattering" and "anti-relationality" might allow for the transcendence and subsequent reorganization of social structures (1995: 94–5, 164). Working along similar lines, Lee Edelman has connected queerness to a "death drive" so as to establish its "resistance to a Symbolic reality," one that unnecessarily privileges children and a too coercive focus on the future (2004: 3, 18). Like many other critics, I find such destructive idealisms seductive and exciting, but I also think that they relinquish, to too great a degree, the temporal, social, and political systems in which we are enmeshed and in which queer individuals are inextricably and quite usefully invested. I find then convincing and practical Darieck Scott's inquiries into race and queerness, neither of which he wants to disrupt entirely, which enables him to demonstrate how "suffering seems, at some level or at some far-flung contact point, to merge into something like ability, like power (and certainly, like pleasure) without losing or denying what it is to suffer" (2010: 15). While the tendency of bad beatitudes to acknowledge the profane in the sacred and the sacred in the profane obviously has correlations with these valuable lines of inquiry, I generally avoid their psychoanalytical underpinnings and sustained focuses on abjection and stigmatization to imagine how aesthetic, cultural, and historical contexts engage destructive pains and pleasures in a more balanced, if still inevitably uneven and unavoidably tense, fashion. Through the trope of angelic outlaws, those inherently hybrid figures, bad beatitudes hedge or compromise Bersani's, Edelman's, and Scott's radical idealism, yet they achieve a longer lasting, and more presentist, I think, viability by establishing more clear-cut joys along with clear-cut pains in already established social systems. On the down side, this approach risks losing out on or at least dampening the queer utopian energy fortified by José Esteban Muñoz, who pushed for a "rejection of a here and now and an insistence on potentiality or concrete possibility for another world" and yet it nonetheless adheres to Muñoz's desire to see "queerness as collectivity" as I consider how angelic outlaws reassess, decry, and revalue the pleasures and ethics of eroticism, romance, and queer communities in a decidedly nonutopian, postlapsarian, but none-too-quickly changing world (2009: 1, 11). If pleasure and pain lead to transcendence in the works I study here, it is always in a deeply flawed and pragmatic, never quite yet utopian sense. It is not defeatist, I think, to recognize pleasures where we can in the past, though it would be so to be satisfied with such pleasures amid degradation in the present and future.

Last but not least, I want to note upfront that this angelic approach to bad beatitudes focuses primarily on depictions of queer and gender nonconforming men. On the one hand, angelic outlaws and collaborators, with their hybrid, connective, and bridge-building connotations, as outlined above, uniquely enable and constrain a diversity of post–Second World War queer masculinities. The embodiment of bad beatitudes in figures of angels, ranging from young to old and combining and shifting elements of effeminacy and butchness, weakness and strength, health and physical and mental illness, anxiety and self-assurance, nationalism and celestial-ism, allows for a spiritual eroticism that suffuses in order to celebrate and to critique a multiplicity of queer masculine and effeminate identities. Angels rising and falling, meanwhile, provide a key allegory for how such characters can evolve over time, historically, culturally, aesthetically, sometimes all in one narrative, sometimes all in one evening, as characters move from parks to bars to private apartments, and back again, environments that each come with their own shifting freedoms and constraints. From delicate muscle men akin to Arnold's angels, to the more feminine and the more beefcake connotations of the slang "angel" versus "iron angel," from the conservative queerness of angelic men who for ease, for comfort, for fear, or for financial gain bow to powers that be during the day and hire a hustler at night, to the bravery of more willfully "fallen" outlaws who challenge any oppressive religious, medical, and civic status quo even though they may at one time have served in the military or worked for a legal firm, by encompassing all such characters this trope makes literary room for truly queer—in the sense of both strange or out of the ordinary and in the sense of nonconformist genders and sexualities—masculinities. Yet, and this is a big yet, on the other hand, this focus inevitably leaves out biological women and trans men.

While authors from diverse racial and religious backgrounds use angelic characterizations to describe variously masculine and effeminate queer men and occasionally trans women, I have not found angelic imagery to be associated quite as frequently with lesbian or with trans male characters, and when such imagery does arise, it does not focus as extensively on the neo-Miltonic or neo-Blakean tropes that provide a key theme to the literature examined in this study. This is not to say, though, that such female-centered angelic imagery does not occur. There is the occasional reference to be found in letters, for instance, such as in Mary (Mamie) Burrill's note to Angelina Weld Grimké in 1896 wherein she describes herself as "like an angel bending o'er you" to "breathe into your ear, 'I love you'" (qtd. in Beemyn 2014: 94n117). Angelic figures also arise occasionally in the art of lesbian poets, such as in Adrienne Rich's "This Beast; This Angel," "Lucifer in the Train," and "Gabriel," and in Audre Lorde's "For Each of You" or "Movement Song." In Kushner's *Angels in America* Hannah Pitt, an elderly Mormon woman, has an eroticized encounter with an angel who exhibits primarily a version of femininity, as much as an angel with multiple genitals can be gendered. To do justice to angelic outlaw tropes in lesbian writing or in that of trans men, however, would take another study, one which might deal with how queer authors reimagine Victorian associations with the overdone "angel in the household" motif or the tendency, as Jacqueline Foertsch has observed, for contemporary authors to "angelize" women in AIDS fiction "into irrelevance," rhetorically disempowering them (2001: 154). Yet while I focus on angelic outlaw images in male-focused literature, I want to acknowledge my debts to lesbian and trans writers' work on profane within allegedly sacred and sacred within allegedly profane queer traditions. I think here of Gayle Rubin's observation that "[m]inority sexual communities are like religious heretics. We are persecuted by the state, the mental-health establishment, social-welfare agencies, and the media," rather than like participants in a different morality system, and Leslie Feinberg's reformulations of a queer "sacred" past in *Transgender Warriors* (Feinberg 1996: 23, 38; Rubin 2011: 135). If this study focuses on queer male angelic outlaws, it thus discusses only one limited yet poignant aesthetic or cultural facet of queer bad beatitudes at large.

An Angelic Outline

Even with these limitations, the rest of this book will evidence how angels and angelic outlaws provide a theme that resonates across a still quite wide variety of queer American writing. While the literary bad beatitudes I discuss will vary among almost casual passing slang references that indicate an ostensibly simple beauty or an ethereal quality; references steeped in religious debates; references to S&M that emphasize pain and pleasure and queerness; more general metaphors used to counter expectations regarding queer individuals; and references that draw heavily on "high art" traditions so as to queer an established Miltonic and Blakean cannon; all of these bad beatitudes activate, if to differing degrees, each of the others and so engage the social, cultural, medical, spiritual, and political concerns presented in this introduction. In the following chapters, I will demonstrate how this wide-ranging and influential critical queer trope was enhanced by a diversity of racial, ethnic, spiritual, and socioeconomic approaches.

In Chapter 1, "John Rechy's Angelic Outlaws: Surviving the Desire for Salvation," I argue that in his breakthrough novel *City of Night* (1963) Rechy draws on his Mexican Catholic heritage as well as Milton and Blake to formulate an aesthetic celebration of queer angelic outlaws. By means of this argument, I set the critical angelic framework for this study and I emphasize how aesthetic and cultural references far outweigh any rigorously theological engagement with angels or Christian beatitudes. As Rechy considers versions of rebellious and more collaborationist bad beatitudes, he depicts same-sex hustlers, johns, drag queens, and effeminate men enacting a self-affirming transcendence of their seemingly profane experiences by perceiving their illegal and socially taboo lives in rebelliously angelic terms. In particular, Rechy has his narrator, a hustler with a Mexican-US heritage, draw on the Hispanic-Catholic narratives of his childhood and his cosmopolitan lineage to cast himself and his acquaintances as rebel angels fighting against too narrowly constructed divine and legal strictures forbidding same-sex intimacies and cross-dressing. In doing so, this narrator reevaluates such supposedly degraded pleasures by appropriating for them the exalted symbolism of the church and a religiously influenced state. Rechy thereby formulates angelic outlaws circulating in cruising areas and in drag into manifestations of bad beatitudes as his characters acquire an unconventional grace through reimagining ostensibly profane and criminal actions as sanctifying. This enables his characters to think beyond religious promises of salvation after death and beyond a spiritual or legal sense of justice or morality to pursue what self-validating pleasures they can while alive and in US underworlds.

To complement this analysis of Rechy, I expand the period of time under consideration by showing how Countée Cullen, Langston Hughes, and especially Richard Bruce Nugent deploy angelic characters in order to exalt the generally marginalized same-sex desires of both masculine and effeminate mixed-race men with predominantly African American identities. In this second chapter, "Richard Bruce Nugent's Angelic Erotics: Rebellious Spirits in Multiracial Same-Sex Romances," I argue that while these writers resonate with Rechy, they more emphatically expand a Miltonian and Blakean angelic-ness to encompass a more detailed picture of the tense multiracial makeup of the United States and its queer populations. More covertly in early Renaissance writers such as Cullen and more overtly in later writers such as Nugent, these authors evolved a spiritualized angelic rhetoric to admire the nobility of critically rebellious, queer African American men, with Nugent explicitly extending his critique beyond discrete categories of race and color. Indeed, I show how Nugent, in particular, uses a spiritualized angelic rhetoric to reassess same-sex desiring and gender nonconforming men from across the racial and color spectrum of US citizens, from African- to Puerto Rican- to Italian-Americans, who pursue mutual erotic intimacies. He does so to recast multiracial and sexual outlaws as morally valuable and brave, despite their allegedly degraded, decadent, or vice-ridden circumstances. He evolves this angelic literary trope to insist on the hybridity of modern American identities, which merge and keep in tension the complications and the insufficiencies of diametric terms such as macho and effeminate, normal and queer, black and white, pagan and civilized, familiar and foreign, and even monogamous and promiscuous. In doing so, Nugent presents sympathetic reinterpretations of rebel angels who challenge and transcend the status quo of a conservative, ostensibly religious US culture in the pursuit of a noble individuality and of more tolerant and varied forms of same-sex romantic relationships and gender expressions.

In Chapter 3, "Allen Ginsberg's Angelic Economies: Sex, Spirituality, and a Queer Anti-Imperialism," I change tracks slightly to foreground the economic and anti-imperialist connotations of queer angels raised in the previous two chapters. Ginsberg, like Rechy and Nugent, uses queer angels to imagine how an unconventional morality can emerge from a conventionally profane spiritual eroticism just as normative forms of religious and social sanctity can themselves become profane as they trample on unconventional but consensual same-sex sexual encounters. Yet whereas Rechy uses queer angels to emphasize rebellions against external and internal homophobic oppressions and Nugent to critique diverse same-sex relationships amid cultural and state-sponsored racism, Ginsberg focuses on how such erotic spiritual intimacies can encourage a rejection of the aggressive heteronormative and patriarchal Judeo Christian economics of the American middle classes. In doing so, he connects same-sex desires to the freedom to reject the exploitative socioeconomic exchanges underpinned by America's excessive capitalism and imperialistic overreaching. While Rechy and Nugent also touch on such topics, I refocus economic issues here by analyzing Ginsberg's queer socioeconomic critiques from across his long public career, which stretches from the mid-1950s until his death in 1997. Ginsberg, I argue, imagines an eroticized angelic mysticism drawn from Jewish and Christian literary traditions, as well as his own version of Buddhism, to fashion a rhetoric that merges equitable economic exchanges with nonviolent erotic and spiritual exchanges. In *Howl and Other Poems* and *Kaddish and Other Poems* and in his less-studied yet still valuable later work, Ginsberg connects spiritually joyful and mutually beneficial same-sex encounters to rebellions against self-destructively avaricious capitalist excesses, particularly a mechanically unspiritual American imperialism at work both at home in the United States and abroad.

Rechy, Nugent, and Ginsberg all developed angelic outlaws to value men who rebelled against conventional religious, legal, social, and even medical repressions of same-sex desires and gender nonconformities, and in my final chapter, I explore how such themes work in literary bad beatitudes that address the traumas of HIV/AIDS. In "Angels amid Affliction: Angelic Immigrants and an Expansive Americanism in the Era of HIV/AIDS," I explore how the rhetoric of bad beatitudes shifted as writers struggled to make sense of an often senseless influx of pain and death. To conceptualize the effects of the virus, these writers often infused eroticized human bodies with spiritual graces alongside and even at times because of these bodies' physical sickness. They insisted on the spiritual and physical value of sick queer individuals and of the caretakers of sick friends and lovers by imagining both groups as courageous angelic outlaws. Rather than naively idealizing or romanticizing illness, these authors use angelic tropes to acknowledge the physical, mental, and spiritual fortitude and the communal ties that developed through fighting the disease, fighting unhelpful authority figures, and fighting a larger, often uncaring American society. After outlining the empowering prevalence of angelic tropes in HIV/AIDS era literature, with a focus on how angelic images evoke a spirituality achieved through pursuing rather than avoiding psychologically disturbing and physically dangerous sex in the 1980s and 1990s, I focus my discussion on Rabih Alameddine's *Angel of History*. Alameddine, I argue, engages HIV/AIDS to evoke how memories of repression, shame, and the destruction of queer bodies signal why queer individuals must prevent these traumatic memories from overtaking queer joys in the present and in an imagined future. At stake in such slippages of memory, Alameddine insists, are conceptions of citizenship in both the national population and more localized queer communities, as queer people living with or alongside those with HIV/AIDS get caught in battles over recalling or remembering who has what rights within any body politic. Mainstream responses to HIV/AIDS in the United States, Alameddine suggests, too often fashioned queer individuals as analogous to unwanted immigrants, outcasting both demonized groups from institutional and legal socioeconomic protections. Queer affirming responses to the virus, conversely, encouraged effected and certainly infected individuals to reimagine painfully and pleasurably hybrid, never monolithic national and subcultural identities—identities that despite all the suffering refused to abandon the potential for spirituality within queer physical pleasures.

Through his analysis of pain and pleasure in the era of HIV/AIDS, Alameddine's novel offers an ambivalent, even melancholic analysis of queer life in our contemporary US society. I want to maintain this melancholy and yet emphasize a cautious optimism regarding queer inclusions in almost all facets of our emerging conceptions of Americanism. To close this study then, I offer a brief conclusion, "Angelic Anxieties and Outlaw Expectations," which functions primarily as an ambivalent and arbitrary endpoint. As the angelic outlaw trope continues to resonate in queer literature, art, porn, and culture, and I see no reason why it will not, it will sustain its role as a key component of queer bad beatitudes. While having to search for the sacred or beautiful in the profane and the sordid is undoubtedly a sign of troubled times, I cannot help but think that hoping to establish, much less to enforce, any *too* stable notion of the profane or the sacred, or the ugly and the beautiful, would present its own problems and tyrannies, which would then themselves have to be rebelled against. As such, literary bad beatitudes, while inevitably a sign of religious, medical, legal, and social failures to understand the diverse values of humanity, are also a sign of cultural, aesthetic, and erotic strengths. If this latter is the case, then I hope to keep finding queer angelic outlaws in writing, painting, and film.

1

John Rechy's Angelic Outlaws: Surviving the Desire for Salvation

In a heightened scene in *Millennium Approaches*, Tony Kushner's misguided Louis claims that "there are no angels in America, no spiritual past, no racial past, there's only the political," only human interactions (2014: 96). Louis, as it turns out, is wrong. In Kushner's play, angels are in America and they are militantly conservative, denouncing migration, invention, and minority equity, including for people of color and with HIV/AIDS. Louis is also wrong, if more metacritically so, as US literature is rife with angels, specifically with angelic outlaws who challenge any such conservative stasis by advocating for the progressive economic, social, and queer politics that Kushner himself champions in his humanist heroes Prior Walter and Belize. Kushner's dramatic representation of an angelic stasis thus counterpoints a notable trend of post-1945 US literature, one that manifests an overtly forward-looking and leftist sociopolitical angelic agenda. One influential example is Allen Ginsberg's *Howl* (1955), wherein "angelheaded hipsters" seek human connections that challenge conservative middle-class family ideals (2007: 134). These angelic hipsters achieve this by getting "fucked in the ass by saintly motorcyclists," as they "screamed" not with pain but "with joy," acquiring cross-class, gender nonconforming, and nonreproductive pleasures for free (136). Ginsberg's queer angelic contexts evoke healthy beneficial communions linked not to straight-laced conventions but to a more openly inclusive American sexual culture. Presenting two poles of a metaphoric spectrum, Kushner's angels, which offer a conservative reimagining of Walter Benjamin's backward-looking "angel of history," represent elite conformists pushing for a hierarchical stasis, while Ginsberg's angels embody ecstatic advocates for the sanctification of diverse queer individuals (1968: 257).

Ginsberg and Kushner help both to illuminate and to bookend the largely overlooked queer trope that I discussed in this book's introduction: namely, the rise of queer angels' associations with left-leaning spiritual, sexual, racial, and socioeconomic politics in the 1950s and the evolution of these figures as a means to consider the trauma of HIV/AIDS in the late twentieth and early twenty-first centuries. As quasi-divine figures fashioned in often beautiful human forms, angels represent most clearly a blurring bridge between divinity and humanity. In doing so, they refigure the often degrading identifier "fairy," and, thanks to John Milton and William Blake, they come with a venerable literary tradition that messily encompasses both collaborators with and rebels against divine and secular repressions.[1] In US literature of this period, authors often expanded such a unique mixture of sacred and profane angelic imagery, with its quasi-inclusive, quasi-salvific associations, to fashion certain queer characters, primarily gay men, as embodiments of what I call bad beatitudes. By "bad beatitudes," I mean states-of-being that embody an unconventional grace obtained through engaging and reconceptualizing conventionally degrading behaviors or identities, such as same-sex sex or nonconformist genders. Same-sex sex, for instance, could spark a sense of degradation as well as a noble, transcendent, and lasting pleasure only achievable for a queer man with another queer man. This behavior then creates a hybrid state-of-being in which the conventionally profane signals the unconventionally sacred and the conventionally sacred signals the unconventionally profane, with both inverted concepts held in tension in the minds of the participants and of their subculture. While in subsequent chapters I discuss this trope in works by Countée Cullen, Langston Hughes, Richard Bruce Nugent, followed by a closer look at Ginsberg, and then Rabih Alameddine, I want to start with a discussion of John Rechy. While chronologically, Rechy fits somewhere between all these writers, his influential conception of an "Outlaw Sensibility" (1991) and its earlier manifestations in his first novel *City of Night* (1963) provide a fine framework for understanding the proliferation of queer angels in their conservative and their rebellious embodiments in US literature from the second half of the twentieth century.

Rechy is also a useful case study because, like Ginsberg and Kushner, he not only valuably queers past literary traditions regarding sacred and secular virtues but his writing can also inform current critiques of queer communities across the United States. While scholars such as John Howard and Scott Herring have advanced studies in rural US queer cultures, contemporary critics continue to build on early investigations into the varieties of post–Second World War queer urbanities and their relationship to normative cultures, from Martin Levine's elucidation of macho "clones" to Marlon Bailey's investigation of queer black balls to Jack Halberstam's investigations into butch and trans subjectivities. These communities and their skirmishes with normative societies can all find some resonance with those that Rechy reimagines in an "Outlaw Sensibility" and in *City of Night*. Indeed, scholars have long emphasized the ways in which Rechy portrays such diverse queer subcultures interacting with each other and with the larger heteronormative urban world. Steven Ruszczycky, for instance, has highlighted how Rechy depicts a "racially mixed conglomerate of drag queens, dykes, gay men, runaways, hustlers, and scores," all persecuted by homophobic police, to emphasize the ethical problems inherent in queer "subcultures of leather and kinky sex" that perversely fetishize such repressive authorities (2014: 232). Ruszczycky usefully extends early critiques of how Rechy fashioned queer communities into a metaphor for American neuroses writ large. Fifty years prior, for example, Stanton Hoffman argued that in *City of Night* the "'gay world' and all its parts," such as "queens" and patrons of any given "queer bar," "overwhelm not only the possibility of any relationship implying [individual] human involvement" but also serve "as a metaphor for a destructive and despair ridden American reality." Painting with too broad a brush, Hoffman argues that the "America" of Rechy's first novel presents "the possibility of a vast hell always defining a smaller and intense personal hell" (1964: 195–6). While this argument may hold true for passages, to understand Rechy's complex interest in tyrannical forms of secular and religious, external and internal repressions, we must also notice how he fashions noble rebels who defy such historical constraints and who angelically bring out heavenly virtues even in unjustly hellish US circumstances. These figures are Rechy's angelic outlaws and he uses them to signal a particular version of the larger cultural manifestations that I have been calling bad beatitudes.

The Bad Beatitudes of Angelic Outlaws in "The Outlaw Sensibility" and *City of Night*

In "The Outlaw Sensibility," Rechy critically considers how two key figures in his writing from *City of Night* onward, angels and outlaws, can signal the profane sublimity of queer rebels who consciously reject religious, social, and political repressions. In an inverted Miltonic vein, Lucifer and his angels serve as Rechy's first examples of heroically admirable outlaws.[2] "Were Lucifer and his band of angels," Rechy wonders, "the first questioning outlaws, defying autocracy and the decreed singing of assigned hymns?" (2004: 150). The "outlaw sensibility" that Rechy describes via Lucifer first questions and then resists absolutism as well as any imposed artistic expressions that might buttress the spiritual, social, and political repressions of a despot. Additionally, Lucifer signals Rechy's sense that any true outlaw must consciously and proudly choose to resist tyranny: "Defiance, pride, choice to remain estranged, an acceptance of risks, a constant questioning of limiting assumptions" are vital to any self-determining outlaw. While this sensibility risks confusing an outlaw with a mundane "criminal," Rechy argues that one must consider any broad imputation of criminality or sacrilege in light of "limiting" or unjust statutes. This is especially so considering that Rechy's outlaw sensibility insists on a "nobility of intention, respect for the individual life, and, in the artist as outlaw, a dedication to unique creativity" (151). Rather than breaking laws for financial gain or rebelling without a cause, much less due to an innate immorality, Rechy's outlaw represents a culturally contested and yet graciously determined morality founded upon a combination of tolerance for individual self-fashioning and for uncensored creative efforts. As such, if from a conventional perspective Rechy's outlaws appear to be degenerate criminals, with this metaphorical use of religious terminology they become unexpectedly angelic. They become analogous to those whom Rechy labels "*beatas*," people proximate to the "glamorous … angels," who exist on the "peripheries" of Hispanic Catholicism and evoke not dogma but the mysterious "wonder" of the world, of an exalted material life (156, 157).

Usefully, this blurring of boundaries, which risks confusing a principled outlaw with a common criminal, and an angelic *beata*, signals how Rechy capitalizes on the instability of cultural conceptions of morality and legality or sacredness and profaneness to promote a respect for human diversity. Thus while certain outlaws' "nobility of intention, respect for the individual life," and "dedication to unique creativity" are socially lauded and at times even sacred virtues, outlaws can leverage these virtues to question and to reject "laws" that are "wrong" or "repressive" of individual life and innovation. To rebel against immoral laws, these outlaws often employ subversive tactics such as "infiltration," "sabotage," and "camouflage." While these tactics risk veering into what Rechy calls "collaboration" with authoritarianism, they also enable outlaws to reveal contradictions or conflicts in accepted religious and civic ideals, particularly when such ideals as morality and immorality or freedom and oppression are taken to an extreme, as in the contexts of heaven and hell (2004: 151). Lucifer's rebellion, for instance, infiltrates religious aesthetic traditions as he uses his role as a chief angel in God's chorus to promote liberty and as in doing so he becomes an epic liberal hero who evidences and then challenges God's autocracy and his divine repression of alternative art forms, creating his own version of heaven in hell. Lucifer's and his angels' decisive, noble resistances initially sabotage heaven via camouflage as these rebels use their beauty, their theological reasoning, and their liberal individualism to blur sacrilege and virtue until they overtly reject God. These angelic outlaws serve Rechy well because they evoke contradictory or paradoxical images of gorgeous, blessed beings rebelling against an unjust and selfish authority by appropriating merits it reserved for itself, such as power, self-determination, and creative independence. Rechy uses such subversive angelic outlaws across his writing to reconceptualize superficially monolithic and discrete notions of morality and immorality, of beauty and ugliness, of satisfaction and suffering, of community and alienation, of power and impotence, and of salvation and degradation, particularly in the context of allegedly profane and nominally criminal queer rebellions against sexual and gender norms.

Indeed, to characterize more abstract outlaw rebellions in twentieth-century contexts, Rechy connects them to queer and to Hispanic minorities, which he argues have drawn productively on contradictory or blurred conceptions of virtue and vice. Rechy refers to a "gay sensibility" and a "Hispanic sensibility" partly because he was "personally familiar" with them, but also because they inform his conception of an admirable "outlaw" (2004: 155).[3] These sensibilities manifest an analogously rebellious hybridity, one evidenced by iconic images that sustain cultural tensions, sometimes "reconciled" and sometimes not. Such a hybridity comes to the fore in the prominent combination of "muscles and mascara," pointed signs of masculinity and femininity in the queer community, or in Hispanic Catholic churches' images of "blood drenched statues of saints writhing in exhibitionistic agony, bodies stripped only when they're suffering," a mixture of anguish and eroticism, which "glamorous ... angels" watched over, a convergence of tropes that merges and holds separate glamour and degradation (155, 156). Masculinity and femininity, sanctity and profanity, mortification and elevation held in tension, courting and resisting synthesis, all generate the hybridity of outlaws, especially those angelically queer outlaws who for much of the twentieth century defied simplistic binaries of sex and gender and engaged in diverse sexual practices that brought agony and ecstasy along with connection and exile due to their noble violations of repressive religious beliefs and secular regulations.

"The Outlaw Sensibility" usefully clarifies and reaffirms Rechy's earlier fictional analysis of such an outlaw hybridity in *City of Night*, wherein he depicts same-sex desiring and gender-nonconforming hustlers as angelic outlaws, tortuously alienated from salvific, civic, and social rituals. The narrator of *City of Night*, a queer hustler, serves as an especially poignant outlaw because he represents what Rafael Pérez-Torres refers to as a "doubly marginalized position," an echo of Rechy's phrase "dual outsiders," for he engages with the margins of and yet remains alienated from the center of both hetero- and homo-normativity, for instance, queer circles that seek relationships based on middle-class straight ideals (Rechy 1989: 157; Pérez-Torres 1994: 209). This very marginality, though, inspires the heroic element of Rechy's characters, who illustrate what Zamora has called Rechy's "motif of *non serviam*," such as the narrator's refusal to conform to religious or social repressions, despite their attractive safety, due to "his commitment—heroic in its dimensions in view of the odds arrayed against the possibility of its realization—to life in its fullness as that-which-ought-to-be" in a world attenuated by death and decay (1979: 57). More seekers of new moralities and new freedoms than sinners or criminals, Rechy's queer outlaws, predominantly men, enact a self-affirming transcendence through their flaws and through wounds acquired during their willful, often proud exile from an unjust society. By depicting these men in angelic contexts, Rechy works to reevaluate these characters' supposedly degraded pleasures by appropriating for them the exalted symbolism of the absolutist tyrannies that these communities chose to rebel against for denying their individual desires. Rechy thereby formulates angelic outlaws into manifestations of bad beatitudes as these characters acquire an unconventional grace through reimagining ostensibly profane or nominally sinful actions as sanctifying while revealing queer-phobic laws to be immorally repressive.

Angelic outlaws situated throughout *City* also offer a substantive structuring motif that Rechy uses to critique and to valorize a multitude of queer characters as they veer between self-destructively collaborating with and more heroically rebelling against repressions of counterculture identities. Collaborating, for instance, with even a loosely Catholic notion of divine salvation too often brings disappointment. For, as Rechy has suggested elsewhere, "[w]hen we pull away from religion," rejecting too tyrannically limiting creeds, we discover that there is "no substitute for salvation," no precise replacement for the stable completeness of a sacred elevation into a heavenly community however ultimately dehumanizing (qtd. in Rechy 2003: 42). Rechy uses angelic figures in *City* to critique how inadvertently collaborationist queer characters too facilely transfer the idealism of a divine salvation to injuriously intoxicating fantasies of perpetual youthfulness, economic power, drugs and drink, or purgatorial sadomasochistic encounters, which can only briefly redeem one from isolation and loneliness. These substitutes never pan out because the characters' conception of idealism stems from either a despotic divine inertia that destroys the living individual that it promises to save or from the fantasy of an impossibly perfect fulfilment of egotistic desires, which proves unsustainable. Moving beyond conceptions of a stable divine salvation allows for a more earthly self-determination, including new communities and enjoyments of queer sexual pleasures and nonconforming gender identities.

As such, if there is no strict substitute for divine salvation, a radical revision of its imagery can conceptualize a more humanistic, more individualistic consolation or even aspiration. In response to critics of Rechy's "sensational" countercultural themes, Ben Satterfield once argued that "Rechy is a moralist" who reveals "the absolute necessity of love in a world without [divine] redemption, a world of franticness and death" (1982: 79). I agree, but to take Satterfield's argument one step further, Rechy in fact uses a sensational queerness to highlight how human desires can manifest a new form of redemption, one that makes the world less self-destructive and more vital. For if angelic associations can misleadingly camouflage self-destructive intoxications as a heavenly "salvation," when this seduction proves tragically compromised outlaws can use angelic characterizations, replete with their images of human bodies in glorified contexts, as a critical symbolism that can be levered to break off morality or glory from divinity in order to attach them to more individualistic validations of human beauty, of same-sex encounters, and of queer genders. If these virtues risk inspiring self-destructive excesses, for instance, a healthy love of male beauty degraded into an obsession with fading youth, these queer angelic characterizations can still inspire nobler rebellions that stimulate a self-love and a love of others. Even Rechy's tragic queer characters exemplify how seeking an impossibly perfect fulfilment of egotistic desires or turning from more affirmative validations of queer lives inevitably undermines actually achievable, more pragmatically partial fulfillments or redemptions of the value of marginalized human lives. Rechy uses his most successful angelic queer outlaws then to celebrate inevitably yet usefully imperfect hopes for peace, community, and happiness.

Angelic Outlaws in *City of Night*

In the prologue to Part One of *City of Night*, Rechy quickly introduces his first angelic figures as emasculated embodiments of a static and failed religious ideal. Rechy has his unnamed narrator recall a cabinet in his family home in El Paso that his mother had kept since his childhood and that contains "figurines of angels, Virgins," and "dolls." Reflecting on that cabinet, the narrator notes, he recalls his mother as "a ghost image that will haunt" him perpetually (2013: 21). This memory evokes a recurrent tepid echo of an immemorial Catholic beatitude, a ghostly enervation of the epic stature of the "glamorous … angels" presiding over torture and ecstasy that Rechy himself remembered from Hispanic Catholic churches. In the novel, the figurines sit impotently closed off from a small domestic world in a container that resembles a reliquary or even a prison. The "Virgins" imprisoned with the angels indicate a willful naiveté regarding sexuality, while the "dolls" evoke a juvenile context that merges sacred objects with the half-remembered toys of a loved but aging, superstitious guardian. These figurines unintentionally undermine religious seriousness and authority.

This memory likewise connects these angels to the narrator's mother, herself a representative of imperfect religious nurturing as she could never quite protect her son from his father's sexual abuse and violence. The narrator's father would occasionally "fondle" the young boy and allow his timeworn friends to do so too (2013: 21–2). The father would also grow violent, as when he forced his children to help set up a Christmas nativity scene complete with its "angels on angelhair clouds" until someone made a mistake and the arrangement fell apart and the father would fall into a "rage" throwing tools and shouting (22). The mother retaining these angel figurines at home highlights the ineffectual, antiquated religious ideals of gender hierarchies and parental authority, which actually hinder the religious older generation's ability to safeguard or to guide its children sufficiently. Indeed, Rechy has lamented how the Catholic Church had held his own mother a "prisoner" and had "stifled" her creativity and any will "to get out of [her] marriage" to his father. This stifling, Rechy suggests, connected to church officials' "hypocritical attitudes toward sexuality," which provide "the major cause for sexual repression," particularly "feelings of antihomosexuality" (Casillo 2002: 53). This context for the novel's angelic figurines highlights the repressions that will cause the narrator in *City* to revolt by reimagining the religious imagery that haunted him from his childhood.

Throughout the novel, the narrator's conjoined recollections of angels and of his mother offer a comfortingly familiar yet repressive ideology, one that "haunt[s]" him even as he reimagines it to validate his own same-sex desires. As such, Rechy shapes a nameless narrator who, despite drawing on his Catholic Hispanic heritage and the marginalized queer contexts of his time, represents an "everyman" reflective of many queer individuals', really many individuals' desire to be desired combined with fears of vulnerability due to loving someone else. Rechy reinforces this tension with the narrator repeatedly longing for and yet rejecting images of his mother resting near her cabinet with the "angel figures…"

as she hopes to repossess her son (2013: 166). Rechy's use of ellipses evokes an unsuccessful reclamation by this mother's fierce but inevitably imperfect love, itself a "ghost image" of the failed perfection of a divine maternal love, akin to a mater dolorosa, whose angelic entourage remains feebly enclosed behind her. The narrator rejects these maternal and divine authorities, in part because of their stagnancy and failed promises, such as for protection and a convincing route to salvation, and in part because they implicitly stifle his same-sex desires and his career as a male hustler. The narrator's hustling career provides him with an enjoyable freedom for exploration and for self-fashioning. He repeatedly leaves home to search for the self-determination to make the most of his youth through sexual encounters and to find "some substitute for salvation," some salvation that seems actually achievable and worthwhile (28). The narrator's repeated recollections nonetheless emphasize a troubling longing for these domesticated Catholic angelic contexts, with their connotations, however misleading, of peace, stability, and deliverance from tribulation.

Pointedly, Rechy connects these depictions of the narrator's childhood home, dominated by a moribund repressive religiosity, to grander and queerer versions of a despotic angelic stagnancy across the United States. Indeed, from early in his composition process, Rechy used tropes of angelic representatives of tyranny and rebellious angelic outlaws to give order and an epic distinction to the narrator's chaotic, picaresque journey from El Paso through queer underworlds in New York, Los Angeles, New Orleans, and elsewhere. Discussing early revisions, Rechy recalls sitting on a roof in Los Angeles, smoking weed and listening to church bells tolling, as he reconsidered the structure of an early excerpt that described the drag queen Miss Destiny's craving for an ornate wedding. These musings conjured a "frozen" world that reminded Rechy of a childhood game in which one player would throw the others about, releasing them without notice and causing them to "freeze" wherever they happened to fall, although players would always resituate their bodies "for effect." The confluence of these stimuli—the weed, the church bells, and the recollected "statues" game—inspired Rechy to revise this excerpt around a perfidious image representing an "entrapping angel" who served as the thrower in a fictional version of the "statues" game. This image, he notes, had existed out of sight, in the back of his mind, and in revisions he wanted to bring it to the forefront to signal Miss Destiny's impeded dreams. As such, Rechy rewrote the excerpt, investing the relevant passages with the form of this game and reordering the scenes to have Miss Destiny fear the advent of this horrific angel (2013: 5–6). While an ostensibly permanent situation determined by marriage or by a divine representative might offer a comforting certainty, in Rechy's revisions this "entrapping angel" suggests a violent fate that unilaterally throws marginalized individuals, such as Miss Destiny, into uncomfortable positions and expects them to stay there, much like the narrator's mother's attempts to reclaim her son for her home or like God's expectation that Lucifer stay subordinated in Heaven. Lucifer, of course, refused to stay put, and pragmatically rearranging himself "for effect," he took his own imperfect independence in Hell, providing an angelic archetype for Miss Destiny's rebellious desires.

Indeed, in the finished novel, Rechy's narrator emphasizes Miss Destiny's angelic resistance to a divinely ordained fate that threatens to limit her social and intellectual aspirations. Soon after the narrator meets Miss Destiny in LA, she tells him that at certain moments when she is extremely stoned and hanging out in one of the local queer dive bars or on one of the cruising avenues, she pictures "an angel" that arrives unexpectedly and declares, in a perverse annunciation, that an apocalypse is coming, with the result that "Heaven or Hell" shall constitute existing in perpetuity exactly as one happens to be existing at that moment and in one's exact present environment with one's exact present companions. Rebelliously trying to rearrange herself, Miss Destiny describes how she envisions herself fleeing but this "evil angel" spots her and restrains her where she is (2013: 142). Miss Destiny has been to "College" and longs for a glamorous intellectual queer life, being particularly fond of discussing "Shakespeare" and his cross-dressing leading ladies, whom she sees as predecessors to her own drag or trans existence, and she fears being stuck in the cruising spaces in which she now circulates, such as the dive bars with their patrons "searching" for love and one-night stands or the "frantic" world of cruising parks filled with other effeminate men and "vagrant" prostitutes who hope that someone will pick them up, or even her own apartment filled during debauched nights with people whom she considers, at times, to be "*tuh-rash!*" (141, 132, 122, 124). Miss Destiny detests the idea of existing perpetually in these spaces even as she knows that in them she can live her life most freely, dressed in women's clothing without getting hassled or arrested due to sartorial laws, and in which she can search for a man to whom she might be espoused via a wonderful "wedding," a ceremony that wondrously and improbably promises a permanent love (135).[4] The angel's cruelty stems then not from a judgment against her gender variance or same-sex desires, as the angel even acknowledges that for some people these queer places might be "Heaven" (143). The angel's cruelty stems from enacting a permanency that will lock Miss Destiny into a life that cannot progress, sticking her with places and with people belonging to only one leg of her journey to refine her independent identity, and it is this enforced inertia that she rebelliously protests.

Notably, however, Rechy balances Miss Destiny's fear of inertia with a clear value of the Shakespearean cross-dressing and even revised Miltonian relativities that LA's cruising grounds enable. Recalling Satan's realization in *Paradise Lost* that the "mind is its own place, and in itself / can make a Heav'n of Hell, a Hell of Heav'n,'" Rechy's narrator insists on the comparative benefits of his underworld. One dive bar, for instance, is filled with "trapped exiles" and yet it also provides a relatively safe space in which to drink, to socialize, and even to seek sex work for diverse "queens," for overtly effeminate men, and for the male hustlers, who outside it are "fugitives" from the mainstream lives of the outside world and the smaller town from which they came (2013: 125). LA's Main Street is similarly a place to find work and for "queens" from small towns and generally more intolerant rural American regions to promenade in pursuit of their particular type of "sexplay" and of their hope for a "permanent" relationship, as well as a place for hustlers to enjoy a sexual "anarchy" that embraces their intense physical desirability (124). Lastly, Pershing Square, where the narrator first sees Miss Destiny, provides a relatively safe space for her to joke and to talk with friends while "swishing" around as she fashions her feminine persona and chats up passing men (123). Refusing to idealize this underworld, Rechy describes how these spaces often evoke "[t]error," "depression," and "guilt" and that personal connections made there are rarely "permanent"; but he also indicates how in visiting these environments his male characters seize the opportunity to cross-dress, to find a quasi-welcoming community, and to pursue diverse same-sex encounters, all behaviors that normative social and legal restrictions would deny to them (221, 42, 136, 124). As such, the very degradation of these spaces and their inhabitants becomes mitigated and revalued, in however qualified a fashion. If the grime, terrors, and marginality of such spaces add to Miss Destiny's and her associates' frequent depression and loneliness, these outlaws also achieve a rebellious euphoria by returning to such venues to find greater possibilities for self-reformations, for erotic pleasures, and concomitantly for forging meaningful romantic connections unavailable to them in the mainstream world.

These very values of course often inspire a desire for still more freedom, and so bolstering her revolutionary fervor with the sartorial and erotic subversiveness valued in this outlaw community, Miss Destiny imagines resisting the angel's paralyzing decree and actively invading heaven in order to challenge a static divine will. After a night at the bars, Miss Destiny invites her companions to her apartment, which allows the queens enough privacy to change into more complete drag. Inspired by putting on a defiantly resplendent evening dress, and by regret for her home's squalor and her company's unintellectual banter, Miss Destiny reveals her own plan to invert notions of the sacred and the profane by refuting the hell of the crude surroundings in which she fears God's "evil angel" will stick her forever. Lamenting her position to the narrator, she shows off her new beautiful clothing, then decries the shabbiness of her present environment, and announces her fear that she will get stuck there. So rejecting this as an eternal option for herself, she declares that at some point wearing "the most lavish drag" one can imagine, she will "storm heaven and protest!" insisting on her existence to celestial hierarchies as she will "shake [her] beads" toward God causing the divinity to "cringe!"[5] Inversely imitating God's angel's invasion of earth, Miss Destiny imagines herself as her own avenging angel who will defy heaven, succeeding where Lucifer failed. Her drag and her insistence will become an aggressive armor that will force God to "cringe," to recoil from her, and thereby to cede her some room, if only in a limited fashion. Although exhibiting a "franticness" that the narrator intuits is produced by her own horrific isolation and alienation, Miss Destiny imagines an active rebellion against a world that should but that does not allow her to pursue her glamorous femininity, her sexual interests, and her desire for intellectual social peers all at once (2013: 144). In the meantime, she takes what pleasure she can in her dramatic dress within surroundings that she hopes will be a stepping stone to a more sophisticated worldly life.

If Miss Destiny's implied elevation into an attacking, self-avenging angel inverts the narrator's flight from his mother's religious home, it also echoes the narrator's earlier encounter with a Professor in New York who aggrandizes his hiring beautiful hustlers by referring to them as angels. Like Miss Destiny, the Professor suffers from a near debilitating loneliness and he hopes to thwart this fate, but whereas she uses angelic rebellions to counter an inhuman freezing of humans' self-fashioning, this bedridden intellectual imagines himself as consorting with angels to camouflage his commercialized eroticism. "God," the Professor laments, "deals out" human "destinies," and he laments that his fate was to manifest a particularly unattractive and physically undesirable body. The Professor thwarts the romantic loneliness that his fated unsightliness produces by pursuing what he calls "Interviews" with the hustlers to whom he gives labels such as "earthangel" or "Guardian" "angels" (2013: 77, 84, 76). These angelic characterizations draw partly on what María DeGuzmán identifies as a "Swedenborgian sentimentalism," a theological "rhetoric about love and the central notion of people as angels," and partly on beautiful and rebellious

Miltonic and Blakean angels (2014: 130). The Professor adapts these theological and literary contexts to distract from the economic nature of his encounters with prostitutes by valorizing their relationships as loving, ennobling, and beautiful rebellions against the unjust gambler-like "deal[ings]" of God.

This angelic rhetoric also cloaks the Professor's own sophisticated egotism. He conceives of these grandiose "Interviews" as transcendentally tender relationships between himself and each individual "angel," which over time coalesce into a pseudo-sanctified congregation of desirable men with himself as a regal intermediary. He tries to understand these angelic hustlers "intimately," he tells the narrator, and he discusses with each allegorical angel the additional angels whom he has encountered so that each young man has a sense of the Professor's own experiences and so that the Professor has a sort of imaginary brotherhood of angels about himself. The Professor imagines, moreover, that these young men fashion a dreamlike "angel-crown" for himself, as he thinks when being "poetic." With this "poetic" license, the Professor claims that these "intimat[e]" nominal "interviews" allow himself and his angels to examine each other in depth through shared psychological explorations, but in practice they center on his own importance rather than on a shared knowing or an actual reciprocal familiarity (2013: 78, 77). The Professor, for instance, dominates his sessions with the narrator by lecturing about his travels, his philosophies, and the previous boys he has bought. He fashions a masturbatory intellectual monologue, after which he fellates the narrator and then dismisses him. Exchanging money for temporary intimacies that he directs, the Professor camouflages his commodified connections by imaging himself as gloriously exalted by his collected community of "angels."

While occasionally acknowledging the ridiculous pompousness of this mythology, the Professor nonetheless argues that these angelic encounters serve as real rebellions against any uncritical conceptions of God. If the Professor intermittently cuts his sublime egotistical talk with subtly self-deprecating banalities, as when he refers haltingly to "what I—uh—Like—To—Do," a queer allusion to preferred sexual acts that is so crudely clichéd that after saying it he "giggled" in a sophomoric fashion, he predominantly considers himself a serious rebel against illogical and dangerously estranging notions of divinity (2013: 78). He argues to the narrator, for instance, that our earthly surroundings easily refute any conventional faith in a "good God" and so we reject God, whereas if contemporary humanity had developed a faith in an "evil" chief divinity then our surroundings would support our faith in such a God as well as cause us to reject this God, "rebelling" but in such a way that might lead us to a more humanistic "Good" (83). The Professor claims that humanity rejects God as unbelievable when it perceives Him as benevolent because so much avoidable horror, pain, and viciousness exist in the world He created. This rejection can cause a perilous alienation because humanity grows confused as a traditional divine moral guidance falls short of the particular versions of a chaste, peaceful, and beneficent "Good" that it so often promises. Humans should more rationally conceive of God as vicious, the Professor argues, which should inspire them to band together to fight Him through the pursuit of a "Good" inclusive of kindness, social welfare, and sexual freedom, and even the discovery of a different deity altogether, one that might manifest a more realistic "Love" (81). A human manifestation of this ideal divinity, the Professor preaches, involves acknowledging "mutual" human surroundings and reciprocally engaging each other so as to seek out and to encounter "Love" (83). The Professor uses this second reference to loving "mutual" encounters to represent his "interviews" with the "angels" as outlaw acts that reformulate divine concepts of Good and of Love based on mutually satisfied yet differing desires, such as his desire to talk to and to touch beautiful young men, and the hustlers' desire for money and admiration. Individuals with differing desires help one another in briefly shared moments and leave one other at least partially satisfied with their exchange, which evidences one valuable form of mutual love and an outlaw morality.

If at times, of course, this moral mythology works to camouflage a reinscribed hierarchy of power, the Professor is no meek collaborator and he never comes close to attempting the cruel authoritarianism of allegedly divine and in practice state-sanctioned repressions. He constructs rather a self-centered but still relatively noble and moral rhetoric of outlaw-ship that validates both brief and long-term same-sex encounters and nonbinary genders. One overarching "immorality," the Professor argues, is the injurious concept that the majority of society labels "morality," a "morality" that cruelly forces people such as himself and desires such as his to remain hidden when they should in fact be out in the open so that they can be seen as "beautiful" and acknowledged to be not intrinsically harmful. "Why," the Professor asks, "is what I do Immoral, when it hurts no one?" (2013: 88). The Professor offers here, as Thomas Heise argues, a "heretical theology," but one that makes a humanistic moral sense (2011: 182). For compared to "poverty, repression, the blindness to beauty and sensitivity," and the covert, dishonest, and misleading trickery of any anti-queer, fascistic "vice squad!" the Professor's interactions with the angels are fairly benign (2013: 88–9).

To pay to lecture about one's life and then to fellate the auditor comes across as fairly nonthreatening on both individual and larger social levels compared to the post–Second World War US government's and society's denigrations of queerness as a conflation of sin, sickness, and crime. Quite immorally, these denigrations often helped to force unconventional pleasures and identity expressions into murky rooms or private apartments.[6] The illiberal tactics of vice squads and their associates hunted sexual and gender nonconformists even into private spaces, serving to repress and to destroy the livelihoods of the individuals whose names they could maliciously report to the public, to families, and to employers, often causing individuals who had simply sought beautiful companionships and shared pleasures to lose their social positions and their incomes.[7] If the Professor seeks primarily to satisfy his own desires, he simultaneously facilitates and exalts his angels' queer activities, at times even financing their eventual rebellion against him in pursuit of their own independent desires. The Professor consequently represents an imperfect yet still relatively admirable outlaw morality.

Still, despite advocating for this iconoclastically moral outlaw mutuality, one based upon only partly shared or reciprocal desires for sex and for money, the Professor himself longs for a comprehensively reciprocal long-term relationship. Since any substantial sharing of lives and desires is severely limited between the Professor and his young men, he tries to bridge these gaps by cloaking his favorite hustler, Robbie, with grandiose religious and literary narratives that exemplify flights from convention. Ironically, this one-sided strategy elides almost any conception of the young man as an independent being even capable of sharing and it thus replicates a divinely inspired alienating coerciveness just such as the Professor hoped to resist. Drawing upon his professional research into aesthetic reimaginings of Lucifer's rebellion against God by "Blake, Milton, [and] Dante," the Professor insists to the narrator, that when he first encountered this young hustler he identified "[t]he Archangel" (2013: 89). The Professor uses this willful misrecognition to force Robbie, a professional "call boy," into literary narratives of Luciferian "rebels" who reject "a jealous God" who gave his angels "wings" and then forced them into submission, curtailing the very privileges that he had given to them, the freedoms enabled by "Flight" (88–9). The Professor appropriates these fantastical literary re-significations by characterizing his "angels" as rebels against social taboos, religious doctrines, and even laws against same-sex encounters. This rebelliousness encourages the Professor to imagine that Robbie may also rebel against the life of a call boy. The Professor jealously insists that in their relationship this hustler shared with the Professor "his body *and* his soul" and that Robbie claimed to do so for "*love*" rather than for money, even as he shrewdly "expected" financial payment for sex, engaging in an emotionally manipulative "Robb[ery]" (92, 94, 100). Although Robbie soon claims his right of "Flight" and leaves the Professor, the latter discounts the desires of the boy he knew only superficially in favor of a procrustean literary re-signification: Robbie as the angel who sought independence from the norm and the call boy who loved his score. This allows the Professor to pretend that he and Robbie have shared the same physical, psychological, and emotional desires and that each had satisfied the other.

The Professor works hard to maintain this facade of a comprehensively mutual relationship with Robbie, but his egotistic fantasy finally proves not only false but masochistic. Despite having not seen Robbie in person for several "years," the Professor frequently invokes Robbie as his "Guardian Angel" and claims that in return he himself remains "Loyal," evidenced by his refusing to pay other angels more than Robbie's old rate (2013: 95, 76, 90). This carefully imagined spiritual and financial constancy between the men, however, breaks down when the Professor, sick and fatigued, reports "dully" that he has heard that Robbie works presently in an LA "bar" (95). By admitting that Robbie would rather work in a bar than be with him, the Professor effectively dulls the angelic glory of their relationship. He reveals the pain this causes when after having clasped the narrator to him only to have the narrator reactively shove him off, an echo of Robbie's flight, the elder man asserts himself as more than simply a score, the narrative figure into which his angels conceptually force him. The Professor demands that the narrator read his resume, which includes his diplomatic positions, awarded distinctions, "publications in scholarly reviews," and other writings, and he insists that this is part of his life as well and that in the larger world he is "Admired" and able to command the attention of a public audience, even if the hustlers he hires have no clear interest in these sorts of achievements. The Professor laments that although he has an international and institutional reputation for political, intellectual, and literary achievements, the hustlers consider him only as the "ridiculous" figure who paid them so that he could fellate them (99). At times then the Professor recognizes that rather than share any communion with him, his angels predominantly reject any intimacy save for circumstantially coerced sex. These men needed money and so, in a logically inverted fashion, they "drained" it from the Professor and accepted his lust but, he cries, they never tried to know him as a complete human being (100). As the Professor realizes, his attempts to actualize a complete or even a partial mutuality with these hustlers consistently fail to achieve his ideals. These failures, moreover, only intensify his pain, humiliation, and self-denigration as he feels his accomplishments repeatedly shorn off from his own private and public identity.

Rechy goes on to show how, worse still, the Professor allows his angelic fantasies to dissuade him from pursuing the practical possibility for a reciprocal relationship with his caretaker Larry, who sustains a sincere infatuation with him. Unlike the hustlers, Larry's involvement with the Professor goes well beyond his paid position. Having taken care to learn to discern the Professor's faintest "moods" and his fluctuating "tastes" in young men, Larry has acquired a specialized knowledge that he uses, at his own romantic expense, to please his bedridden employer by procuring "angels" for him (2013: 75). Larry seeks out the hustlers despite his "hatred" for them, which derives both from his jealousy over the Professor's desire for them and from their disregard for the great man's achievements (100). Larry himself sits perusing a substantial tome by the Professor, whom he knows has composed myriad "great" works, while the latter eagerly fellates the narrator in another room (91). Larry's attempt to share an intellectual intimacy with his employer complements his pursuit of physical contact with the older man well beyond that necessitated by a professional responsibility for his physical well-being. When the Professor briefly reveals distress at his superficial encounters with the angels, Larry "hugs" the professor, initiating the same gesture rejected by the narrator, as a means to protect him, to love him, and to be physically close to him, going so far as "kissing" him, gestures both affectionate and amorous (100). The Professor notes nonetheless that this caretaker does not count as an "angel" and that there is an "Uncomfortable" air about him (91). The Professor disparages Larry's advances in favor of brief affairs with indifferent prostitutes whom he can engage sexually, even as he realizes that they are a form of fantasy and that these angels will "fly" off to other environments and to new scores (438). This escape, however, enables the Professor to recreate them in his own narratives according to his relatively independent designs. Yet if the Professor escapes the uncomfortable risks or responsibilities of acknowledging a lover's humanity, of making oneself vulnerable, and of trying to satisfy someone else over time, his angelic illusions cost him the intellectual, emotional, and psychological pleasures of the reciprocal sharing that he so deeply desires.

Rechy details how the Professor's outlaw morality benefits and harms him, but he also describes the angels' ambivalent use of this morality as they too seek imperfect reciprocations of complementary desires. In reaction to socioeconomic circumstances partly beyond his control, Robbie, for instance, chose to create an identity that caused him to be desired without tying him to romantic responsibilities beyond his brief encounters with scores. The Professor recalls that he had met Robbie at a masquerade party where the latter wore a chic "uniform" that he had "improvised" to show off his lithe body and his seeming "purity" (2013: 82, 83). Robbie had assumed this clothing not so much as a veil or a disguise but as a form of self-fashioning akin to a priest's gown or an academic robe or a drag queen's dress. Tailored to his purpose, Robbie's costume "uniform" emphasized his social role as a fantasy, rather than a purported reality, and his very real physical desirability, the latter manifesting a "purity" despite its being used to commodify lust and sex. Robbie retained his "purity" because he honestly or virtuously signaled an "improvised" fantasy of duties, of loyalties, and of a conventional manliness designed for the precise purpose of attracting men to pay him for sex, which in turn would satisfy his own desire to be desired enough to be paid for it. This young man, the Professor explains, had fashioned his personal version of "heaven" in seeing other men appreciate and desire him, and while this might seem suspect coming from the Professor, his assessment echoes the narrator's admission of his own "craving" for other man to act upon their desire for him as he remains relatively unresponsive (90, 69). Robbie's "heaven," then, may have been an unconventional one, as it rejoiced openly in lust and sensuality, but it is not unique to him and it maintains a value precisely for being based upon an acknowledged fantasy made briefly concrete and tangible. This "heaven" then benefitted both Robbie's clients, who could pay for satisfaction, and Robbie himself who gained validation and purpose from men's lust for him without his being beholden to sustaining a long-term illusion or to a jealous partner who might inhibit him from accruing the erotic interest of a great variety of men.

This heaven gives Robbie a valuable but all too temporary strength. Seeing Robbie's picture in the Professor's photograph album of his angels, the narrator observes Robbie "smiling" as if all the pleasure of the earth were his to possess, yet the narrator suspects, in a likely instance of projection, that Robbie also looks as if he might "resent" that the sun itself might outshine him, just as Lucifer resented how God's power in the heavenly firmament outshone his own (2013: 98). Drawing confidence and a sense of power from the admiration of other men, men whom he can leave when he wants to find fresher forms of adulation, Robbie finds a vision of his splendor reflected in the eyes of his admirers. If this proves tragic in Robbie's presumed overreaching jealousy for an angelic luster or a brilliance that he cannot achieve, an echo of what Zamora has recognized in a separate instance as Rechy's use of "the myth of Icarus," Robbie is nonetheless far from as tragic as he might have been (1979: 55). If Robbie falls because he fails to pursue a career and an identity that might outlast his alluring youth, which deteriorates much like Icarus's wings, he nonetheless has a hell of ride, enjoying parties, meeting new people, and traveling. As such, in an age of queer hiding and legal and social repressions of "fairies," Robbie's Icarean or angelic self-fashioning and his consequent achievement of at least some of his rebelliously lofty goals signal a qualified success, even if he ends up in a relatively low-income job, bartending in LA.

To complement his balanced critique of the Professor's and Robbie's angelic outlaw-ship, Rechy also stresses how a too naive egotistic eroticism can end much more disastrously. In LA the narrator spends an evening with an older hustler named Skipper and two scores. The narrator learns that Skipper had once met the Professor who to get the hustler's picture for his "angel" album had introduced him to a photographer who in turn had introduced him to a famous "Director," an increased exposure to admiration that heightens Skipper's appetite for fame and fortune (2013: 195). This Director takes advantage of Skipper's "*Craving*" for cinematic celebrity, an echo of the narrator's "craving" for men's lust, by telling him that he is extraordinarily "*Beautiful*" and by promising to put him in the movies (197, 198). Both these men pursued parallel desires, the Director to have sex with a handsome young man and Skipper to be a desired object within Hollywood's perhaps too fabulous environs, even if this means he must "*reciprocate*" sexually with someone to whom he himself is not at all attracted (198). Skipper thus pretends to fulfill an ideal akin to the Professor's romantic notion of mutually shared love. Despite this effort, his film career fails to take off and the Director abandons him, with Skipper finding solace by sleeping with increasingly less influential men until he ends up having to hustle in LA bars where he meets the narrator. Having depended upon his youthful beauty for his rise, Skipper now lingers in downtrodden dives as "he flexes" his limbs, "studying" his physique, as if to determine how little potential to earn a living by his physicality he has left (191). This anxious posturing undermines Skipper's longing to be admired in the present, as does his reference to his past to inflate his value to scores, as he shows them old "photographs" of himself in the glory of his ascendant youth. Rechy portrays Skipper, much more so than Robbie, as a tragic form of death in life, as a "ghost" who mourns his lost youthful allure and who sells himself as a palimpsest of what he once was, in the photographs, as he faces the insulting indifference of scores who doubt that they want him as he currently is (191). Part of Skipper's tragedy is that he turns himself into Miss Destiny's "evil angel" by freezing himself in the remembered and photographic images of youth. His photos evoke an especially tragic melancholy because they rely in the present on a past that has failed to live up to his dreams of fame, fortune, and companionship.

As Skipper offers an explicitly tragic echo of Robbie, one obese score who obsesses over him embodies an intensely bitter and cruel echo of the Professor. The Professor mourned his angels' refusals to know him completely but he still took joy in his self-centered erotic engagements and he had a healthy self-respect for his own intellect, as well as respect from his peers and his social circle. With distinctly less intellectual and social suavity, the "fatman" in LA wallows in his dissatisfaction over his own erotic deficiencies. The fat man claims that he had the opportunity to have purchased Skipper's company when the latter was fresher and better looking, as when the Professor had pursued him, but this claim rings hollow. The fat man's failure to have actually done so, despite his clear wish that he had, implies either that he could not have afforded Skipper earlier or that his offer to purchase Skipper's time and body would have been bested by offers from more attractive or more powerful men. Additionally, by cruelly observing that Skipper is much older and much less attractive than he once was, the fat man reveals a nasty tendency to attack others to counter his own self-loathing. The Professor remembered his peers' companionship fondly, but when two other bar patrons of presumably this score's age and class mock his obesity, their alienating jibes cause him to react violently to cover his own insecurities, as he drops his cigar and smashes its casing "angrily" with his foot and then critiques with fresh "venom" how Skipper has aged (2013: 186). This anger merges with self-degradation when the fat man insults his slimmer yet still unattractive associate, insisting that if the latter wants sex he will have to "pay" to have it just as he does himself (188). This bluntness emphasizes the fat score's own crude shame regarding paying for sex by divesting the hustling world of even the little glamor or value supplied it by the Professor's literary angelic rhetoric. It also further alienates him from his one unpaid acquaintance, as his thin associate tempers his substantial "indignation" at his companion but only while he thinks the man's familiarity with the hustling world might help to procure him Skipper (189). The fat score intuits this hidden anger but he pursues his attacks even as they masochistically reinforce his own isolation and embarrassment.

If the Professor aggrandized what he desired, the vicious score perversely and with tragic irony degrades his one-time dream man, not realizing how this demeans himself, in part for exacerbating his own spiteful cruelty and in part for desiring someone worth degrading. Using his chief advantage, his money, the fat man plies Skipper with drinks, encouraging Skipper to detail his rise and fall and shouting "[l]ouder" when Skipper grows quiet, evidencing his reluctance to embarrass himself (2013: 194). Drunkenly craving even this mockingly prurient attention, Skipper proceeds until the fat man intuits that Skipper is depressed enough to accept his offer to hire him for the thin score. Displacing his fantasy of an orgasm with Skipper into a vengeful "climax" of the hustler's degradation, the fat man mockingly rejects Skipper's proposed fee of "thirty" dollars and pretends to look "indifferently" at the old photos from "body magazines" that Skipper shows to justify his price (202, 203). When the skinny score recognizes that the fat man has one of these photos "framed" in his room, the fat man's embarrassed vitriol increases and he "pitilessly" demeans Skipper through offering him only a third of his original price for both his services and for his photographs (203, 204). The fat man takes pleasure in himself buying and rejecting an older Skipper for the younger narrator, claiming to Skipper that he no longer desires him for himself, a facade he reinforces by further insulting even the photographic recollections of Skipper's glory days by valuing them so cheaply. The fat man simultaneously works to cheapen or to devalue symbolically the obsession he himself had long nurtured for Skipper and thereby to diminish his own failure to satisfy his longings. The fat man's present fierce "hatred" of Skipper comes from his own thwarted satisfaction and his resentment that his "framed" inspiration for lust, a photograph of Skipper, has been betrayed, albeit unwillingly, by its subject's aging (204). While there is an undeniable tragedy in desire getting overwhelmed by a self-consoling rage and revenge, Rechy heightens the self-destruction of the fat man's egotism as his abuse briefly re-galvanizes Skipper who grabs back his "photographs," pushes the score away from him, as the narrator had the Professor, and for the first narrated time explicitly rejects him by calling him *"fatso"* (204). Skipper's ability to reject the man even while at his own lowest point finds support in the narrator similarly telling the man to "[f]uck" himself as the skinny man repeats the insult "fat." These provoked final blows leave the score utterly humiliated and he flees what could have been, even for him, the comradely environment of the bar into the now protective dark outside alone, while even Skipper has a drag queen admirer who offers him consoling company (205).

Angelic Outlaws as a Model for Action

Taken together, these diverse queer outlaws provide problematic but comprehensible models through which the narrator can assess the benefits and the dangers of diverse rebellions against a world that generally rejects queer relationships. Conditioned by this world, the narrator discounts his desire for men even as he finds solace in men desiring him. This solace provides at least some thrill from same-sex sex, while evidencing his financial and his erotic value as well as his control over his needs. When he begins his career, the narrator notes that "[t]o reciprocate" sexually while hustling would have worked against his longing to be desired and to be pursued by men willing to work against almost all odds to have him, while he himself maintained at least some facade of social and psychological safety, retaining some grounds to consider himself not queer even as he accepted same-sex erotic encounters (2013: 69). In a society in which laws, medical experts, and social taboos predominantly condemn same-sex encounters, comprehensively reciprocal same-sex relationships—two men showing desire for each other—represent a heightened version of perversity that the narrator rejects. Instead, he seeks an unhealthy narcissistic compromise between a heteronormative capitalist society and his same-sex desires through hustling.

Although the narrator knows of men who enjoy successful relationships and knows of furtive environments that facilitate their efforts, he avoids these because a non-commodified same-sex closeness would force him to acknowledge the extent of his own queerness, namely that he too desires sex and even possibly relationships with men, and these desires would force him to compromise more extensively with another man's "terms." The narrator notes that he avoids certain bars because they were gathering spaces for numerous men of his age who sought possibly friendship, but certainly noncommercial sex, companionship, love, and possibly long-term partnerships, such as the mutual romantic reciprocity envisioned by the Professor, and as such these spaces made the narrator "nervous" (2013: 72). While Heise sensibly calls such possible "mutual" partners "lovers," critics generally avoid such descriptions to focus on condemning or admiring Rechy's uneasiness with love and romance (2011: 192). Stephen Adams, for instance, has argued that "Rechy's implicit thesis" is that "to love, to reciprocate sexually, is to admit weakness and 'feminine' vulnerability, to court the possibility of rejection" (1980: 88). Conversely, Jennifer Moon points to the "pleasure of partial knowledge" gained by Rechy's cruising characters who become "united through bonds of queer intimacy and ambivalent belonging" (2006: 55, 56). Extending Moon's argument, I would suggest that Rechy values even partial, non-romantic sex acts because they offer at least some validation of the allure and the social functionality of a queer body, which religious, medical, and legal commentary consistently portrayed as sinful, as sick, and as deserving primarily to be locked up either in an asylum or in prison. Partial encounters, properly used, open up the possibility of a self-love that could ease the way toward loving other same-sex desiring men. Still, Rechy subtly critiques these "partial" cruising pleasures as too partial, as too incomplete. He has his narrator consistently note the existence of men reciprocating sexually and he does so to lament his narrator's reluctance to pursue such options for himself.

After all, commodified and predominantly one-sided sexual encounters with the numerous scores whom the narrator meets during his travels never quite satisfy him. Rather, the narrator all too slowly discovers that his rebellious, self-focused desire for scores to pay him for sex can be as injuriously futile as it is healthy. Charles Tatum has argued "we sense fully," in *City of Night*, "the pain and desperation of the male, who, while believing he controls his own destiny, is propelled from encounter to encounter by the whims of others who dictate his behavior through financial manipulation" (1979: 49). Pain and desperation are certainly here but the narrator's growing understanding of the stimuli behind these traits, his ability to gain legitimate "job[s]," and his rejection of ceding any control to a long-standing lover's "terms," all give him a qualified sense of self-control (Rechy 2013: 70). This self-control, combined with the narrator's realization of the dangers of egotism and his increasing consideration of romantic sex-sharing, lends the novel what Karen Christian and Carlos Zamora identify as its "*Bildungsroman*" characteristics (1979: 53; 1992: 98). Their emphasis on the narrator's maturation usefully signals how he slowly adjusts his self-injurious behavior even if his progress remains rocky and uncertain.

The narrator's dilemma regarding his maturation is that in refusing to reciprocate sexually with other men, he both bolsters the traces of sexual shame left over from his morally unsound Catholic upbringing and conjointly loses the companionship and the support that a sustained erotic relationship can provide. Associating his faded religious upbringing with the transitory nature of hustling, he observes that with his "ego poised flimsily on a structure [the Catholic Church] as wavering and ephemeral as that of the streets," arenas where men could be met and abandoned, his sense of self-worth consistently required bolstering through the reaffirming desire of more men. Brief sexual encounters in metaphorically and in literally dirty spaces, such as darkened cinema "balconies" and "heads [toilets]," bring him some temporarily firm validation but the limitations of these encounters remind him of their insufficiency in countering his sense of alienation. An "[o]rgasm" with another man could lead to the temporary obliteration of selfhood and egotism that might reveal the potential for new social organizations, as theorized by Leo Bersani, but as Rechy points out such an obliteration serves this purpose only "momentarily" and fades away all too quickly (2013: 70).[8] These insistently momentary validations of same-sex desire are multi-edged: they offer solaces, but solaces so ephemeral that they actually emphasize a preceding and successive loneliness rather than overcome it. Simultaneously, these encounters reinvigorate the narrator's early encounters with religious and social "guilt," which repeatedly causes the narrator to abandon and then to return to hustling (71). He would accept a more conventional "job," he reports, and then once more he would feel "guilt" (152). By reporting the "guilt" as recurring after his legal employment, the narrator indicates his remorse for his same-sex encounters but then his still greater remorse for abandoning the limited value and companionship that even hustling can provide. He feels culpable for rejecting a vital part of his existence as a living sexual being.

To avoid queer sex, and the contemporary risks of degradation and of institutionalized oppression that come with it, fills the narrator with "guilt" because this also eschews the comforting validations of a community, of an erotic solace no matter how transitory, and of the moral and intellectual nobility of sustaining an outlaw status. In his more law-abiding abstemious phases, the narrator realizes that he misses his noble "rebellion against an innocence" that is unwarranted due to a broad reality that facilitates widespread pain, suffering, and injustice (2013: 71). Trying to measure out the value of the reality around him as well as its horrors, such as its inability to justify a calm, innocent perfection, the narrator admits his own long-standing desire for the divinity of his youth and its "Heaven" filled with "angels and peace," much like the stagnant calmness of his mother's cabinet of figurines, even as the alienation and franticness he experiences across the United States denies such a celestial existence, such that he now imagines Heaven as a terrifyingly dark "cave" (152, 153). Echoing the Professor, the narrator rebels against a conception of a perfect God, or indeed any God, for which the world provides no evidence. Yet if the narrator remains terrified of the resulting imputation of an inescapable Platonic "cave" or an uncertain amoral free-for-all, he also begins to reconceive of and then to pursue the beatitude or the noble angelic qualities that can still exist in a degraded world, if initially through one-sided same-sex encounters that provide only a partial satisfaction.

The narrator's chief predicament then is to discover how he wants to live outside the realm of heteronormative strictures. He must, in part, avoid a sexual rebellion against a homophobic world that echoes the latter's devaluation of queer individuals as youth-obsessed and shallow. While the narrator values relatively anonymous sex with myriad scores, he realizes that men's adoration of his body will be time limited and that this pleasure alone ultimately diminishes his sense of self. The narrator, for instance, sees in Skipper a warning, for Skipper had attained only a transitory "beauty" that relied on a young body unravaged by time, and as Skipper ages he becomes little more than an unhappy, desperate "caricature" of his former perfection, as his photographs of his past physique resonate unflatteringly with his present self, signifying both the fleetingness of the former and the decline of the latter (2013: 191). The narrator critiques not Skipper's hustling but his over-dependence upon a transitory value that minimizes intellectual or emotional consolations. Although the narrator increasingly searches for value in "Youth" and a desire for "Youth," having witnessed Skipper's overreliance on his physical attractiveness, the narrator also begins to fear that his own immature or unrefined reliance on the desire of other men will remain stagnant and he will no longer be able to obtain the unsophisticated "gratification" that he needs (158, 259). Even Miss Destiny, after all, took solace in her intellectual reflections on Shakespeare as much as in her good looks. As such, the narrator wants to have as much sex as he can while young to enjoy other men's confirmation of his appeal but he knows that he must find other satisfactions in order to evolve and to avoid becoming a debased "caricature" of himself, like Skipper (191). The narrator, who has enhanced his own innate intelligence with a college education, realizes that he is not stuck in the hustling world in the same ways as are Skipper or even Robbie, for he can find more intellectual work and philosophical consolations. He suspects that he must use these abilities to reconceptualize a multifaceted intellectual, psychological, and physical rebellion and a more enduring acceptance of his evolving identity and sexuality.

One healthier form of an angelic outlaw rebellion comes from establishing a stable self-satisfied identity less threatened by external forces or a fleeting youth. Rechy's narrator encounters one example of this through Chuck, a hustler who fashions a stable, self-sufficient identity that he uses to enjoy the relatively unconstrained cruising environment of Pershing Square in LA. While the narrator often mourns his lost certainty in a stable yet restrictive divine order that he had discerned as a child in the "sky," Chuck recounts easily his own youthful challenge to a God-like authority by describing how one day he and his older brother launched "rocks" into the air to see if they could connect to "the Sky," to see if they could either touch heaven or get a result from their attempt to nudge it (2013: 154–5, 167). In the context of Rechy's connective tropes, Chuck's actions serve as a minor insurrection against heaven. Heaven, however, the "Sky" with a capital "S," fails to respond to Chuck's incursion, whether due to distance, to apathy, or to nonexistence. Faced with this nonresponse, Chuck reimagines his own fate by appropriating an ideal of paradise, as he tries to get "Heaven roped" as one might rope a steer (171). With this image, Rechy merges in Chuck his ideal of an angelic outlaw with the US ideal of a cowboy as a cool, composed, independent figure, one not particularly reliant upon a youthful allure. Chuck evolves both these ideals when he learns that due to industrialized farms, the convention of a freely roaming US cowboy was by the 1960s as fictional as Milton's rebel angels, while the queer cowboy dressed up for independent cruising was relatively real. Rather than rage against circumstance, Chuck draws on all these tropes to rope in and to reimagine his favorite heavenly concepts of calm and of pleasure in the cruising range of Pershing Square. While smaller than a cattle range, the Square allows Chuck to reject regimented patterns of industrial commerce. Using his cowboy drag to hustle, Chuck makes money easily and only when he wants to, "happily" having few if any real responsibilities and to be able to enjoy watching the world go by him (155). Compared to the often violent roping of cattle and to cowboys ruled by farm managers, Chuck considers his queer hustling to be flexible and fairly satisfying for all parties involved. He represents then, by far, one of Rechy's most relaxed and happy characters.

Chuck's contentedness stems in large part because he has acknowledged his needs and found a practical environment in which to fulfill them. Consequently, stability or a lack of substantial movement fails to bother him to the degree that it does those characters who fear getting trapped with their daily associates. Chuck, the narrator observes, is like a "statue" in Pershing Square but his contented stability opposes the fixed stagnancy that Miss Destiny fears from her "evil angel," which Rechy associates with his childhood game of "statues" or the melancholic tragedy of Skipper remaining fixated on his old photographs. The narrator imagines that Chuck likely remains content because his version of an "angel" kindly invites him to a welcoming repose as compared to Miss Destiny's "evil angel" who she fears will confine her. Chuck generally remained calm and collected inspiring the narrator to imagine that a "compassionate angel" had once advised him to "[r]est," following which he had not taken life too seriously and had experienced little to no serious distress (2013: 158). While heeding this angelic advice, Chuck also refuses to stay completely still, as Miss Destiny fears that she would have to, as he shifts to make himself more comfortable, much like Rechy remembers players rearranging themselves "for effect" in his childhood "statues" games. Chuck accepts "[r]est" rather than restraint. Through his self-fashioning then Chuck attains in Pershing Square a version, at least, of the heavenly calm that he had hoped to find in earthly Western ranges, despite all the anxieties and terrors surrounding him. By pragmatically revising his ambitions, and his methods for achieving them, he developed a healthier, more satisfactory approach to life.

Chuck bolsters his quiet self-assurance, moreover, with a general tolerance for other individuals' cultural transgressions, which he refuses to perceive as threats to his masculinity and his nonnormative sexuality. Broad-minded, he encourages rather than gets angry at men who desire him, and this helps him to maintain the angelic calm that he has roped in and reshaped for his own purposes. His enviable calmness comes, the narrator fantasizes, from a "compassionate angel" but this angel symbolizes his own best intellectual, emotional, and psychological responses to the world around him. The narrator notes that Chuck generally accepted and at times enjoyed the diverse reality around him, including the values of desires different from his own, such that though "sexually" Chuck preferred women, he happily rents his body to men because it was "easier" to make a living and to be social this way in the casual bohemian urban environments in which he chose to live (2013: 159). Chuck's relaxed acceptance of same-sex hustling recasts the otherwise dirty, dangerous disorder of the park around him by evoking its more affable commercial potentials. He exchanges sex for money, preferring this to other physical or intellectual careers, and he pursues this trade in a companionable rather than in a judgmental, violent, or shameful fashion. As the narrator notes regarding the hustling scene of Pershing Square and its environs that this urban cowboy remained "one of its best-liked citizens," admired by men looking for sex and other young men who sold themselves and drag queens, in large part because Chuck seemed to have just the easy and carefree life that he wanted, that perhaps most American citizens want if with different methodologies and end goals in mind than Chuck's (156). Unlike the narrator, who hustles to find some value in same-sex attractions that he is too ashamed to claim for himself, Chuck's tolerance allows him to shape a masculine persona that rejects a tyrannous religious guilt and the constraints of middle-class commercial heteronormativity. His tolerance and his own comfort allow him to establish an affable, community-building identity that has a human-determined angelic ease to it. While Chuck would rather be riding horses on some mythical frontier and he neglects to think of his financial future, of what he will do when he grows "*old*"—Rechy's italics emphasizing the possible social, sexual, and economic horrors of old age—Chuck nonetheless achieves a self-accepting and a self-contented identity outside of conventional norms, an identity such as the narrator craves but cannot quite attain for himself (174).

This craving signals how the longer the narrator spends in the United States' queer underworld the more he values the bravery and the transcendent self-possession of individuals who engage critically the complex realities of their erotic lives and their self-fashioned genders. Traveling to New Orleans, the narrator visits ostensibly degraded environments that through their very alienation from social norms provide fertile ground for identities to blossom that would elsewhere get crushed by convention. In the murky atmosphere of a New Orleans queer dive, for instance, the narrator meets Kathy, an extraordinarily attractive "queen" who appears looking like "she had materialized" out of the "smoke" that pervaded the room around her (2013: 372). As Alan Sinfield has remarked, while the narrator reveals "uncertainties" about his gender and sexuality, the "queens" he meets "come into their own in the later, Mardi Gras chapters" (2012: 99). This queenly self-assurance stems not just from Mardi Gras but also from the outsider environment that Rechy's queens inhabit. A dark, ostensibly dirty bar allows Kathy, who has been disowned by her family, the freedom to embody an exquisite identity that defies any insistence on a reality or an unreality grounded in rigid expectations. Discussing contextual realities in "more than five decades" of a more refined yet loosely analogous Ballroom culture, Marlon Bailey has argued that a concept such as "realness," which signifies the performance of a perceived reality, can work as "a guide" to "construct, rehearse, and hone" a conventionally "'real' gender performance" that helps individuals "to choose and fashion their gender and sexual subjectivities through performance" and thereby to subvert gender and sexual norms. Often though, Bailey notes, "realness" also functions as a protective and a repressive technique used by minorities "to blend into the larger heteronormative society to avoid homophobic discrimination, exclusion, violence, and death" (2013: 55–6). Bailey's discussion sheds light on how and why Rechy's characters, such as Kathy, enact or embody "realistic" characteristics of diverse sexualities and genders to engage in a vital, if at times defensively constraining, self-fashioning.

Indeed, Rechy quickly develops Kathy's self-fashioning performance of "realness" by describing her unique hybridity of unstable realities and actualizing affectations. He describes this hybridity, moreover, by using his trope of the angelic outlaw to heighten its glamor and spiritual value. This strategy suggests how Kathy transcends both normative and nonnormative stereotypes for gender, sex, and sexuality, and it acclaims the effectively subversive nature of her complex individual existence. The narrator notes of Kathy that in this costumed, carnivalesque environment filled with nonetheless "real faces," from "the studied toughness of the malehustlers" to the careful if somewhat "unsuccessful" effort of the "queens" to manifest "femininity," Kathy seemed to be "as unreal as an angel: a monument to the utter perversity of her violated sex" (2013: 374). The narrator existentially disrupts simplistic notions of stable realities and unrealities that perversely discount more complicated yet nonetheless authentic lived experiences. He presents this disruption through his juxtaposition of only ostensibly opposing terms: the "real faces" of the "malehustlers," for instance, are in fact realized through "studied" (not innately felt) and then performed masks of "toughness," while the queens' painstaking and yet "unsuccessful" presentation of femininity through cosmetics is likewise "real" in its empirical existence. Kathy, a biological male recognized readily through the feminine pronoun "her," embodies a particularly heightened challenge to such labels as she transcends any rigid violators of her daily self-understanding. Her existence is only "unreal" amid the stereotypes that the hustlers and queens try to personify and to evade. Amid this background Kathy appears "as unreal as an angel" because she self-confidently accepts her unique manifestations of her physical, psychological, and spiritual being.

Kathy's angelic transcendence of human pressures, however, is troublesomely emboldened and qualified by an illness through which Rechy indicates how outlaws can perversely and yet triumphantly use trauma to generate a beautiful dignity. Sickness is a common trope in queer writing, which I will address in more detail in Chapters 2 and 4, but I will note briefly here that Kathy's illness serves to symbolize a social alienation that, despite its apparent degradation, can produce a form of glamor. Attempting to contextualize Kathy's exquisiteness, a friend of hers reports that Kathy has been abandoned by her relatives, that she lives in squalor all alone, and that she is "dying" (2013: 375). While the narrator finds the logic of this contextualization of her glamor mysterious, it is in fact practical rather than convolutedly theoretical, psycho-analytical, or spiritual. Kathy's repudiation by her family and her unidentified fatal illness explains her attractiveness as these traumas accelerate her pursuit to live her life as she wants to while she can. Her difficulties likewise intensify her friends' need to appreciate her and to admire her perseverance despite adversity while she remains alive. Rather than a slow transition, Kathy must embrace her sense of herself, and this self-assurance combined with her physical features and her style makes her alluring and charismatic. Her very illness, moreover, while hastening her calm self-acceptance, also isolates her socially and romantically, as she tells the narrator that she refrains from going "out" much in her present condition, though when she is "out" she is "out" unreservedly as herself (374). While she will occasionally shop for clothing with friends or appear during carnival season, her public communal interactions are largely curtailed and the revelation that she lives alone suggests a correspondingly private isolation. As scarcity so often sparks interest, her frequent social absence, combined with her other virtues, exponentially heightens her friends' awareness of her value.

As Rechy praises Kathy he also sets her up to show how even a particularly noble angelic outlaw risks collaborating with an oppressive queer-phobia. He posits a masochistic potential within a rebellious transcendence, a version of a bad beatitude, as Kathy pursues revenge against repressors rather than more self-fulfilling longings. During Carnival, for instance, Kathy dresses as a bride, a thematic echo of Miss Destiny's desire for a wonderful "wedding," and thereby launches a melancholic rebuke to social norms by pursuing her desire for a longer-lasting mutual familial love, a new version of the love denied her by her biological kin. Wearing a traditional wedding-style gown and a "bridal veil," Kathy subversively enacts a normative ritual signaling a romantic and familial permanency (2013: 413). If she can do so only in a hustling bar indicative of transient and commodified sex during Mardi Gras, which allows for such subversions, this rebuke still proves effective. Joining with a temporary "groom," a hustler named Jocko whom she desires, Kathy strikes back at a lustful, supposedly straight man who aggressively and misogynistically compliments Jocko on Kathy's beauty. In return, Jocko invites the man to "kiss" Kathy, an invitation that Kathy echoes by "smiling" at the man and allowing him an extended kiss before she "ferociously" grabs his hand and places it near her crotch (412, 413). The man "eagerly" touches her until he realizes that Kathy has a penis and he withdraws himself quickly in surprise, clearly unhappy. The man had inserted himself into Jocko and Kathy's environment, a holidaymaker come to ogle the degraded nightlife, and he had allowed himself to be enticed by Kathy's femininity, even as the queer setting should have made him wonder about Kathy's sex. As revenge for his incursion and for the hypocritical norms that he represents, the couple "ferociously" reveals to the man the ambiguity of his own erotic desires. While this revenge against a representative of norms that actively destroy long-term queer bonds may seem satisfyingly just, the narrator observes it and feels enormously "sad" for all involved (413). For in pursuing this revenge, Kathy and Jocko taint the valuable symbol of a love bond between themselves by using each other, albeit willingly, for retaliation against the outside world rather than for their own pleasures.

As such, if Kathy's angelic outlaw status represents a variation on Chuck's noble self-assurance in his own identity, she exhibits a clear melancholy due to her unfulfilled dream of finding someone to share herself with in a mutual, if not necessarily monogamous, romance. Kathy stays with Jocko for a while hoping perhaps for the love, honor, and protection traditionally promised by a groom. Yet despite the virile health and physical prowess evoked by his athletic appellation, Jocko has no more capacity to safeguard Kathy from her fatal illness than from her loneliness even amid the incursive, too often queer-phobic carnival crowds. Their union is too tenuous and too partial. It is a cold Mardi Gras masquerade, one shaped by and reflective of the larger emotional environment about them. Their relationship exemplifies what the narrator thinks of as an emotional "ice age," a phrase he recalls from the Professor who used it to describe an epoch with little romantic or psychological sharing, where individuals will have sex with someone but not truly offer affection to them, somewhat akin to artists who work "without heart" or empathy (454, 92). Through these parallels and echoed phrases, Rechy connects transitory relationships and quick apathetic couplings to empty artistic creations, all of which involve a self-centered posing that results in frustrated attempts at communication, whether by erotic or aesthetic means. Rechy shapes Kathy then to signal how emotional and psychological relationships, self-fashioned identities, and art each engage, to varying degrees, aesthetic and erotic representations that can lead to meaningful, mutually beneficial connections or to a frozen isolation as people use each other for parallel yet not really shared reciprocal purposes. While aesthetically and erotically preparing herself for the former, the repressive normative culture that surrounds and even invades Kathy's immediate environment steers her toward the latter, as evidenced by her alienating interactions with Jocko.

On Fairies and Angelic Outlaws

As the scene with Kathy and Jocko indicates, Rechy rarely underestimates the power of a normative US culture to rout romantic relationships between angelic outlaws. The evolving angelic rebellions that the narrator associates with the Professor, Miss Destiny, Chuck, and Kathy each evoke, to varying degrees, a successful acceptance of oneself and an enjoyment of one's sexual and gender variances. In all these cases, however, the rebellions fall short of transcending normative repressions to a degree that enables the formation of mutual, long-term, if not necessarily permanent or monogamous relationships. While the narrator astutely critiques the successes and the shortcomings of these queer outlaws and learns from them, as evidenced by his appropriation of the Professor's angelic rhetoric, he nonetheless clips his own wings by uncritically accepting common misogynistic associations of same-sex relationships with effeminacy. When the narrator first begins to hustle in New York City, he meets another young man named Pete, who advises that if men engage in same-sex sexual encounters for payment then the man getting paid is not "queer" but if men engage erotically with other men without payment, and so presumably for actual pleasure, then such men will begin "growing wings" (2013: 53). Like the narrator, Pete sidesteps admitting his queerness while nonetheless covertly pursuing it through hustling men. Pete keeps his tough masculine facade and he avoids "growing wings" or becoming a fairy, someone seen as effeminate and fragile, but he lives a lonely existence, pursuing only brief same-sex contacts emotionally and psychologically distanced by age and commodification. His longing for a meaningful connection eventually becomes too much and he tries to connect with the narrator by holding his hand "tightly," a fleeting, fearful romantic gesture that the narrator rejects to protect his own illusion of his self-sufficient, tough, heterosexuality (66). The young men so firmly accept stereotypes that they ignore their own feelings of a mostly masculine longing for each other and they abandon even their friendship to avoid any temptation.

Rechy increasingly offers, nonetheless, a positive connotation to the notion of "growing wings" as his narrator gradually converges fairies with so many noble angelic outlaws and begins to long for a relationship of his own. The angelic outlaws whom he critiques and admires, including queens, all try to share their sexual, emotional, and psychological lives with others, however unsuccessfully or contingently. From Pete's tepid attempt to hold the narrator's hand to the narrator's repeated anxious references to masculine men who seek a longer-lasting companionship to Kathy's symbolic longing for a wedding, Rechy raises the possibility of reenvisioning degraded fairy figures as powerful angelic rebels. Both fairies and angelic rebels work analogously to fly away from or to transcend the social and religious tyrannies that more effectively repress such exceptionally alienated sexual outlaws as Rechy's narrator, Pete, and their scores. As the novel progresses, these convergences of winged fairies and angelic outlaws incite the narrator to recognize the tenuous facade of his own tough, independent heteronormativity and the appeal of a same-sex relationship.[9] Indeed, Rechy structures the narrative to spur his protagonist to reimagine what might be as he conflates these categories of fairies and angels into an uninhibited ideal that might lead to the multifaceted pleasures of a same-sex, same-gender relationship.

This reimagining comes to a head for the narrator in New Orleans during Carnival week with its appropriation of Catholic rituals permitting a release of pent-up desires. Here, the same-sex intimacies associated with fairies merge explicitly with rebellious angelic encounters in the fantastic excesses before Lent. The narrator's critique, for instance, of Kathy's and Jocko's "marriage" amid his own destabilized drunk and high state-of-being jolts him into envisioning the mutual connections that two outlaws might achieve. These ostensibly tragic or debauched circumstances beneficially disrupt his limiting self-categorizations and inspire his attempt at an unaffected connection with another man. Very quickly after lamenting how Kathy and Jocko betray themselves to mock the tourist, the narrator notes that his personal "mask" began to fall, much like that of an intoxicatedly honest carnival-goer, and having attracted two scores with his aloof butch facade, he tells them that he is "not tough" and is in fact as frightened and as sensitive to critique as everyone else around them (2013: 414). Like the Professor, these scores had wanted a fantasy, not shared honesty, and so they abandon the narrator. But this verbal release attracts a healthy-looking physically fit, "masculine" young man a bit older than the narrator who invites the narrator to accompany him to his room, which the latter does without having "mentioned money," signaling his increasing desire for an emotionally shared rather than a commodified sexual encounter (418, 417). After sex, the two men talk together and the man reveals his full name, Jeremy Adams, inspiring the narrator to respond with his full name, a post-coital revelation that brings them closer together as individuals rather than as anonymous bodies. Rechy emphasizes this closeness but he continues to withhold the narrator's name in the text, thereby recalling all that readers still do not understand about the young hustler while also keeping him as an "everyman" representing most people's desire to be desired and their fear of romantic vulnerabilities. Simultaneously, Rechy makes use of an epic aura and a potential for paradise—signaled by the everyman narrator and the Edenic "Adams"—to allow the narrator to grow his wings by merging the romantic desires of the fairy and the rebellion of the angelic outlaw with his noble self-determination.

Jeremy himself represents a still more mature and a more optimistic convergence of the fairy and the angelic outlaw in a desirably rebellious queer masculine embodiment. Kevin Arnold has argued that in Rechy's writing "[r]eciprocation implies submission … a threat to the masculine identification that Rechy's dominant characters cannot seem to do without" and that because of this "it is *representationally* impossible for a subject to occupy both masculinity and homosexuality in the discursive space of Rechy's novels" (2011: 124, 127). Arnold's claims seem generally accurate save for several significant exceptions, including Jeremy who breaks free from this conservative rhetoric of masculine dominance and who suggests a path forward for the narrator. Jeremy rebels against stereotypes by remaining both "masculine" and eager to reciprocate sexually and emotionally with the narrator, as evidenced by his compassionate response to the latter's confession in the bar where they meet and through their subsequent sexual and conversational intercourse. Juan Bruce-Novoa persuasively suggests that Jeremy serves as "an alter-ego" for the narrator, one "who represents stability, permanence, and love, but who must be rejected for the sake of fidelity to the dream of intense life" (1986: 71). If we do take Jeremy as in part the narrator's older alter ego then their similarities raise at least the possibility that the narrator may eventually take on Jeremy's learned preference for a long-term romantic constancy rather than the Professor's fading fantasy of value accumulated by the parallel and yet unshared erotic intensities sparked between the so quickly estranged hustlers and scores.

The narrator certainly considers seriously Jeremy's claim that even an attempt at reciprocated affection between two men can create a value unobtainable by either on their own. He stays and thinks over Jeremy's insistence that what "makes life livable" is "the attempt itself ... or, even, merely the remembrance of that attempt to share—*in* sex and *beyond* sex" (2013: 444). This desire to at least try "to share" so complexly with another man places Jeremy in Pete's broad category of a fairy, and earlier this would have caused the narrator to flee. But with his defenses down during Mardi Gras and with Jeremy's help, the narrator proves willing to transcend misogynistic and not always accurate equations of effeminacy with homosexuality, as well as common perceptions that same-sex and same-gender desires are vicious and self-defeating.

The narrator's accumulated experiences allow here for more comprehensive perceptions. These learned perceptions resonate with the maxim of a wise French Quarter resident who reports that all individuals construct a "mask" throughout the year but that during carnival in New Orleans people frequently show their true faces, whether they be "Devils! Cannibals!" or, more rarely, "*angels*," even if through studied behaviors or cosmetics, much as Kathy showed her femininity (2013: 352–3). Echoing this resident's insight, the narrator realizes that the majority of people who typically camouflage themselves with normality desire a profane, sensual rebellion almost as much as do society's more habitually rebellious and consequently more alienated members, its angelic outlaws. Yet willing to dissent only in short bursts, so-called normal individuals prey on angelic outlaws, metaphorically and literally cannibalizing and sucking the life out of them, using them for devilishly selfish sex fantasies before discarding them. These uncritical collaborators with heteronormativity end up blending into mainstream society but they also end up un-partnered. More open outlaws, meanwhile, particularly the queens, fairies, and queers, including men like Jeremy and the narrator himself however briefly, reveal themselves to desire the angelic calm that comes from making the moral and yet marginalizing choice to admit and to pursue their own identities. Despite suffering a broader alienation from the US mainstream, these individuals at least open themselves up to the life-enhancing and self-transcending recollection and present possibility of a long-term companionable romance.

Rechy uses the evolving narrator and Jeremy then to consider the benefits of two queer angelic outlaws embracing a romantic affair. Following his own logic, Jeremy invites the narrator to move in with him so that they might "share" their existences with each other. This proposed sharing causes the narrator to wonder whether his own corresponding physical and psychological desire for Jeremy might present a "substitute for salvation" (2013: 444). The narrator, in other words, considers whether an "attempt" to sustain an innately desired human partnership founded "*in*" and extending "*beyond*" an ecstatic eroticism might substitute for, although never precisely replicate, his childhood longing to connect to a divine sublimity, to a being outside of himself. The benefit of any in-equivalency is, of course, that even a long-term human communion could eschew the heteronormative repressions, the physical and emotional distance, and the divine tyranny that the narrator associates with the permanent Catholic "salvation" of his childhood. The narrator's connection with Jeremy thus might allow both to transcend their own divine-like egotism. This mutual transcendence could nourish a stable yet evolving relationship that mutually benefits both partners by providing them with companionship, at the very least, and a dependable if not perfect or even entirely permanent support. Even if their relationship fails, Jeremy argues, the very memory of the attempt, the temptation of the attempt (to reword Milton), would evidence their ability to hope that a relationship could succeed. For the narrator, the very self-affirmation of queerness implicated in even a failed same-sex relationship would entail a bittersweet memory that with its gesture toward optimism and a more liberated romantic union could counter his more haunting, "ghost"-like memories of his youthful rejection of the repressive tyranny of the Catholic Church and its heavenly hierarchy.

Yet these lovers also indicate the difficulty of accepting a shared long-term intimacy, which necessitates surrendering some of the individualism that they have won by struggling against social norms. Having fought to interpret his alienated identity as a "strong" solitary masculine hustler, the narrator fears relinquishing his "self-love" and self-sufficiency, thinking while with Jeremy,

"I have only Me!" (2013: 433, 432, 444). He still has his youthful appearance, he reflects, and so he can still enjoy his solitary identity through pursuing an easier and more immediate physical and detached psychological pleasure with innumerably more men, while also making money. The narrator's dilemma is that his accumulated social rebellion has allowed him to feel secure, desired, and valuable in a queer underworld and Jeremy asks him to undergo a new rebellion that curtails these successes in the hope of obtaining a stable romantic union, a more desirable version of heaven on Earth, reminiscent of doll-like "angels" in his mother's cabinet (153). Like this childhood version of Heaven, however, the narrator suspects that what Jeremy offers might be tried only to be discovered too late to be a "deadly myth," romantic "[l]ove" itself being a destructive deception designed to "seduce" one "away from the only thing which made sense—rebellion—no matter how futilely rendered by the fact of decay, of death" (444, 445). The narrator encounters a horrific catch in that having attained some independence from religious, social, and legal tyrannies by rebelling against them, he maintains a holdover sense of guilt. This guilt evokes a dread of futility due to an eventual "decay" and "death," and this shame and this dread make him suspect the value of a shared relationship, which could re-subordinate him within a repressive hierarchy and cheat him of youthful pleasures.

Ironically then, the narrator pursues a nobly rebellious sexual and physical intimacy with men but only in the briefest of encounters, as he ultimately cuts his rebellion short by refusing to risk more complex emotional and psychological relationships. Bruce-Novoa has suggested that "the prestige of the socially acceptable path, the goal and symbol of the good life—'true love'—attracts the outlaw, but the protagonist prefers to remain uncompromised and free" (1979: 39). While perhaps underestimating the outlaw potential of a "good life" inclusive of a conventional "love" in same-sex form, Bruce-Novoa is right that the narrator eventually finds Jeremy's proposition too tied to social restrictions. Rechy simultaneously intimates, though, that a continuous rebellion can itself become compromising as it begins to work against the narrator's surfacing desire for romance. Consequently, any ideal of freedom is as much a "myth" as "[l]ove." The narrator will never be free to follow all his desires because he both desires Jeremy and what Jeremy offers and at the same time he desires the easy and easily dispersed of lust of anonymous scores. The narrator cannot be entirely free because there is no freedom that does not restrict some of his wants. As a result, rather than feel "triumph" over his decision to leave Jeremy, he feels only an "abject, crushing defeat" (2013: 446). In rejecting all forms of romantic love and its restraints, the narrator unhappily qualifies and impedes his own rebellious aims.

Conclusion

Read in conjunction both "The Outlaw Sensibility" and *City of Night* show how Rechy uses tragic angelic associations to throw into relief human outlaws who pragmatically reject authoritarian heteronormativity and gender norms in order to create communities more beneficial to queer individuals. To imbue these latter angelic characters with less self-destructive bad beatitudes, Rechy highlights how his nobler angelic characters negotiate with rather than egotistically dominate the individual desires of others. In the novel specifically, Rechy's narrator and many of his angelic associates willfully exile themselves to ostensibly degrading spaces such as illegal and often dirty and dark queer bars, movie theater toilets, and cruising parks that nonetheless valuably allow for some sexual freedom and for diverse manifestations of dress and erotic costuming. These spaces, through their fairly extreme alienation from dominant norms, facilitate queer angelic outlaws' resistance of social, religious, and legal tyrannies and of aesthetic stagnancies while also enabling a pragmatically partial fulfillment of myriad desires in a communal fashion. If these communities are never utopian and are frequently problematic, offering similar potentials for social and economic exploitations as more normative US environments, they do permit healthier, less authoritarian, and more human versions of sexual satisfaction and self-fashioning. Rechy's angelic outlaws, moreover, empower bad beatitudes that radically revise a desire for an impossible salvation and instead signify a desire for a calming excitement or a stimulating peace. These states-of-being cannot replace the staggering loss of a complete divine salvation. But they allow individuals to survive this loss and help them to thrive as best they can by allowing for a critical negotiation of hybrid human desires made up of physical, psychological, emotional, and spiritual needs, many of which can best be fulfilled in mutually beneficial, sharing, and self-limiting relationships. Subsequent chapters will explore similar examples of a queer American pragmatism in works by Richard Bruce Nugent, Allen Ginsberg, and Rabih Alameddine, among other authors.

2

Richard Bruce Nugent's Angelic Erotics: Rebellious Spirits in Multiracial Same-Sex Romances

While the last chapter explored how John Rechy's bad beatitudes draw on both the author's Hispanic Catholic upbringing and European literary tropes, I argue in this chapter that several African American writers created queer angelic outlaws that work within analogous and yet uniquely expansive cosmopolitan traditions. Countée Cullen, Langston Hughes, and, most notably perhaps, Richard Bruce Nugent used queer angels to challenge repressions of same-sex sexuality and nonnormative genders that likewise challenged a specifically anti-black cultural and state-sponsored racism. If Rechy's work reimagines Hispanic Catholic contexts, Protestant religious rhetoric provides a significant background for these angelic outlaws found in writing by Cullen, Hughes, and Nugent. Specifically, these authors draw on the unique Protestant-influenced hybridities in twentieth-century African American writing, which both W. E. B. Du Bois and Alain Locke classified as naturalistic and Christian spiritual influences on communities that identified both as black and as American. In *The Souls of Black Folk* (1903) Du Bois famously analyzes how black US citizens maintain a "double-consciousness" consisting of "two souls" and "two warring ideals" in one body. This double-ness causes a "spiritual striving" often supported by the "Negro Church," the "historical foundations" of which are likewise doubled, stemming from an African "nature-worship" and a less natural "Christian" belief system (1961: 17, 144–5). In 1925, Locke similarly remarked on the intertwining "Christian" and "sensuous," "almost pagan elements" in "Spirituals," those "unique spiritual products of American life" that became "nationally as well as racially characteristic," with such secular and spiritual elements subsequently manifesting in "Negro poetry" (2012: 105, 53). This intertwining of paganism and Christianity, spirituality and secularity shape the context within which literary queer angels—beautiful, even sensual spiritual beings with natural human characteristics that blur the boundaries between heaven and earth—exist and in which they challenge racial and sexual as well as religious, socioeconomic, and legal repressions.[1]

For many of the writers who took part in the Harlem Renaissance, spiritual, socioeconomic, racial, and national concerns were explicitly interconnected with sexuality and gender. The Renaissance, as Henry Louis Gates Jr. influentially observed, was "surely as gay as it was black, not that it was exclusively either of these" (1993: 233). In concurrence with this line of thought, Gregory Woods has convincingly shown how it "is often possible to read a particular" Renaissance "poem as referring … to either racial or sexual oppression," and A. B. Christa Schwarz has concurred, demonstrating that while "[s]uch issues as oppression, struggle, and liberation would, in the context of Renaissance writing, almost automatically be read in a racial context … the space writers left by often not explicitly identifying race as their poems' topics" facilitates "a transference between race and sexuality, enabling both racial and gay readings" (Woods 1993: 127; Schwarz 2003: 144). Quite often, a thread of spirituality works alongside these political and socioeconomic issues of race, sexuality, and gender. Alden Reimonenq has noted that "[b]ecause sexuality is inextricably wound up in the very experience of being human, it often shares turf with deep religious experience or political conviction" and this interconnectedness comes through in the literary bad beatitudes of Cullen, Hughes, and Nugent (1995: 361). Much like Rechy, these writers used angelic imagery to reframe issues of same-sex attractions and nonconforming genders but also of black multiracial individuals in the United States in exalted terms. More subtly in Cullen's and Hughes's writing and much more overtly in Nugent's, all three of these authors evolved a spiritual angelic rhetoric to present sexual outlaws and critically rebellious queers of color as admirably noble.

Indeed, the angelic outlaws fashioned by Cullen, Hughes, and Nugent function comparably to a queer "talented tenth" *and* to those "great" figures from history cited in anthologies praising same-sex love, such as Edward Carpenter's *Ioläus*, which Locke had recommended to Cullen.[2] These writers adapted both Du Bois's art-as-propaganda approach and Locke's progressive aestheticism to affirm the value of subtly and more explicitly queer facets of the African American community, which were too frequently sidelined from the public rhetoric of racial uplift or condemned as "decadent."[3] Scholars have often pointed to the only ever qualified tolerance in 1920s and 1930s Harlem for a spectrum of same-sex desiring and gender-nonconforming individuals. Claude McKay's *Home to Harlem* (1928), as Gary Holcomb observes, depicts a "diverse" scale of queer life with an "ambit running from [effeminate] pansies to [masculine] wolves," such as the "proletarian, mannish" Billy, and the novel experienced a fairly prickly reception (2003: 721). For despite the tolerance in some cabarets, speakeasies, rent parties, buffet flats, public restrooms, and the famous drag balls that at times welcomed a range of same-sex eroticism and gender expressions, queer individuals remained a source of public scandal, particularly when they transgressed interracial boundaries. While articles on "homosexuality were regularly run in the black press," for example, Schwarz notes that this publicity did not "necessarily" indicate "a new sexual freedom, as it also constituted a reaction to what was perceived as the negative development of Harlem into an entertainment center catering to white visitors' sexual/homosexual interests" (2003: 38). Many such same-sex interactions took place in what Kevin Mumford has called "interzones," "black/white sex districts, termed vice districts by urban authorities," which while "located in African-American neighborhoods" functioned for many races in both "spatial and ideological" terms as sites of home and exoticism, of safety and crime, as well as of economic, social, and erotic exchanges and exploitations (1997: 20).[4] Considering that such hybrid interzones were a prominent space for homoeroticism, an angelic rhetoric served well to exalt those remarkable queer black or multiracial individuals who rejected conventional notions of vice and used such physical and ideological spaces to construct an eccentric, rebellious grace of their own.

Cullen, Hughes, and Nugent, for instance, used a spiritualized angelic rhetoric, fairly Miltonic in its scope and characterizations, to recast multiracial same-sex desiring and gender nonconforming men from across the color spectrum as morally, even as patriotically, valuable for courageously surviving and sometimes thriving in their nominally degraded and socially alienated circumstances. Nugent in particular extends Cullen's and Hughes's Miltonic overtones to invert and to hold in tension concepts of inclusions and exclusions and of the sacred and the profane, blurring the boundaries of African, Caucasian, Italian, and Puerto Rican US citizens, especially soldier-citizens. He evolves this angelic literary trope to reinterpret the hybridity of modern American identities, which merge and keep in tension the complications and the insufficiencies of diametric terms such as black and white, macho and effeminate, normal and queer, pagan and civilized, familiar and foreign, and even monogamous and promiscuous. As does Rechy, these writers all present sympathetic reinterpretations of rebellious angels, ones almost akin to Lucifer, who challenge the status quo of a conservative, ostensibly Christian culture in the pursuit of noble individuality or a more tolerant, harmonious society. In doing so, they created a key strand of what I have been calling bad beatitudes in American literature and culture.

Cullen's Miltonic Critiques of Race and Sex

When it came to merging African and European spiritual literary traditions into African American queer contexts, Countée Cullen offered some of his most complex art through his reimagining of Lucifer's rebellion and fall. With Miltonic resonances, Cullen references this iconic angelic outlaw to allude to an epic striving stifled by autocratic hierarchies and to draw implicit connections among spiritual, racial, and queer rebellions. In "The Shroud of Color" (1924), for instance, Cullen uses Luciferian imagery to describe resistance against a racist society, reputedly condoned by God, which murderously rips apart the mystical and physical splendors of the world. While the homoeroticism in the poem remains veiled, Alden Reimonenq has pointed to its presence by noting that it was initially entitled "Spirit-Birth" and that "Cullen often used the word 'spirit' and its derivatives as a codification for homosexuality" (1993: 151, 153). As an additional queer layer, the retitled version was dedicated to Llewellyn Ransom who, Reimonenq notes, was likely "Cullen's lover" (153). Cullen thus links a covert same-sex attraction to a spiritual rebellion against European-American conceptions of God and the state as they lead to violence against black communities.

In addition to these peritextual pointers, spiritual, racial, and homoerotic rebellions shine through in Cullen's verse as the speaker finds a model for resistance in Lucifer. Contemplating earthly, physical, and homoerotic pleasures, the narrator recalls how his naked dark legs could capture the light and how he had once thought of humanity in an idealized sense, as a mirror wherein beauty seemed to manifest itself (2013: 57). Using a neo-platonic dialectic that soaks in and reflects an erogenous physical pleasure to imagine an ideal world, the narrator had initially posited a brown male body as a refined mirror that reveals an abstract human beauty. Over time, however, his experience revealed a less-exalted actuality, for he remarks that presently he finds himself wavering over Veracity's substantial canyon, a break between an ideal truthfulness and a seeming truthfulness, a division that strips mankind to its core because of what it had seemed to be and for how it currently exists. The narrator wonders, moreover, whether the fact of his very own or others' breathing and existing could entice him such that he might condemn his own hopes to perdition, and be satisfied to envision the hot sanguinity of his young age redden any sacrificial circumstances dedicated to Veracity, when in fact he could sacrifice himself to an idealized sense of the world (57–8). The speaker's existence in a racially and sexually repressive society sharpens his perception of Veracity. As brown and black bodies, sites of actual and potential pleasure, become bloody red sacrifices to the truth of white aggression, the narrator perceives a conceptual stripping of a humanity clothed in an ideal beauty. Refusing to remain content with inequalities in what could be a better world, the speaker begs for God to allow him to cease to exist (58). Following this request, one marvelous dark "wing," such as an angel's wing, appears and raises the speaker until he gains an epic perspective of the cosmos, of history, and of an epic angelic rebellion against oppressive forces (59). From this perspective the speaker sees Satan shining as if he was the sun as all too loyalist archangels join with God and Christ to cast Satan out of heaven. Yet rather than admit defeat, Satan rebelliously clasps "stars" from his original home and shouts while falling that a star remains itself even if it glows in a damned inferno (61). Cullen echoes here *Paradise Lost*, wherein Lucifer, the "morning star," draws his "starry flock" of rebellious angels down to Hell, where their luster wanes (5.708–09). Inverting Milton's ironic depiction of the Morning Star waning, Cullen uses this revolutionary Archangel to model for the narrator, who himself holds sunlight in his thighs, a rebel who refuses to relinquish a shining beautiful angelic ideal despite extreme attempts to repress it or to mire it in horrific circumstances.

Cullen's Lucifer represents an exemplar that spurs the speaker to remain alive so as to resist specifically racial and implicitly sexual oppressions. The narrator initially hopes to condemn his own hopes as a self-defeating gesture, but Lucifer presents hell as a space of opposition where a beautiful "star" can burn bright to recall what might be possible with a less conservatively hierarchical, more liberal acceptance of difference. To place this in more earthly terms, the mystical dark "wing" reveals a harmonious belief in humanity, and the speaker notes that everything he could see and hear and each element of his people worked in concert with this human symphony, a clear shift from divinity to humanism. This aesthetic spiritual humanism composed of a harmonious multiracial music of the spheres evidences for the speaker the value of struggling against racial violence and causes him to realize that surviving the agony that white society causes brown and black individuals evidences more bravery than even that exhibited by heavenly beings who adhere to or rebel against God (2013: 62). Juxtaposing Lucifer's rebellion with brown or black people striving to overcome white violence helps the speaker to reconsider supposedly hellish conditions as both an impetus and an environment for a courageous will to live. Cullen thus allows his human speaker to outshine any actual angels by endowing him with a greater share of the qualities usually attributed to allegedly higher beings, such as courage, beauty, devotion, and moral fortitude. As such after the speaker returns to earth, he starts resisting such social aches and he notes that in his grasp he held on to a faithful hope, one still burning clearly, hardened into an element akin to a dog's bright fang, which he says he will equate to veracity (63). Like Lucifer's "star" and most particularly like African Americans' persistent bravery, the narrator's fiery hope for a better humanity can still glow as he compares his dreamlike Veracity to the less-favorable veracity or actuality of his violent world. Indeed, he does surpass the angels in courage as the speaker suggests that even a sharp fang, such as one from the hounds used to hunt escaping black rebels, will offer inspiration to create the Veracity of equity and equality. He hopes that this harmonious Veracity will one day equal, in the sense of both to challenge and to equal the validity of, the empirical world in which he currently lives.[5]

While this dreamlike vision has obvious connotations for resistance of racial inequality by defining dark or black or brown in terms of rebellions against unjust hierarchies and courageous critiques the poem functions simultaneously to revalue a specifically brown homoeroticism. For a bit of sunlight still paints with gold the speaker's nude legs just as he sees Lucifer shine like sunlight, and just like Lucifer's collection of stars, themselves sorts of suns, the speaker's warm, bared thighs will continue to shine in hell and on a repressive earth (2013: 58, 61). I am not arguing, of course, that Cullen directly equates Lucifer to black and queer rebels. But in this poem, Cullen draws on what scholars have long noted was his pagan sensibility, referring to his skepticism of Christianity and his celebration of a queer sensuality, to use the story of Lucifer's fall as authors have since Milton as a means to frame reevaluations of earthly rebellions in a cosmically epic rhetoric.[6]

Cullen more painfully advances his merger of spirituality, race, and homoeroticism in "The Black Christ" (1929), wherein the speaker undergoes a more affirmative Christian conversion after white men lynch his adored brother Jim. Initially, the speaker struggles to acknowledge a God who seems to ignore the prayers of black people in the South, observing that black communities long to have "angels" even as they themselves no longer rear "Jacobs" and that he hopes to see noble rebelliously angelic and Jacob-like humans fight against the decrees of unjust heavenly forces even though they may perish in the attempt (2013: 163). Cullen's speaker implicitly longs for or even longs to become a new Jacob to wrestle against a heavenly indifference to black suffering, a desire that resonates with the humanism of "The Shroud." Of course, rather than confront just Heaven, this humanism challenges a specifically racist Americanism. As

Herman Beavers has noted, the biblical Jacob battled an angel and became Israel, thereby becoming a "signifier" of "himself" but also "of nationhood," and this angelically inspired reimagined nationalism applies likewise to Cullen's poem (1995: vii). Struggles against spiritual, racial, and national subjugations function conjointly here, and Jacob's speaker longs for noble black men to struggle with him to reshape heaven's national influence, which permits white Americans to murder them. Cullen intensifies this specific desire through forcefully sensual imagery, as his speaker imagines that he himself might grapple from sunset until morning with one of God's angels, the two figures clinging together in various formations until at last the heavenly angel gasps out an admission of defeat and grants a blessing to the Jacob-like, even rebelliously Luciferian man who has beaten him. The goal of this eroticized grappling is to gain the angel's blessing and thereby to encourage God to acknowledge the benefits of American black rebellions and a useful same-sex sensuality. Manifesting an uncomfortable ambivalence that both critiques God and seeks heavenly support for black and queer communities, the speaker even suggests that this battle *may* have been angelically thrown, subtly, in his favor, for the speaker reflects that God's winged heavenly army would on its own join those fighting for racial justice but that this help is somehow refused or thwarted (164). Criticizing both an unfair divine hierarchy that seems to prevent angels from helping oppressed black and queer Americans as well as Americans who resist striving for divine support, the speaker simultaneously longs for a heavenly grace and condemns it for its insufficient earthly engagements.

Yet the speaker nuances his blasphemous critiques after Jim emerges as a divine figure and kindles his faith in a homoerotic Christianity. After local white men murder Jim, lynching him like "[q]ueer" produce from some enraged or horrified plant, Jim returns from the dead as a contemporary and ghostly *imitatio Christi* (2013: 183). Christian and pagan frameworks mix with a homoeroticism that surpasses fraternal love as the narrator calls Jim his Lycidas, an allusion to Milton's elegiac pastoral for his beloved friend Edward King, as well as his Jonathan and his Patrocles, men frequently associated with same-sex love rather than with brotherhood (190). The speaker rejoices, moreover, when Jim returns to life with such vitality that the speaker's hands can fumble along Jim's lithe body, feeling his moving, vibrant corporeality (191). The eroticized black Christ-figure who proudly returns symbolizes what Amitai Avi-Ram has called "the clearest instance of how the desires for liberation from racial and sexual oppression coincide in the same figure" (1990: 42). The produce of this lynching is thus diversely "queer." It provides a violently ironic image of natural maturation cut perversely short, thus the enraged or horrified natural setting, while it more positively invigorates the speaker's faith in God and in his black community's potential to heal after being brutalized.[7] Simultaneously, it evokes a homoeroticism that alludes less to fraternal incest than to the self-affirming beauty of black male bodies in general and one in particular that shares traits with the speaker's own. Despite the violence then, there is both erotic and self-love here. Together, the narrator and Jim form an angelic bridge between heaven and earthly communities by offering a hybrid humanist and religious reevaluation of Christian tenets. With the return of Jim, the speaker reevaluates his faith in God and he finds himself ready to grapple with God's angels for a heavenly blessing for his community's value and for same-sex love.

In several shorter poems, Cullen more subtly combines an angelic humanism with queerness to undermine certain discrete divisions between commonplace conceptions of sin and salvation. In "Dictum," the speaker laments his break from a lover with an unspecific sex and gender and he wonders whether God ever longs for the angel he condemned so harshly. He questions whether God ever called out over angels' and other loyalists' hymns, remembering how "Lucifer" had once been magnificent in his winged glory (2013: 150). The speaker imagines that just as he misses his former lover, God must miss the beauty of Lucifer's spirit made manifest in his heavenly bodily form. Damnation for such analogous queer attractions must be too strict if even God can still desire Lucifer, missing at least to some degree his pleasing presence. More playfully, in "She of the Dancing Feet Sings," a female dancer wonders what she might do in "heaven" among the various angelic hierarchies who are too dignified to lower themselves to enjoy the "faery" music that she loves. Sympathizing with and seeing as almost salvific a less perfect but more humanly pleasurable hell, she observes that the melancholy, thoughtful "angels" who reside in Satan's inferno will be happy to see her and understand her preference for hell over heaven because these angels likewise could not stay in a too rigidly precise celestial paradise (84). This poem evokes the tension between the staid, too rigid ostensible perfection of heaven and the deliverance of a more comfortable, even fun imperfection of hell, which more readily accepts free-spirited women and "faery" culture, implicitly including fairies, individuals with same-sex desires and nonnormative genders, and the men who love them. In this reading, "faery" signals a less rigid and a more exalting term for fallen angels. Analogously, in "More than a Fool's Song," Cullen warns against a fallible humanity arrogantly asserting condemnations based on preconceived notions of right and wrong as his speaker reflects that the "souls" people think may be falling fast to hell are perhaps in fact rising high to heaven (101). Cullen's dedication of this poem to Edward Perry, who Molesworth notes was "likely on sexually intimate terms" with Cullen, calls for a reconsideration of human conceptions of sin, including same-sex encounters, which might actually be forms of salvation (2012: 127).

Langston Hughes's Troubled Angels

Cullen engaged the bad beatitudes of a black subculture of which Hughes seems to have been an only peripheral participant, yet Hughes likewise used angelic motifs to draw on queer spiritual sensualities that challenged too rigidly conservative racial and sexual identities. Hughes's role in queer traditions has, of course, long remained vexed. Reporting Hughes's "first homosexual episode" as a sailor and his few "heterosexual" experiences, Arnold Rampersad concludes cautiously that Hughes had a "complicated sexual nature" (2002: 77, 449). Schwarz similarly observes that because Hughes "was—perhaps on a sexual level—involved with women and at least on one occasion with a man, the possibility that he did not perceive himself to be included in any category such as homo-or heterosexuality seems given," even as due to his associations with Cullen, Nugent, and others, "Hughes was presumably aware of contemporary models of same-sex love" (2003: 70). Bolstered by these biographical insights, readers might agree with Shane Vogel's persuasive claim that Hughes's writing often "suggests something in excess of the narrow winnowing of desire into a binary of sexual object choice" (2006: 418). To add to Hughes's complexity, a related "excess" also works with regard to his depictions of race. Through readings of *The Big Sea* (1940) and *The Weary Blues* (1926), for instance, Sam See argued that Hughes's "aesthetic ironically coincides with the identitarian stereotypes of African Americans and queers that were propagated by early-twentieth-century sexological science and degeneration theory," which alleged that "blacks and queers were unnatural and degenerate because they, unlike whites and heterosexuals, exhibited a lack of racial and gender differentiation through racial miscegenation and arrested sexual development. Yet," See contends, Hughes's use of such stereotypes "countermands their pathologizing aims" (2009: 799–800). See's argument can be adapted for other works, too, wherein Hughes adopts hybrid stereotypes of rebellious angelic outlaws to celebrate as concurrently healthy and holy their seemingly pathological or profane behaviors, such as blasphemy, rejection of white supremacy, and queerness.

Hughes's ironic portrayal of black stereotypes that subvert and challenge hierarchical differentiations comes through particularly clearly in his short story

"The Trouble with Angels" (1935). Satirizing Marc Connelly's once-prominent drama *The Green Pastures* (1930), Hughes describes a "famous white play about black life in a scenic heaven," complete with a cast composed of a conservative black "God" and of variously timid and defiant black "angels" (1997: 124). As the show prepares to travel to Washington, DC, the capital's black citizens grow angry because the host theater refuses to grant them entrance. These citizens complain to the actor playing "God" but "God," Hughes notes, "was getting paid pretty well" for his role and he puts off the protestors by replying that "it wasn't his place to go around the country spreading dissension and hate, but rather love and beauty" (121). Through this God, Hughes caricatures those relatively well-off black Americans who refuse to disrupt the status quo for fear of losing what affluence and influence they have amid a dominant white society. Sardonically, Hughes has God turn the table on this Washingtonian black upper class, which Hughes associated with its own forms of an alienating elitism. In his autobiographical *The Big Sea* (1940), for instance, Hughes would decry this "unbearable and snobbish" group, which enforced a segregation of black society according to education, color, and wealth, even as it seemed "lacking in real culture, kindness, or good common sense" (1993: 206–7). Hughes critiques here what he perceived as the immorality of an African American snobbery that perversely replicated an ostensibly divinely ordained white racism.

In his story, Hughes opposes such self-injurious cultural quietism through Johnny Logan, who performs in the play as one of the underappreciated angels and who serves in the narrative as a heroic twentieth-century Lucifer. Raised in Augusta, Georgia, Logan left when the local self-glorified "white folks" banished him because he "believed in fighting prejudice" (1997: 122). Living to fight another day, Logan carries his independence into adulthood by encouraging his fellow "angels" to "strike" in DC, inciting a rebellion against the play's "God" and God's white backers (122, 123). Taking on left-wing racial and economic connotations, Logan's revolt proves tempting until God silences it with a satanically serpentine "Shss-ss" and the cast recalls the legal and financial repercussions of refusing to perform (124). "Nobody," Logan realizes on opening night in DC, "wanted to sacrifice anything for race, pride, decency, or elementary human rights." Refusing to acquiesce to segregation or to a repressive faux divinity, Logan "went downstairs" from the dressing room toward the stage "to drag the cast out by force" but he ends up getting arrested "for disturbing the peace" (125). Such a deceptively heavenly peace, amusing and financially beneficial solely for white audiences and investors, Hughes points out, can be hell for those on the outside. Hughes thus follows Claude

McKay and other contemporary writers in critiquing the racist term "nigger heaven" as a means to indicate the inferior balcony seating of a theater, as opposed to the more favorable yet hellishly immoral white sections on the main floor.[8] Hughes's geographic directions, moreover, indicate an explicit inversion whereby "God" and his collaborationist angels take on conventionally satanic qualities by willingly descending to hellishly degrading stereotypes down on the stage. Drawing on an inverted Miltonic theology akin to Cullen's, Hughes's nobly rebellious Logan/Lucifer assumes a lonely messianic quality by following his compatriots down to hell to try to redeem them by turning the actor angels into angelic men, albeit unsuccessfully and to his own detriment.

While "The Trouble with Angels" satirizes race politics and quietism, Hughes's earlier story "The Little Virgin" (1927) offers a resonant angelic context that uses implicitly homoerotic relationships to facilitate an adolescent sailor's difficult path toward self-awareness. Hughes's "Little Virgin" is a "blond boy, sixteen or so, probably a runaway from some neat middle class home in an inland village" who went "looking for adventure at sea." He finds it on a ship with a "crew made up of Greeks, West Indian Negroes, Irish, Portuguese, and Americans," most of whom call him "the Little Virgin because they discovered that he had never known a woman and because of his polite manners" (1997: 17). In contrast to the older, widely traveled crew, the "Little Virgin" represents a simplistic naïveté that Hughes aligns with provincial repressions and a one-time economic stability. This inexperience appeals to the jaded sailors who "liked" the "cleanness" of the "boy" even as they enjoy telling him smut, for "the fun of seeing him red and confused was too great to resist" (19). With a sublimated homoeroticism, the sailors work to de-virginize the Virgin, if only metaphorically, by initiating him into their vulgar adult masculinity, part of what Schwarz identifies as the crew's Whitman-esque "strange comradeship" straitened into "a strict fraternity" (2003: 77). With what they intend as an affectionate hazing, the ironic effect of a too regulated sexuality, they make the young man "a subject for ribald wit and ridicule at night on the after-hatch." When the Virgin says "[h]eck, no," for instance, instead of "[h]ell, no," one sailor calls him a "pink angel" (1997: 19). Although effeminizing and mocking, the nickname fits as the runaway sailor represents an angelic innocence and rebelliousness as well as an alluring connection between states-of-being, signified through his pink blushes. In part he connects the rough sailors to their own half-mourned pasts and in part he invokes the occasional humor, pain, and excitement of innocence transitioning into experience. When the hazing gets too harsh however, a "young" sailor named Mike protests, "I'm tired o' you guys ridin' the Virgin" (21, 20). If implicitly queer, with "ridin'" evoking a harassment that substitutes for sex, Mike's rhetoric is explicitly sympathetic. Rather than alienating and demeaning the boy, Mike wants to initiate him in a gentler, more inviting fashion.

The "pink angel"'s relationship with Mike, however, ends up exacerbating the painful corruption of a youthful idealism betrayed by experience. Following his defense of the Virgin, Mike and the boy fall "deep in conversation" and "the young boy looked happy for the first time since leaving New York. He had seemingly found a friend" (1997: 20). This friendship intensifies as the only slightly older Mike pursues an affectionate pedagogy, teaching the boy the business of the ship and about relationships. From Mike the boy learned "the vocabulary of the sea" and "an amusing collection of filthy stories," and for "the village boy this young sailor from Newark seemed a model of all the manly virtues," with a life that the boy "wished to emulate" (21). Mike's relative urbanity, his age, and his knowledge shine for the boy as they enjoy a relationship that echoes, with a narrower age range, the function of Greek pederasty. Their relationship merges a physical, intellectual, professional, and even erotic knowledge that is reputedly "filthy" but in actuality proves mutually comforting. Their intimacy founders though when they abandon the hyper-idealized all-male ship for a port town, which forces the boy to face the occasionally hellish reality of even Mike's adult existence. The friends go drinking with several women and when one spills beer on Mike, he "slaps her" causing the boy to protest that "no gentleman would hit a woman," after which "Mike up and hits him, too." Confronted with tenderness twisted by drink, competing desires in mixed company, and racist hierarchies—"All that fuss over a African gal!" one sailor spews—the boy falls apart both physically and mentally (22). The kid's distress and presumable hangover leave him susceptible to a "severe case of tropic fever" forcing him to the ship's "hospital" room. Attempting to make amends, "Mike picked the boy up and carried him there himself," sitting by him "as he tossed ... or talked aloud when the delirium returned," repeating his distress at Mike's violence toward the African woman (23). The boy's delirium and his obsession over this encounter with the woman reveal his distressed confusion regarding Mike's initial interest in her despite his racist, misogynist abusiveness. The adolescent proves unable to accept his idol's flawed and contradictory humanity. When he leaves the ship to speed his recovery, still not having attained a name to signify his own adult identity, he represents a queer angelic interloper who might not survive his earthly maturation.

The story's queer undertones stand on their own but become clearer still when read alongside Hughes's autobiographical *The Big Sea* (1940), in which he describes his experience as a mess boy in platonic yet heavily eroticized contexts. This ship provided the site for what Faith Berry reports was Hughes's "first homosexual experience" and the "almost certain" inspiration for "[t]he Little Virgin" (1995: 38). In *The Big Sea* Hughes approaches queerness only by implication, recalling a "hot cabin" in which one roommate lay "stark naked" "laughing and gaily waving his various appendages around" and another who "said he didn't care much for women" and "preferred silk stockings" (1993: 4, 7). By the 1940s "gay" and hence "gaily" had ambiguously same-sex and effeminate connotations, which Hughes reinforced by juxtaposing one "gaily" nude roommate with another interested in women's clothing but not precisely women themselves.[9] Hughes insinuates differently veiled queer desires though he never quite confirms them. The happy cabin thus evokes a fragile, covertly queer comradeship that informs the "pink angel"'s early relationship with Mike. The latter relationship, conversely, reflects the potential for violence to erupt in even friendly circumstances when intolerant heteronormative mores crudely repress queer masculinities.

This highly fraught atmosphere works in conjunction with Hughes's other queer allusions, which like the "pink angel" manifest a tension between an uncertain idealism and despair. In "Joy," for instance, the possibly male speaker goes looking for "Joy" and finds "her" being held by "the butcher boy!" (1995: 63). As scholars have noted, "Joy" could be the name of a female lover found with another man or the feminized, possibly effeminizing ecstasy that the speaker himself has found with the butcher boy, a character whose profession disturbingly implies equally nourishment and death, and possibly a butch masculinity.[10] This ambiguously joyful same-sex romance contrasts painfully with the much more explicitly queer "Café: 3AM," which indicates a possible future for the "pink angel" back on land in New York. In this poem, late-night "vice" cops viciously seek out "fairies," alleged medical "*Degenerates*," hunted by legal representatives of society, despite "God" or "Nature" having fashioned these people as they are. This unholy or unnatural hunt occurs in spite of or perhaps to cover over the irony that these secular authorities themselves skirt norms both through their excessive pursuit of queer nonconformists and through their own unusual dress, as indicated by Hughes's question over whether one should call a publicly authoritative woman a "[p]olice lady" or a "[l]esbian" (406). These uncertainties of sexualities and gender expressions and how to interpret them resonate with the uncertain manifestations in "The Little Virgin" and *The Big Sea* of a pleasurable and yet sadly dangerous eroticism.

Hughes, indeed, rarely observes publicly ambiguous genders or sexualities without assigning them tragic contexts. His discussion of the Harlem drag balls in *The Big Sea*, for instance, offers particularly melancholic characterizations of individuals living a visibly queer life. Far from emphasizing a playful fluidity of gender performance, Hughes reports that a "close up" examination of drag participants revealed an unsightly need for a "shave" and he highlights the "pathetic touch" of "former 'queens' of the ball, prize winners of years gone by," stuck reliving their faded glories (1993: 273). Such a "pathetic touch" haunts the "pink angel's" downfall and the homophobic challenges to "God" and "Nature" in "Café." These latter likewise recall, obliquely yet with clear thematic analogues, the suppressed rebellion in "The Trouble with Angels" enacted by the Luciferian Logan against a racist and commercially exploitative secular representation of heaven. Taken together then, Hughes's queer and queerly angelic characters rarely achieve a predominant happiness. But memories of the queens at the ball combined with the idealism of Hughes's queer angels inevitably commemorate multifaceted attempts, however troubled, to pursue festivities, freedoms, and joys by finding the value in racial and sexual outlaws and thereby challenging their degradation.

Richard Bruce Nugent's Angelic Dreams

While Cullen and Hughes both used angelic tropes to reevaluate the sacred and the profane through racial and sexual rebellions, Richard Bruce Nugent most extensively and most optimistically shaped his bad beatitudes to depict grace existing amid and even because of allegedly degrading queer circumstances. A friend of Langston Hughes, Wallace Thurman, and Zora Neale Hurston, Nugent achieved some early prominence through his sensual drawings for little magazines, for his minor role in *Porgy*, and for his overtly pan-erotic prose piece "Smoke, Lilies and Jade," which was published in *Fire!!* (1926). Although Nugent never achieved the fame of his more prolific colleagues, pursuing instead the vocation of a dilettante, his work offers a notable queer critique of normative US art and culture. Cody St. Clair has recently argued for "valorizing" what he calls "Nugent's dilettantism" for its resistance "to capitalist, bourgeois standards of artistic industry and professionalism" mandated by the "politico-aesthetic restraints of uplift and the New Negro" (2017: 274, 275). Resisting the middle-class mores intertwined with Du Bois's and Locke's policies of racial uplift and their rejection of decadence, Nugent's eroticized critiques of bourgeois aesthetics come through in much of the fine work that he did produce.

In the 1980s, scholars and artists began to excavate this work in groundbreaking anthologies and cinema focusing on queer black men, such as Joseph Beam's *In the Life* (1986), Beam and Essex Hemphill's *Brother to Brother* (1991), and Isaac Julien's film *Looking for Langston* (1989), while Wirth added fuel to this new fire through his compilation of Nugent's art in *Gay Rebel of the Harlem Renaissance* (2002) and his publication of Nugent's Renaissance-era novel *Gentleman Jigger* (2008). As these latter volumes illustrate, Nugent's prose ranges across a variety of homoerotic narratives, many of which use a decadent symbolism to depict the sexualities and genders that fashioned new forms of taboo relationships across the color spectrum in 1930s US culture. As Wirth argues, by "refusing to accept the supposition that homosexual themes, modernist forms, and 'decadence' were off-limits to black writers," Nugent fought "to expand his contemporaries' conceptions of blackness" (2002: 45). Indeed, Nugent often blends what David Gerstner has described as a "decadent Orientalist" influence with techniques drawn from "modern arts," often with European and African elements, to create a formally and thematically queer multiracial aesthetic for American fiction (2011: 23).

Nugent's engagement with literary bad beatitudes and his stylistic versatility come across most complexly in "Uranus in Cancer," an all but complete novel that critiques the multifaceted constituents of a queer multiracial America.[11] Composed in four parts, "Exposition," "Lunatique," "Letters into Limbo," and "Sing a Dream," this work uses shifting narrators to examine the evolving love life of Angel Stuartti, a young man with African, Hispanic, Italian, and US heritages, born in Puerto Rico, and raised in New Jersey. Wirth published a slightly abridged version of the highly romantic "Lunatique" in *Gay Rebel*, but a consideration of the whole manuscript illuminates Nugent's thoughtfully sustained prismatic modernism, his representations of continually shifting and concurrent perceptions, simultaneously affirming and disparaging, of queer individuals in the mid-twentieth century from the perspectives of Angel himself, his conventionally masculine lovers or "trade," a female lover, and his friends. In doing so, Nugent more than any of the other writers discussed here intentionally disrupts what Siobhan Somerville has described as the "intertwined" and "simultaneous efforts to shore up and bifurcate categories of race and sexuality" between "black" and "white" and "homosexual" and "heterosexual" during "the late nineteenth and early twentieth centuries" (2000: 3). Nugent creates this disruption and reaffirmation of queer desires and subjectivities through his hybrid characterizations of his queer angelic outlaw, Angel. In thus engaging the angelic motif I have been outlining, Nugent alludes only indirectly to Miltonic and Blakean literary traditions reimagined by Cullen and Hughes, but his bad beatitudes do draw on the cultural and spiritual rebelliousness associated with an ethereal, spiritually erotic queer character who challenges the multifaceted degrading American contexts of queerness and blackness.

While Wirth's abridged publication of "Lunatique" launches directly into Angel's surreal poetic perception, in his manuscript Nugent invites a more critical reading by balancing out this section's dream-like prose with the pragmatic concreteness of an opening "Exposition."[12] The "Exposition" frames the subsequent sections as remembrances of Angel collected by his distant cousin Aeon. Having initially set out to write a history of their family in the United States, Aeon quickly shifts focus to the fascinating life of Angel, thereby centering a family's and even a nation's experiences around a queer multiracial individual. Aeon begins by tracing Angel's cosmopolitan background, describing how his grandfather Alviro left the United States for Italy, rejecting "forever this land of opportunity that somehow could always find the black blood in no matter how pale a person and use the stigmas against him" (c. 1955: i). By introducing the grandfather's pragmatic move to Italy to avoid discriminatory US hierarchies, a move partially reversed when Angel's mother repatriates her own family, Nugent encourages a reading of the grandson's fantasies as an analogous means to decenter a world hostile to individuals with mixed racial heritages, as well as with nonnormative genders and sexualities. If Nugent employs a purplish poetic prose to signal the idealism of an adolescent just beginning to explore the romantic aspects of sensuality, an echo of an idealized Greco-Roman or Italianate paganism, Angel's perspective also encompasses a real world mixed with metaphors and literalism. This perspective angelically blurs the poles of dreams and reality as well as too narrow racial, sexual, and gender classifications. If at times this dreamy, angelic perspective risks lunacy it also evokes a new ordering of existence, one that resists any too static or discrete categorizations and allows for evolving and more affirmative, if at times frightening, identity formations.

"Lunatique" begins with Angel going through puberty, and thus in a physical and psychological in-between state that explains his intense blurring of metaphor with reality, femininity with masculinity, and his natural inclinations with those nurtured by his diversely intersecting communities. At the age of "sixteen," for instance, and living by the Palisades in New Jersey in the 1930s, Angel prefers to think in his mother's "Italian old-country idioms and adages" or in his father's

"Spanish aphorisms," and while "other boys were playing pool" or "learning loitering on the streets, he was living dreams" (Nugent 2002: 251). Preferring to perceive the world through a distancing European poetry, Angel half-avoids the discrete US conventions of blackness, so hated by his grandfather, as well as the unpoetic, rough masculine habits of his mixed-race male peers. Race for Angel functions much as Joseph Boone argues it does for Alex in Nugent's early "Smoke, Lilies and Jade," wherein Alex's "blackness is simply presented as part of his life, rather than as a fact that needs to be spelled out" and as part of the "spectrum" of colors in a cosmopolitan community (1998: 228). Angel's own multiracial background blends in unremarkably with his diverse community, but his relationship to his male peers notably molds his gendered and eroticized behaviors. When encountering girls, the boys usually offer comments on their erotic "possibilities," which while clearly harassment also lends a "more insolent and stiffly-proud lilt to the girls' walk" and so functions as a problematic tribute responded to with a self-assertive pride (2002: 251). A similar process occurs with Angel, who the boys also "bait" in ways that break through his fugue-like state. Although Angel "never" consciously "heard" the boys, the "sight and sound of them caused *his* walk to lilt a little and invested *it* with a touch of the same coquetry that painted the girls" (251–2). Whether Angel's effeminate flirting is innate or learned, like the boys' loitering or conceptions of blackness, the girls' behavior provides a clear comparison for Angel's that emphasizes his combination of masculine and feminine traits.

The boys consequently perceive Angel not as a stranger so much as an erotically charged fringe variant of the more feminine and eccentric facets of their already diverse community. Although at first they consider Angel a "mildly interesting topic," their "conversation" about him accumulates an orgasmic charge as it "spattered around ... into tepid curiosity as to his sex life," as they imagine that Angel "masturbated" and that "[i]f he were a girl, they could all have a good time" (2002: 252). Angel inspires the boys to engage in pleasurably poetic fantasies, not so different from his own, which lead them away from imagining sex with girls and toward an erotic contact with the effeminate Angel. In an already mixed community composed of multifaceted Latino, European, and African heritages, the blurring of sexual and gender classifications by boys already charged with surging hormones seems fairly plausible. As such, the instability of sexuality and gender becomes part of these boys' psychological and geographical multiracial American landscape.

As part of this poetic blurring, the boys' imagined sexual encounters with Angel at times veer toward an aggression analogous to their expected harassment of women. Nugent raises the interrelated degradations of misogyny and queerphobia to acknowledge their reality and to contradict their seeming inevitability. The boys at first consider Angel to be "like a dog to tease (and pet) but never harm. They had known him all his life, but he was different and not important" (2002: 252). This animalistic characterization allows the boys to trivialize an uneasy sensuality, a teasing and petting, with a distancing superiority not explicitly designed to hurt a peculiar yet familiar member of their society. This initial degradation, however, Nugent insists, risks violence when the boys consider whether Angel might be "a *pato* like they had met down at the ferry terminal, who had been in the toilet looking at everybody when they took a leak, and whom they had chased after they had used him. Scared the hell out of him." The boys have a clear conception of a degraded effeminate queer man, a *pato*, equivalent to a fairy, hinted at by the homonym "ferry," whom they "used" sexually and then terrorized. This violence hovers at the edge of the boys' relationship with Angel. The boys resist seeing someone close to their age and in school with them as a *pato*, but they enjoy imagining that Angel is "so nuts" that he might be tricked into touching them for a cheap trinket, "for an apple-on-a-stick or a dime. That would be fun. And convenient too, if it worked. That was how it all began" (252). To any reader familiar with the conventionally tragic endings of contemporary same-sex narratives, the phrase "[t]hat was how it all began" following the juxtaposition of the story of the ostensibly normal boys who "used" and then abused the *pato* raises an ominous cloud, which the rest of the narrative resists. This scene thus evokes a consistent yet not always fulfilled potential for male violence against effeminate and supposedly psychologically abnormal men, as well as the limits of using mannerisms and sexual practices as the sole basis for queer identifications.

This scene broadens an exploration of Angel's effeminacy and same-sex desires to include the desire of these explicitly masculine boys to entice an effeminate male without considering themselves to be at all queer. George Chauncey has noted that though effeminacy rather than same-sex erotic attractions generally connoted queerness in the 1910 and 1920s, some queer men insisted on their masculinity, and Eric Garber has detailed how a similar interpretive process occurred in African American culture, specifically in blues songs and in Harlem in the 1920s and 1930s.[13] Nugent draws on these contexts in his depictions of these boys in New Jersey. Rather than just courting girls, these willfully masculine boys often visit local spaces that represent provincial versions of the homoerotic urban "interzones" discussed by Mumford. The boys first visit the ferry/fairy bathroom and then spend hours voyeuristically watching one another flirt with

Angel: they "watched while one went over and talked to him. Watched while he tried all the obvious tricks unsuccessfully, watched him cradle his crotch," and watched him "take a curving leak into the river far below and ... with a little difficulty put his semi-hard self away again and ostentatiously zipped his fly." The physical and psychological excitement in these scenes flows most strongly through the boys who find it "fun" and like a "game" to try, and to watch each other try, to seduce Angel "night after night" as he remains distracted by "other things entirely" (2002: 252). This process continues, courting and avoiding both same-sex sex and violence in unexpected ways, until most of the boys' interest in Angel wanes.

Nugent offers a romantic twist, however, by having Adorio, the local heartthrob, continue to pursue Angel, initially using this "game" as a means to prove his own superior attractiveness and subsequently as an excuse to pursue a loving same-sex intimacy. Nicknamed "Cano," a reference to "his pale hair," which contrasts "provocatively with his Puerto-Rican being and complexion," Adorio exudes a magnetism that makes him the boys' "acknowledged leader" and that causes a "vision of him" to linger in the "girls' eyes" (2002: 251). After the boys fail to seduce Angel, Cano bolsters his allure by claiming that "*he* could get" Angel. Cano's motivations though prove far more complex than simply enhancing his public reputation, for "[e]ven after the others lost interest and stopped watching, he continued" to meet with Angel, as this had become "a habit" for him, "like praying" (252, 253). Cano and Angel's relationship quickly takes on a highly romantic, emotionally charged, and spiritual idealism. Rather than crudely exposing his "crotch" to Angel, Cano uses more poetic techniques in their nightly encounters. "Look at the sky," he tells Angel, "then the stars will be in your eyes, and I can have one for the asking. And if you look closely enough, you'll see them in *my* eyes, taken from yours." Rather than starting with lust, the two share romance and poetry, using metaphorical techniques and identities, which through repetition normalize their relationship and communicate their shared desire for closeness. Cano becomes the "Moon" for Angel and this poetic fancy enables Cano to share with Angel what "a man smothers inside himself and has lonesome feelings about" while Cano learns to listen to Angel, who likewise now feels as if he "had no secrets" (254, 253). If such poetry prevents them from overtly acknowledging their love both to themselves and to each other, this distance also allows their companionship to develop a shared spiritual rhetoric that facilitates their psychological and emotional intimacy.

While this poetic perspective allows both boys room for private exploration, Nugent indicates how fantasies drawn from secrecy and illusion can lead to psychological trauma. Angel's romantic vision of the "Moon" offers Adorio an alter ego through which he can question how far his interest in men might go, "I couldn't love you, could I, Chicito?" In this persona, Adorio tests this hypothesis as "the moon kissed [Angel] sudden-and-long" and then "spoke on in tentative tones ... half frightened and half calculating, half conqueror and half conquered" as they "made love," with Angel fellating Adorio (2002: 257). This semi-private space on the Palisades perceived through anthropomorphic celestial mythologies allows for a negotiation and even a battling of frightening and deeply longed-for connections, as well as a strategic and spontaneous surrendering to romantic and sexual desires on both sides. Cano moves past his resistance to romantic same-sex sex by emphasizing Angel's youthful gender ambiguity, calling him *chiquito*, and Angel responds to Cano's sensuality by turning him into a celestial figure that would not mock him at school or chase him as a *pato*. A conventional reality, however, unfortunately intervenes. After sex, Angel falls asleep, and Cano leaves, perhaps not wanting to disturb Angel but in practice leaving his lover alone and naked in the Palisades. When Angel wakes, he succumbs to the psychological trauma of abandonment after physical and romantic closeness, and his body and mind respond with a fever that makes him "[d]elirious" and causes "hallucinations," which a doctor warns might lead to a "[n]ervous breakdown" (258–9). Only when Cano visits Angel in his sickbed, in a public light, in the presence of his lover's mother, does Angel break the bounds of his fantasy heightened into fever to acknowledge that "the moon was Adorio" and begin to grow "well" (259). For a relationship to succeed in a healthy fashion, Nugent implies, it must be based on honestly acknowledged subjectivities rather than just nighttime fantasies.

Critiquing the borders between health and illness plays, of course, a significant metaphorical role in much early twentieth-century queer literature. Such sicknesses represent the influence of contemporary European and US religious, medical, and legal authorities that continued to damn, to pathologize, and to criminalize same-sex desires and gender nonconformities, a perspective that individuals had to discount in order to consider themselves healthy and sane. As Wallace Thurman demonstrates in *Infants of the Spring* (1932) through the depressions of Stephen and Raymond, and through Paul Arbian's suicide, racial inequalities frequently intensified any large-scale senses of dis-ease for same-sex desiring or gender nonconforming people as racism seeped into even the most accepting of homoerotic "interzones," such as parts of Harlem. Vaguely defined maladies and volatile nervous conditions represent the effects of this pathological thinking as sexual and gender nonconformists of all races were made to feel feverish or delusional as repressions and as the threat of arrest combined with the very real risks of losing jobs, families, status, and one's liberty could all easily cause a "nervous breakdown." The best cure in these cases would have been an inclusive and equitable role in a more diversely welcoming subculture or social circle. Along such lines, the ability of mental illness, in particular, to signify unconventional dreams of social reorganization helped to validate queerness and to facilitate the formation of more welcoming subcultures. The stakes of these mutually influential cultural comparisons among sickness, queerness, and race would change drastically in the 1980s with the advent of and societies' shifting reactions to HIV/AIDS across American racial spectrums, a subject I will examine in Chapter 4. But in early instances a shift to an unconventional, only seemingly sick psychological perspective, unfortunately more easily conceptualized than achieved, could paradoxically help to begin a cure to misconceiving queer individuals to be ill.

In "Lunatique," Nugent draws on these representational traditions, but he emphasizes the creative value of queer thinking. He stresses how Angel's poetical perceptions and his reputation for being "nuts" stem from his valuable refusal to accept static categorizations and classifications. Extending the plurality of an already cosmopolitan American society, formed out of African, Puerto-Rican, Spanish, Italian, and English cultural and linguistic influences, Angel blurs the lines restricting what constitutes a permissible romantic relationship. Granted, this refusal to abide by accepted relationship structures can go too far, as when Angel excessively distorts actual identities and mistakes metaphors for actualities. Angel's lover is only ever like the moon and is not actually an anthropomorphic celestial body, although his identifying characteristics shift to reflect "Adorio" in more personal circumstances and "Cano" in more public ones. Taking this flexibility too far, as Nugent illustrates, can lead to the very real pain and suffering of physical and psychological illnesses, but appreciating the elasticity of seemingly discrete categories valuably recognizes the expansiveness of both individual and communal identities.

Nugent illustrates this elasticity by having Angel and Adorio establish a relatively healthy balance of private and public classifications. If far from an ideal openness, the boys adapt to their age and environment and shift pragmatically between a personal romance and a public friendship. These shifts prove mutually influential for all involved: "When Angel was well, he went with Adorio to the block and the guys soon accepted him, because he was Cano's friend. They grew to know him some and to like him" and they grew to appreciate that Angel "saw things they didn't see until he showed them and said things they never said until they heard them from him" (2002: 259). If initially the boys accept Angel because of his friendship with Cano, a familiarity expands to a welcoming acquaintance, and the boys incorporate into their consciousness Angel's thoughts on the sights, sounds, and people around them. True, these poetic perceptions are limited, for the boys never recognize or accept explicitly a mixed-race same-sex romance. They do, however, learn to accept a softer, less crude version of male friendship and a perhaps ignored open secret that enables the continuation without social ostracization of Angel and Adorio's relationship. If problematic from the point of view of inclusion and equity for queer individuals, the situation presents a pragmatic solution for two teenagers, one that enables Angel to feel less isolated and that allows his romance with Adorio to continue fruitfully if never quite safely in the too slowly changing world of 1930s New Jersey.

More troublesome is the effect of this social assimilation on Angel's personality and sexuality as his public persona adopts some of the boys' hardened and misogynistic crudeness. Nugent signifies such troubling differences in evolving private and public identities through names that indicate the importance of and yet resist the totalizing effect of classifications. Alone, Adorio and Angel call each other by their given names, yet their friends recognize them as "Cano" and "Chico," respectively, nicknames that hide the softer, more loving, spiritual intimacy associated with their private romance. As such, Nugent writes, "Chico went with the guys … when they stood and watched the girls" and "Chico watched and said things, too" (2002: 260). Nugent presents this more problematic "Chico" harassing the girls to critique the learned misogyny so prevalent in most male cultures. In doing so, Nugent signals how despite Angel's effeminacy, his biological maleness offers him some access, no matter how partial, to dominant social groups should he sufficiently conform to masculine norms, however crass, which he does as Chico. Whether Angel does this for a protective camouflage or to gain a sense of masculine power, the effect makes him a harsher individual.

As this analysis suggests, Nugent uses "Cano" and "Chico" to explore the compromises that queer men make with themselves and with each other as they variously sustain and deviate from deeply rooted paradigms of heterosexuality and masculinity. In many ways, their private and public relationships provide an early example of the "down low," which Jeffrey McCune relates to a "sexual discretion" in black American communities that has acted historically "as an epistemology—a knowing and doing outside of the common eye, or more aptly the scenes of surveillance" (2014: 6). Indeed both Angel and Cano use their sexual discretion to study and to learn about new forms of masculinity and same-sex eroticism. Despite Angel's general disinterest in erotic relations with women, he allows Cano to teach him

> what it was that a woman wanted a man to be and how to be it—how to make love to women ... because [Cano] wanted everything for Chico that he wanted for himself. For Adorio loved Angel ... more completely than he had ever loved anyone before. Loved him the same way he wanted to love a woman, but at the same time differently, too, for he loved Angel as he loved *himself*, and there was manhood to share and have with him. (2002: 260)

Nugent indicates how Adorio and Angel give and take in their careful shaping of their innate desires for gender and sex. This considered process echoes what Boone has called "Nugent's achievements" in "Smoke" wherein he represented "an African-American character under the sway of libidinal desire that avoids the pervasive racist equation of the Negro with instinctual, 'animalistic' sexuality" (1998: 223). A similar process happens in "Uranus," albeit with additional concessions by both boys to a learned heteronormativity. Reinforcing heterosexuality as a quasi-demeaning model and cover for their relationship, Cano demonstrates on and for Chico what he thinks women want from men, which provides an initial way for Adorio to justify having a libidinal intimacy with Angel. This also enables Adorio to teach Angel about a form of masculinity that he wants for himself and for his lover, much like Angel once encouraged Adorio to converse poetically. As they learn and adapt to each other's needs, these pedagogical sessions offer both boys a path to self-love. Such adaptations also enable new discoveries of what might constitute same-sex love and diverse versions of masculinity that enable them to enjoy both natural and learned desires.

This compromising process nonetheless entails several severe drawbacks. It often, Nugent implies, verges on abusive manipulation as both boys use unwitting women as a means to draw closer to each other. It also self-destructively coerces the boys into socially ordained roles that they only gradually learn to modify for their own purposes. Adorio "wanted to love a woman," presumably due to social pressure bolstered by some innate heterosexual attraction, but his chief intellectual and emotional needs draw him toward the quasi-effeminate, quasi-masculine Angel/Chico. "Chico" agrees to pursue women but largely to satisfy Cano's expectations, as Nugent reports that "Angel lived only for Adorio" (2002: 260). Being coerced into pursuing women places Angel in a morally uncomfortable and emotionally hurtful position. Lastly, while the vagueness that surrounds their relationship offers opportunities for togetherness, it also enables them to avoid considering themselves in larger social terms. While initially a greater acceptance of their queerness might prove psychologically difficult, it could eventually offer them a comfortingly stable, intellectually and emotionally useful tool to understand themselves and to prepare themselves to connect to an effective sociopolitical queer network, likely in a larger city.[14]

Angel and Adorio thus adapt to and suffer from the requirements of their larger community, even as they contribute to it on local and national levels. If Angel usefully expands the town boys' perspectives, Nugent signals the value of queer individuals to the nation by having Angel and Adorio enlist together when the United States enters the Second World War. During the war, the lovers find their relationship obliquely idealized within the intense male bonding enabled by the mass movement and mass mingling of men in the armed forces. In the military, the couple engages both ideals of Hellenic lover-soldiers, which Nugent would have been familiar with from his interest in late-Victorian aestheticism, and contemporary US circumstances. Their fellow soldiers, for instance, think of them enviously in terms of the "buddy system" that developed in the US army. Allan Bérubé has observed that this system accorded a "respectability to devoted male couples, whether or not they included gay men," and allowed the manifestation of an "open affection" between socially and institutionally valued companions (2010: 187–8). In Nugent's novel, this publicly respectable affection enables the intensification of the young men's private romance. After a "decimating encounter" in Italy, the survivors watch Angel and Adorio wander off together and reflect "what buddies Cano and Chico were and how always when any of them needed help, one of the two would appear as if by magic, and then the other would be there, too" (2002: 260). As these men admire Angel and Adorio's public personas, the two men privately enact symbolic marriage gestures. Angel gives Adorio his mother's ring, thereby initiating him into a larger family relationship, after which Adorio "made his kind of love to Angel" (261). Nugent overloads this scene with irony as the soldiers praise the pair's friendship, their value to the unit, and by extension to the nation, even as the lovers have to hide the nature of their intimacy, which the military frequently considered to be disruptive to a unit's cohesiveness and worthy of a dishonorable discharge and/or confinement.[15] Race, of course, adds an additional irony since multiracial citizens, such as Angel and Adorio, often fought for the United States only to be exploited in the military and back at home.[16]

As such, the violence that Nugent introduced and then resisted early in "Lunatique" resurfaces with broader symbolism and a more adult and thus more culpable disavowed guilt. If the local boys refrained from terrorizing Chico and Cano like the more overtly queer *pato* whom they used and then hypocritically abused, an analogously hypocritical violence resurfaces in world events as the United States deploys same-sex desiring and gender nonconforming soldiers to fight European fascism while abusing these soldiers and their larger communities through its own legalized authoritarian repressions. This underlines the horrific connections, though not equivalencies, between US tyranny and the very fascism that the United States sent its queer and racially diverse soldiers to fight.[17] Nugent illustrates this duplicitous national exploitation on both queer and racial levels by describing how Adorio gets killed in battle and Angel subsequently returns to New Jersey, "where he was honored as a hero, and Cano was honored posthumously," with everyone being "proud and sad," for "they all knew that Angel was alone" (2002: 261). These townspeople, like US society at large, benefit from and often take pride in the achievements and sacrifices of individuals whose rights they restrict and whose identities and relationships they marginalize or disavow even as they intuit, if they do not entirely admit, the intensity of the distress, the sickness, and the loneliness that this alienation causes. Rather than acknowledge the actual reason for Angel's sadness, however, inclusive of missed opportunities due to the young men having to hide their taboo romance, the townspeople offer pacifying honors and then go home, dodging any admission of their own responsibility for Angel's mourning or their own hypocrisy.

In his edition of "Lunatique," Wirth valuably ends the narrative at this point, thereby stressing Nugent's salient but sad critique of US hypocrisy, with the state and society willingly benefiting from but refusing to give full equity to racial minorities and to sexual nonconformists or to memorialize honestly the latter's losses. In his manuscript however, Nugent finishes this section with a greater progression by detailing how Angel moves beyond this provincial and national impasse. Rather than return to the slow dreamlike consciousness of his provincial life prior to the war, Angel continues a wartime frenetic pace that refuses to give in to a Keatsian dreamlike fascination with death and static-ness. At twenty-one he starts to receive a small allowance from a trust established by his ex-patriot grandfather and he uses it to leave the Palisades for New York, where he "lived rapidly." In New York, he adopts a new gregariousness, such that he "knew everyone after meeting them once and he met everyone at least once. He possessed the kind of charisma that made each person decide he was indispensable ... and unforgettable" (c. 1955: 15). Just as he became "Chico" when he adopted the masculinity of Cano's crew, so in New York he continues to mature by establishing a sociability to combat the crude and violent world around him, moving from a dreamy spiritual existence to one focused on a more earthly strength. To signal this, he takes the name Riccie Ricordi, Chico becoming Riccie, a shortened version of Ricardo, signifying a firm leader who remembers his past, *ricordi* meaning "memories" in Italian. Without forgetting Adorio, Riccie takes control of his own life at a new pace that explores the opportunities available to queer young men in New York in the 1940s, a city whose culture and large populace present him with new relationships and more varied points of view.

Nugent's Queer Prismatic Modernism: An Angelic Avant-Garde Aesthetic

Key to understanding Nugent's rhetorical project in "Uranus" is to observe how his manuscript creates a plentitude of structural narrative scopes, which he uses to represent queer lives from a multitude of perspectives. In the "Exposition," Nugent constructs a frame narrative with Aeon as an editor who works to excavate Angel's life through his compilation of reflections written by diverse characters. "Lunatique" is the first of these after the "Exposition," which turns out to be an autobiographical letter sent to Aeon and signed "Riccie Ricordi nee Angel Stuartti." As such, the final manuscript page of "Lunatique" requires that readers shift their understanding of it as a decadent or surrealist story to a fairly favorable retrospective impression of how Angel/Riccie perceived his early years, albeit from the nostalgic perspective of the now more worldly, more socially mature Riccie. Nugent pairs this with a diametrically adverse account of Angel/Riccie in the next section, entitled "Letters into Limbo," which comprises letters written by Riccie's acquaintance Aldo. In these letters, Aldo asserts his normative masculinity by opposing himself to Riccie, whom he presents as effeminately facetious and as predatorily promiscuous. Aldo characterizes Riccie's behavior as socially disruptive to the communal house in which they live with a group of cross-class, multiracial individuals, including several of Riccie's lovers whose voices Aldo quotes. Still, as in "Lunatique" Nugent forces a reassessment of motivations as Aldo gradually reveals that he once had an affair with Riccie, which he both regrets and pines over. In addition then to offering a new impressionistic perception of Aeon's subject in terms of time and space, these letters also depict the love-hate complications of queer relationships from the perspective of "trade" or ostensibly straight men who occasionally make themselves available for or even subtly pursue same-sex sex with more effeminate men.[18]

While this narrative structure might seem otiose, these letters expand the epistolary form of the first section to create a prismatically indeterminate intimacy. Convolutions and voices encountered always at a narrative remove, via second- or third-hand retellings, reflect erratic modernist identities indicative of the fragmented state of twentieth-century Western societies, such as those explored by Djuna Barnes or Sam Selvon. In "Letters into Limbo" Nugent uses such fragmentations to explore the various frustrations, phobias, disparagements, desires, and the general mental acrobatics engaged in by "trade" or masculine men who desire effeminate men but who often only admit this indirectly so as to retain their sense of a superior, predominantly heteronormative identity. The "Limbo" of this title then refers both to the incompletely understood space into which we send any communication directed toward one another and also to the indeterminate attractions between these men and Riccie. Simultaneously, this "Limbo" alludes indirectly to Riccie's psychological state after the death of Adorio and to Riccie's continued evolution from Angel to Chico to Riccie.

To establish some continuity amid change, Nugent patterns Riccie's immersion in his New York milieu on Angel's social evolution in New Jersey, only from a more sardonic, bohemian angle. In "Lunatique," Riccie recalls his younger self in the Palisades as a familiar yet isolated effeminate boy who merged into dominant male groups by adopting a pansexuality that he learned from his lover and by becoming a popular soldier. In "Limbo," Aldo likewise characterizes Riccie as an outsider in New York but Aldo continues to present him as such with increasingly cruel sarcasm even as Riccie gains friends. In his first letter, Aldo denigrates Riccie by observing to a mutual friend,

> I don't think you ever liked him much but *I've* always found him amusing. He is still the same sort of stinker he was back when all three of us were working together on the same paper. You know, the Hero from World War 2. He still does nothing but what he feels like doing and still seems to be able to make enough money doing it. And as usual, he always knows people,

presently "pacifists," "who amuse or interest" (*c.* 1955: 18, 25). Aldo's account signals a critical shift in perspective from Riccie's self-presentation of Angel. Whereas Riccie emphasizes how Angel was gradually accepted into dominating multiethnic male societies, largely because of his close if not fully disclosed relationship with Adorio, Aldo accentuates Riccie's only partial inclusion in any group, suggesting that Riccie is actually disliked or only marginally tolerated because of his easy independence, his veteran status, or his "amusing" peculiarities and nonconformist acquaintances.

While claiming a patronizing affection for Riccie, Aldo nonetheless undermines his social standing by using the same sarcastic rhetoric for which he increasingly attacks him. Aldo's reference to Riccie being a war "Hero," for instance, reads as unduly sarcastic when preceded by Aldo's reference to him as a "stinker" disliked by a former friend. Then, after Aldo admits that he has accepted Riccie's invitation to share a house with himself and Riccie's acquaintances from New York's bohemian enclaves, Aldo mocks this "communal gathering" wherein "all races and kinds of people can live in perfect and happy juxtaposition ... Living in a Divine Plan" (c. 1955: 25, 26). Aldo suggests that like pacifism, Riccie's interest in a heavenly inspired inclusive and just society serves as a frivolously "amusing" pastime. Granted Aldo might not know about Adorio's wartime death, but this implication openly devalues Riccie's experience with war as a serious motive for his political stance and Aldo likewise disregards how Riccie's African-, Hispanic-, and Italian-American heritage could lead to his interest in social inclusivity. In a subtle fashion, Nugent evokes what Roderick Ferguson has identified as the "multidimensional" nature of pre-Stonewall queer politics, which subsequently got flattened into a more one-dimensional movement (2019: 3). Indeed, Aldo performs a flattening social and intellectual denigration of Riccie, which intensifies as Aldo refers to Riccie as a "bitch" and reports that their housemates often dislike his "flippant manner" (c. 1955: 21, 23). Sexual, gender, and racial politics come into play as Aldo recounts certain white or lighter-skinned associates' aversion to Riccie's effeminacy and flippant outspokenness. Aldo clearly dislikes Riccie's assertiveness and would prefer him to remain submissively quiet, as if to adhere to a perversion of the politics of respectability advocated by New Negro intelligentsia such as Du Bois and Locke, who hoped to enhance rather than to inhibit the influence of black citizens.

Nugent himself, as many observers have noted, resisted any polite politics of respectability, often by refusing to repress his effeminacy. As forerunner to Aldo, Wallace Thurman half-admiringly and half-critically caricatured Nugent for such resistance in *Infants* via the scandalously queer Paul Arbian (a homonym for RBN, Nugent's initials). Notably, in the novel Arbian's friends initially admire his brazen resistance to a Locke-ian call for an aesthetic focus on "African" traditions by insisting on the relevance of his "German, English and Indian ancestors" for his art (c. 1955: 237). But if they support Arbian's refusal to limit himself to an essentialized African past, however valuable, they prove uncomfortable when his cosmopolitanism promotes an effeminate queer identity. After dedicating a manuscript to his dead idols Oscar Wilde and des Esseintes, Arbian dons a crimson robe and commits suicide, inciting his friends to disdain his self-destructive preference for a queer Caucasian decadence. They thus simplistically lament Arbian's displacement of an African American identity for a queer European one rather than see him as exemplifying the expansive multiplicity of black culture. Discussing *Infants*, Michael Cobb rightly critiques Thurman's implication that "the adoption of impolite queer sexualities also means a racial death-sentence" (2000: 332). Analyzing black diasporic identities, Monica Miller persuasively argues that Arbian's suicide "becomes a metaphor of the self-implosion of the Harlem Renaissance, the implied failure of its practitioners to balance individuality and group identity, authenticity and multiplicity in their articulation of a modern African American aesthetic," leaving little room for Arbian's queer cosmopolitanism (2009: 213). Nugent himself, as J. E. Bauer argues, vociferously "advocate[d] a critical agency that, while de-essentializing Blackness," or gender or sexuality, in fact "remains solidary with the minority that has been forced-identified or self-identifies as African American" (2015: 1024). In his writing, Nugent proudly acknowledged his own and his characters' multiracial and pansexual identities and in "Limbo," as a feature of his solidarity with minorities, he declines to kill off his individualistic effeminate queer characters, such as Riccie/Angel, who reject a quietist, racialized politics of respectability.

Offering a revaluation of racial and sexual impoliteness, for instance, Nugent uses Riccie's assertiveness and Aldo's outright nastiness to question who can define the boundaries of civility and rudeness and how these social perceptions inform communal identifications, inclusions, and exclusions. Harnessing his authorial power in "Limbo," Aldo uses his letters to assert his own politely respectable sociability by insisting that other characters share his aversion to Riccie. Nugent's frame narrative, however, implies that Aldo in fact uses a malicious rhetoric to distance Riccie from amiable associations made through his thoughtful reflection on being a queer, multiracial US citizen and veteran. While Riccie's remarks at the end of "Lunatique" that he lived "rapidly" in New York and that his "charisma" made people find him "indispensable" suggest that Angel shifted from a romantic poetry to a campy playfulness, Aldo's letters portray Riccie as a mockingly "flippant" queen, who dilettantishly plays with a social and racial politics of harmony. On the one hand, Nugent hints here at an origin for camp in a curtailed romance, a bitter frivolity that Angel uses to compensate for the death of Adorio and a series of social exclusions. On another, Nugent shows how insecure masculine men, such as Aldo, tend to mischaracterize the achievements and the manners of effeminate men through derogatory descriptions, ironically by employing the very biting, impolite rhetoric that they critique. By twisting Riccie's language into a cruel camp that hurts and isolates him, Aldo consequently becomes a foil for Adorio whom Riccie had portrayed as using poetic prose to draw closer to young Angel.

Particularly mean-spirited is how Aldo, nominally a friendly acquaintance, ascribes to Riccie negative stereotypes associated with queer men, such as being sex-obsessed and callously promiscuous. Aldo spreads these mischaracterizations after Riccie's friend Marcia has fallen in love with Riccie and worries that he has "thoughts" that he hides from her. Riccie clearly relies on an open secret as he did back in New Jersey for his erotic desires remain discreet enough such that Marcia can idealize him romantically despite his having a young man named Anton sleeping in his room. To counter Marcia's fantasy, Aldo distorts Riccie's reputation by reporting that he "has millions of secret thoughts ... all dirty." Aldo's hyperbole regarding Riccie's "dirty" "thoughts" reveals more about Aldo's sexual obsessiveness than about Riccie's. By "Limbo," Riccie's thoughts have in fact become less erotic, even less hotly romantic in a Keatsian or Wildean fashion, and far more pragmatic. He refers to Anton, for instance, as an "attractive rat" and as a "pixie" rather than the "Moon" and such terms indicate that Riccie has grown more guardedly affectionate, distancing himself from his lovers so as not to become too emotionally or psychologically vulnerable (*c.* 1955: 29).[19] Rather than being cruel or salacious Riccie mixes practicality with kindness having found mutual comfort with a somewhat undesirable hustler who needs help. Riccie explains that he found Anton "drifting" at night by Times Square and Central Park, hotbeds of prostitution, amid the "boys who like him—the girls he likes," starving, with an "underdeveloped chest and muscles that the sidewalks of New York never gave him a chance to develop," such that "one would think him sixteen instead of twenty-three" (30, 31). Riccie shares his room with Anton for a sexual recompense, an agreed-upon form of what Samuel Delany has referred to as "contact," or affable, oftentimes mutually beneficial "casual" "interclass" sexual encounters that could be found in Times Square before its gentrification in the 1990s (1999: 122–7). In Aldo's account though, Riccie's crude cavalier-ness underscores the immorality of his supposedly predatory promiscuity. Rather than acknowledge any mutuality or kindness, Aldo spins Riccie as preying upon an allegedly normal but desperate boy who sells his body for sustenance.

Nugent reveals, however, that both Aldo and Anton harbor a craving for Riccie, which they resist by lashing out at him to reassert their ostensible normality. Riccie is handsome, in his early twenties, and so charismatic both in and out of bed that Aldo and Anton fixate on him. Aldo spends pages critiquing Riccie and then admits that they once had a relationship, recalling with pleasure "how adeptly Riccie had learned and could practice the love-techniques learned from the Karma Sutra" (c. 1955: 69). Aldo's scorn for Riccie, Nugent implies, stems from a lingering regret or resentment over their split, from a desire to punish Riccie for accepting same-sex desires so easily, and even from Aldo's need to repudiate any connection to a queer culture. Similarly, Anton tells Aldo, "I don't think I really like Riccie … so what the hell am I still around for? That's the sixty-nine dollar question. … Riccie is a bastard. I don't know how I got mixed up with him in the first place. It must have been the wane of the moon." Anton calling Riccie a "bastard" echoes Aldo calling him a "bitch," although Anton's jealousy likely stems from his uneasiness over his own scrawny physique. Anton reflects that Riccie clearly "knows what he likes" and the men he "likes" are generally handsome and healthy, such as Adorio or Tony and Ed, two strong men introduced in "Letters" (63). Nugent uses Anton's unwitting remark about the "wane of the moon," moreover, to imply that it was only due to Adorio's death that Riccie involved himself with Anton at all and that Riccie perhaps accepted Anton's initial advances because of his placement in the shadows of Central Park or a rare dark corner in Time's Square. Anton's crude "sixty-nine" joke, meanwhile, combined with both Anton's and Aldo's repeatedly recalling Riccie's erotic interests suggests that these men maintain their own predatory fixation on queerness, perhaps hoping to mitigate their envy of Riccie's self-acceptance. Thus, as Aldo represents an inverse of Adorio, Aldo and Anton echo the New Jersey boys who accepted sexual favors from the *pato* and then terrified him, representing a perverse form of "trade." Unlike the *pato*, however, Riccie will stand up for himself, representing an evolution of queer self-assertion.

Nugent balances out these anxious critics with Ed, a handsome man who cherishes his relationship with Riccie despite Aldo's vicious provocations. When Ed needs a place to stay, Riccie kindly invites him into the communal house without any erotic expectations. This setup riles Aldo who works unsuccessfully to undermine Ed's fascination with Riccie. When Aldo mocks Riccie's attention to Anton, Ed defends Riccie, insisting that "[h]e really believes that stuff about people being wonderful and that all they need is a chance prove it" (c. 1955: 61). Riccie, Ed argues, gives Anton a chance to be "wonderful." Yet while Aldo scorns Riccie to distance himself from their previous affair, Ed similarly resists his own same-sex attractions by fashioning Riccie into a moral and erotically untouchable exemplar of friendship. Ed thereby delays and discounts his same-sex desires, although he confesses that the Armed Forces had categorized him as a "4-F," a designation given to individuals deemed not morally or mentally fit to serve, because he had "got caught making out with a fag" whom he "was hustling." Nugent fashions an obvious irony of the Armed Forces' official queerphobia as the more masculine Ed was barred from fighting while the more effeminate Riccie fought and served with distinction. Nugent expands this irony as Ed initially refutes same-sex desires, scorning the "fag" whom he hustled, yet he eventually laments his abstemious relationship with Riccie. "He's never touched me," Ed tells Aldo, while looking "puzzled and proud and in a strange way a little hurt" because "[s]ometimes," he admits, "I want to get with [Riccie] that way so much I ache. I get a hardon and get ashamed he might see it" (66, 67, 68). Ed indicates here his multifaceted dilemma. Ed is "puzzled" because Riccie's restraint undermines his sense of his masculine allure, even as he feels "pride" because Riccie's distance confirms for Ed his own normative masculinity, as if Riccie sees him as unavailable for sex. Ed's "hurt," however, reveals how much he longs to have romantic sex with Riccie even as his facade of normative masculinity self-injuriously contextualizes such romance as shameful.

Nugent simultaneously offers here a critique of self-centered normative masculinities. He juxtaposes Aldo's cynical and Ed's idealistic responses to Riccie to show how they elide his perspective almost entirely. Aldo refuses to consider how Riccie might think of him or to consider that Riccie might appreciate Ed only as a friend. Whether idyllically or contemptuously both Ed and Aldo distance themselves from a queer identity and from a pragmatic consideration of the man whom they desire. Concurrently, they sustain derogative stereotypes regarding the promiscuous lust of overtly queer men as shameful, stereotypes that Riccie clearly resists.

Nugent in fact portrays most of his characters as sexually uninhibited, and this relative physical freedom actually highlights Riccie's intense emotional restraint as an extension of his loyalty to Adorio. By the end of "Letters," Riccie has had sex with Aldo, Anton, a secondary character named Tony, and a woman named Cynthia, thereby illustrating a relatively healthy promiscuity, a willingness to explore myriad facets of his sexuality that echoes his intellectual open-mindedness. These physical encounters though never signify emotional intimacies. Cynthia representatively notes that Riccie can sleep with a person with "nothing personal done" regardless of "how perfect Riccie seems—and is—in bed with that educated mouth and instinctive hand" (*c*. 1955: 98). Nugent validates Riccie's sexuality by emphasizing its learned and innate prowess but this very pairing of pleasure with impersonality, combined with his willingness to move on to new lovers, explains why characters grow frustrated with him. To be sure, Riccie's detached approach to sex with Cynthia might stem from his greater interest in men, but he seems equally unattached to Aldo, Anton,

Tony, and even Ed. From Riccie's perspective, however, and keeping in mind "Lunatique," these failed emotional connections likely indicate the inability of these partners to attract Riccie as completely as did Adorio as well as Riccie's lingering grief for Adorio. In this case, Riccie's reluctance to share a long-lasting mutual connection derives from his enduring loyalty to his first love. Riccie serves then as an ironic and complicated challenge to denigrations of queer promiscuity as he exemplifies a same-sex romantic faithfulness misunderstood by his sexual partners.

Reopening Erotic Avenues: Angel's Return to Romance

Nugent explores the evolution of this queer loyalty in the final section of "Uranus," "Sing a Dream," as Riccie returns to being Angel and refills the emotional void left by Adorio's death through new romantic relationships. As part of this exploration, Nugent's style shifts once again, having moved from the young Angel's romantic symbolism through Aldo's campy sarcastic portrayal of Riccie to land on a quasi-fantastical diagnostic reportage, a loose stylistic synthesis of the previous two sections. The quasi-fantastical element involves Angel's remarkably consistent erotic successes with individuals of varied genders and sexualities achieved mostly through his charm and partly through his wealth, itself derived from his family's wise investments and from his own artistic productions. Generous with his prosperity, Angel invites Aeon to manage a house for him in Puerto Rico, which gives Aeon time to contemplate, with a relative objectivity, and then to write about the intricacies of Riccie's erotic and romantic desires as they play out. Nugent uses this style and beautiful setting, an angelic in-between space, drawn from America, Africa, the Caribbean, and Europe, to depict a rich hybridity of US same-sex desiring and gender nonconforming individuals achieving successful, long-lasting queer relationships that exist outside of a heteronormative monogamy. He stresses the potential success of such relationships by detailing Angel's search for a compatible lover, one similar enough to share his life with and yet different enough to be enticing, someone whom he can love in his maturity as he had loved Adorio in his adolescence.

In "Sing a Dream," Nugent establishes Angel as generally in control of his life and in an exceptionally welcoming environment, all of which enables him to weigh his compatibility with more masculine lovers with an unusual leisure and security. Early in this section, Angel visits Puerto Rico to see his house and his two guests Aeon and Angelo, the latter a distant cousin whom Aeon has invited to stay. As their names suggest, Angel and Angelo have lived somewhat parallel lives, both looking alike, being "as tanned" and "as tall" as each other, being mixed race, and having served in the military. Upon introducing the two, Aeon confirms from his peripheral perspective "how almost exactly alike they were, and how different" (c. 1955: 147). These differences are significant, for Angel is "twelve or thirteen years older" than Angelo, has more money, and has lost his first lover in the Second World War. According to Aeon, moreover, Angel is "effete" whereas Angelo is "macho." This last distinction causes Aeon to suspect that this introduction will also be a "[c]onfrontation" (146). Yet rather than a violent confrontation, these men amiably confront versions of themselves as they might have been and become friends and occasional lovers. Their erotic relationship signals a validation of themselves and each other, celebrating their similarities and their differently unique personalities and experiences, including their service to their country as soldier-citizens. Angelo's primary romantic interest though lies with women and even as he expands his conception of "macho" gender expressions to encompass his desire for Angel, the latter inevitably takes second place to Angelo's relationship with his wife, Debora. Angel, meanwhile, slowly reaffirms that he wants a relationship with a man who primarily rather than secondarily desires men and who accepts this without persistent anxiety, in opposition to men such as Aldo, Anton, Ed, and even, though less vociferously, Angelo.

Nugent celebrates Angel's evolving knowledge of his sexuality by bringing him into a relationship with Angelo's younger brother Jesus. Jesus is "massive," "handsome," increasingly easy with his same-sex desires, and he has the significant benefit of sharing Angel's own interest in nonviolent social justice (c. 1955: 203). To begin with, Jesus insists repeatedly on his preference for same-sex intimacies. When Angelo presses Jesus to admit to a form of pansexuality, maintaining that the "time will come when you want … what is really unavoidably real. … Children and a family," Jesus responds, "I know what I am. What is 'natural' for me. I know what I want—need—[to] have," even if it will not "come packaged and tied in a bright ribbon any more than the things *you* want" (206, 206a). With an admirable confidence, Jesus rejects any limitations of authenticity, "real"-ness or "natural"-ness, to heterosexuality or to the necessity of reproduction and its supposed relation to family. He also challenges the alleged ease of prioritizing heteronormativity over same-sex intimacies, pointing out that Angelo's own complicated domestic relations belie this supposition. To this he adds a particular interest in doing social justice work "with blacks in the south" and his admiration for "some little preacher in Alabama named King," a reference to Martin Luther

King's early career, establishing this section's time frame as prior to or during the famous 1955 bus boycott in Montgomery (204). As such, Nugent expands the interconnection between earlier queer and racial revolts found more covertly or in passing in work by Cullen, McKay, and Hughes, to position Jesus as a near-perfect companion for Angel. As Angel himself has noted that thoughts of men, such as "a memory of Cano" or of Angelo, often dominate his intimacies with women, and that his time in the army and in New York evolved his interest in nonviolent social reorganizations in the 1940s, his reciprocal attraction to Jesus in the 1950s enables a new adult relationship that complements his sexual and racial goals of creating value from otherwise degrading circumstances (155).

The relationship between Angel and Jesus also brings to the fore, quite explicitly, Nugent's use of character names to insist on the spiritual, sometimes fantastical, yet always human values of same-sex romances. While Nugent's Jesus is likely pronounced Jésus, as Nugent at times although not consistently uses an accented "é," he also wants the name to reflect the American pronunciation and reference to the Christian messiah. Schwarz has noted that in terms of "attractive male bodies and sensuality, Nugent's stories are best separated into the largely unspecified depictions of male beauty in Bible stories and the detailed, sensual representations in 'Smoke, Lilies and Jade' and 'Geisha Man'" (2003: 128). In "Sing a Dream," Nugent merges his biblical homoerotic vagueness and his secular specificity through Jesus, evoking a merger of divinity and humanity similar to that of angels. He also loosely connects here these biblical and secular themes to themes of a heavenly revolt, so that not only angelic figures (Angel and Angelo) but also a Jesus-figure revolts against an unjust status quo. As critiques of racial hierarchies become an understood axiom, as indicated by Jesus's admiration for Dr. King, Nugent focuses on the intensity of Angel's and Jesus's same-sex romance. Jesus's incipient pursuit of Angel and their subsequent hours of repeated sexual exertions take to a spiritual level Angel's quasi-fantastical ability to find eagerly available "pretty-boys" and "studs" for sex (c. 1955: 231, 235a). This world spiritualizes a heightened erotic environment comparable to those imagined in later novels by Andrew Holleran or Felice Picano, wherein gay protagonists almost effortlessly find sex partners of all races. As in these more recent works though, Nugent's "erotic" art, as Thomas Wirth has argued, "must be sharply distinguished" from "pornographic" work, not only for the aesthetic reasons of its "elegant style" but also because Nugent so carefully historicizes, theorizes, and shapes his aesthetic contexts (1985: 16).

Nugent's fantasies, for instance, have clear roots in a modernist acceptance that sexual psychologies, like racial or spiritual heritages, cannot be constrained into neat categories. Considering Nugent's "Smoke" and other overtly queer writing from this period, Boone has argued that in these texts "the privileging of the point of view of their gay protagonists subsumes all other nongay perspectives, facilitating a crossing of multiple categories of identity that results in a queer world-vision if not in an entirely queer world" (1998: 217). Analogously, as Matt Brim points out in his study of Baldwin, emphasizing "the term 'queer' can seem to foreclose 'black,'" but "such a foreclosure is impossible" as gay or queer and black are different but intersecting signifiers (2014: 20).[20] While I am thus tempted to borrow here E. Patrick Johnson's well-known term "quare" instead of "queer" to stress a hermeneutic that accounts for "the material existence of 'colored' bodies," Nugent in his own writing uses "queer" to refer to multiracial same-sex and pansexual Americans with diverse geographical heritages (Johnson 2005: 136; Nugent 2008: 113). This racial awareness applies to "Uranus," too, as Nugent's "privileging" of same-sex encounters creates an impressionistic "queer world-vision" where the possibilities for same-sex and cross-sex affairs are almost everywhere in America for almost everyone of any race or color. Importantly, these impressionistic fantasies in fact blurred into realistic modern conditions as queer social encounters became more widely available in the United States after the Second World War, even accounting for the Lavender Scare of the early 1950s and for American racism.[21] Nugent emphasizes this blurring stylistically through his strategic queering of the name "Jesus," for instance, which mainstream black and white US society reserves for references to the Christian messiah but which Hispanic US culture uses as a more quotidian name, much like the names Angel and Angelo. Nugent, for instance, kept pictures of a friend named Jesus who along with a man named Jose, a friend from San Juan, may have been the model for Jesus in "Uranus," and Nugent kept nude photos of a man named Angelo who along with another man named Angel likely served as models for Angelo. In "Uranus" as in these pictures, the spiritually fantastic excitement of a queer eroticism merges happily with its more prosaic although still exciting African, Hispanic, and European American reality.

Complementing this blend of fantasy and reality is Nugent's consideration of how dominance and submission can coalesce lovingly in same-sex relationships. Suggesting the need for some reciprocity of pursuit regardless of sexual roles and acts, Nugent has Jesus initiate the couple's first physical encounter and Angel their second. What complicates their sex is Nugent's description of its loving violence, which holds in tension spirituality, eroticism, brutality and a willing submission not unlike that in John Donne's Holy Sonnet 14, "Batter My Heart." As Angel had earlier with Adorio and Angelo, he allows Jesus to "feel wonderfully male and masterful" during sex to the degree that Jesus works "his will" on Angel's mouth, "practically raping Angel," yet not entirely so, as Angel "respond[s] with his whole being, accepting this master," such that he "helped him along with the rape" (*c.* 1955: 242). This encounter blurs active and passive roles and veers into a consensual yet forceful S&M. While Nugent's use of the term "rape" undermines its reference to actual nonconsensual sex, the encounter signals both the strength and even aggression through which these men sometimes share their mutual love even as it distracts from its calmer intensities. "Every time [Angel] could see into Jesus' eyes," Nugent reports, "he saw only tenderness and wonder and love as Jesus' eyes searched *his* and apparently found there what they wanted to find" (243). This shared physical and visual tenderness echoes in their softer verbal declarations, which diametrically complement their physical exertions. Lying in bed as the novel ends, Angel wonders why they are being quiet and Jesus responds, "We're whispering because—because it's the only way I know to shout 'I love you,'" inspiring Angel to confirm, "I'm in love with you" (252). The whispering is not because of secrecy, for their housemates know about their relationship, and so it rather reasserts their forcefully tender love for each other. Their intensity grows into softness, in their searching to hear and to understand each other, even as they submissively dominate and dominatingly submit to their corresponding romantic needs.

This conclusion offers a usefully realistic acceptance of ultimately messy power differentials and varying desires in male relationships that reject imprecise models opposing effeminacy to macho-ness and passivity to activity. Nugent in fact shows these men working through their various identities, from differences in racial makeup (beyond just black and white) to difference in age, wealth, and gender identities through sex. Following Essex Hemphill, Robert Reid-Pharr has observed the necessity of considering the diverse implications of "what we think when we fuck," considerations that as Darieck Scott has similarly argued can help us to understand the "social political, and *historical* context" of interracial queer desires and erotic actions (1994: 301; 2001: 86). Complicating conceptions of dominance and mastery, Angel explicitly permits Jesus to think of himself as at times physically dominant to sustain some semblance of his masculinity, unfortunately at times a more brutal part, even as Angel maintains the advantages of age, affluence, his charm, and, with Jesus's blessing, a limited sexual independence. After they declare their mutual love for instance, Jesus acknowledges Angel's relationship with Angelo and generously submits to nonmonogamy, observing that Angelo is "in love with Debora ... But he needs you too" (c. 1955: 252). Angel intends to act on Jesus's permission to have sex on occasion with Angelo though his "love" for Jesus will take precedence. In many ways this extends Nugent's early insistence in "Smoke" that "one *can* love two at the same time" (2002: 87). "Uranus" then ends by conceptualizing a nonmonogamous loyalty, as Angel and Jesus work toward a mutual agreement and a shared understanding that they will give first preference to each other. By ending the novel on this note, Nugent suggests that Angel's increased understanding and acceptance of such power differentials, combined with his knowledge that he has found someone whose wants suitably complement his own, allows for a more mature relationship than he had with even Adorio.

Conclusion: A Genealogy of Queer Black Angels

Nugent's project of tracing Angel's maturation over time from the late 1930s until the 1960s complements the more painfully exultant angelic figures imagined by Cullen and Hughes. It also, however, precedes subsequent depictions of spiritualized queer black relationships. In recent decades, critics, artists, and anthologists, such as Sharon Holland, Don Weise, Devon Carbado, and Dwight McBride, among others, have begun to flesh out a queer black literary genealogy.[22] The black and multiracial angelic outlaws that I discuss above present, I think, an important trope within this literary family. Such early heroic neo-Miltonic rebel angels resonate, for instance, with subsequent queer black angelic outlaws in LeRoi Jones's/Amiri Baraka's *The System of Dante's Hell* (1965), Gordon Daniels's *Black Angel* (1972), as well as more modern works that form part of what Darius Bost and others have called a "black gay cultural renaissance," inclusive of Essex Hemphill's *Conditions* (1986), Assotto Saint's *Stations* (1989) and *Wishing for Wings* (1994), and Isaac Julien's *Looking for Langston* (1989) and *The Attendant* (1993).[23] Each of these works, to name just a few, extends the eclectic angelic traditions developed by Cullen, Hughes, and Nugent to emphasize a spiritual physicality that blossoms within and transcends degraded contexts to affirm valuable racial, sexual, and gender variations in the United States. While the similarities and unique brilliancies of these more modern queer black bad beatitudes certainly deserve detailed attention, my primary intent here is to argue for the value of angelic bad beatitudes for a variety of queer American authors across racial, ethnic, and spiritual cultures. As such, I will leave for now these worthy successors to Nugent, and in my next two chapters I will turn to the angelic poetry of Allen Ginsberg and then to Rabih Alameddine's intervention in the uncomfortable angelic art of HIV/AIDS.

3

Allen Ginsberg's Angelic Economies: Sex, Spirituality, and a Queer Anti-Imperialism

As the past two chapters evidence, queer bad beatitudes stem from the 1920s in US literature and hit particular high points in the 1950s, 1960s, and 1970s, decades during which Allen Ginsberg, one of America's most notorious and publicly queer poets, was likewise evolving a uniquely influential series of angelic outlaws. I reference Ginsberg briefly in my introduction and in Chapter 1, but I return to him here to place his most famous images of angelic figures in *Howl* into conversation with his larger body of work and with post–Second World War American culture. Ginsberg, like Rechy and Nugent, uses queer angels to imagine how an unconventional morality can emerge from a conventionally profane spiritual eroticism just as normative forms of religious and social sanctity can themselves become profane as they trample on unconventional but nonviolent desires. Yet whereas Rechy uses queer angels to emphasize rebels against external and internal homophobic oppressions and Nugent to critique diverse same-sex relationships amid cultural and state-sponsored racism, Ginsberg focuses on how such erotic spiritual intimacies can overthrow the aggressive heteronormative and patriarchal Judeo-Christian ideals of the American middle classes and, in doing so, offer the freedom to reject the exploitative socioeconomic exchanges underpinned by America's avaricious capitalism and imperialistic overreaching.

Rechy's and Nugent's bad beatitudes draw, as I have outlined, on their Hispanic American and African American communities, along with their respective Catholic and Protestant cultural influences. Of course Ginsberg never experienced the widespread and seemingly intransigent social and economic racism suffered by Hispanic Americans and African Americans, but his left-wing Russian Jewish heritage did alienate him to a significant degree from mainstream Anglo-Saxon privileges and prejudices. Ginsberg's father Louis was a first-generation American born to Russian immigrants and his mother Naomi was born in Vitebsk, then part of the Russian empire, and came to the United States as a child. Setting themselves apart from mainstream versions of American capitalism, both Ginsberg's father and mother maintained commitments to socialism and communism, respectively, as influenced by their Eastern European and Jewish roots.[1] Although economic and religious prejudice have created far less virulent social alienations in the United States than racism, Ginsberg remained aware that Jews, and particularly leftist Jews, were often set apart from dominant political and social elites both abroad and at home.[2] This sense of his family's marginalized position in the United States due to their relatively recent arrival, their religion, and their socioeconomic ideologies would overtly influence Ginsberg's frequent visions of a multifaceted America intrinsically composed of multiple races and religions, as well as of multiple sexualities and genders. If long uneasy about how his own sexuality fit into this more tolerant America, Ginsberg increasingly acknowledged the spiritual value of his same-sex longings and used these as an impetus to push for more inclusive US communities, merging his indictments of conservative and exploitative political and socioeconomic exchanges with a keen sexual radicalism.[3]

Indeed, Ginsberg's own complicated sexuality, like Rechy's and Nugent's, greatly influenced his reception of religious literary motifs, including those regarding an angelic rebelliousness. From his college years onward, when Ginsberg had his first visionary experience while masturbating and reading William Blake, he used eroticized Blakean religious imagery to fashion prismatic conceptions of morality through a multi-perspectival poetics. Much like Blake's *The Marriage of Heaven and Hell* or his *Songs of Innocence* and *Songs of Experience*, Ginsberg wanted his poetry to undermine ostensibly clear-cut certainties regarding physical and spiritual existences, virtues and vices, as well as just and unjust economic exchanges.[4] In doing so, he used angelic figures to bridge his diverse social and intellectual worlds, linking his personal desires for an angelic Neal Cassady and Jack Kerouac to his broader desire for a more spiritual, more socialistic, yet never quite unified, heterogeneous America. Ginsberg thus illustrates what Maria Damon has recognized as the queer community's use of angelic tropes to evoke "an ethereal sense of belonging to multiple worlds, multiple planes of existence, of inhabiting space somewhere between the human and the divine" (1993: 169). Although Damon convincingly distinguishes between "Beat usage" of "angelic imagery more for the joy of high contrast, for oxymoronic shock value," as opposed to "non-Beat gay usage" for an "actual or sustained sense of otherworldliness," I would argue that these connotations often merge in Ginsberg's queer Beat writing (168–9).

In his poetry from the 1940s onward, Ginsberg overtly engages the "joy of high contrast" in order to highlight a spiritually "ethereal" validation of queerly unconventional erotic and economic exchanges. Specifically, he engages a spiritual and psychological rebellion against a conservative heteronormativity tied to American capitalist excesses, perhaps most nastily demonstrated through the associated Lavender and Red Scares of the 1950s. In doing so, he creates hybrid queer angels that signal the spiritual potential of the material world and of individual lives, no matter how marginalized by mainstream society. By 1949, as Morgan reports, Ginsberg had already considered that the "work of this world is the work of Heaven. The love of this world is the love of Heaven" (2006: 120). The love of "this world," for Ginsberg, frequently included its more marginalized spaces and people. As Thomas Merrill has pointed out, Ginsberg thought that for "the sake of authentic existence, one must retreat from the citadels of unreality," such as the sparkling facades of institutionally lauded social heights, "to the catacombs of Bohemia where the angelic existence at least has a chance." Of course, as Merrill points out, such retreats could offer "a delaying tactic" or an appeal to "dubious adherents" of Beat philosophies, such as the oft-derided Beatniks who seemingly wanted only a simplistic hedonism (1988: 24). Ginsberg, however, consistently distanced himself from such uncritical decadence. In his early poetry, he rejected hedonism by embracing a spiritual materiality, offering a reaffirmation of Blakean contraries and a dialectical sense of heaven and hell, and in later poems, such as "Going to Chicago" and "Thoughts Sitting Breathing," he critiqued unphilosophical, self-indulgent debaucheries. Often Ginsberg fashioned this critique by evoking homoerotic angelic Beat figures who bridge worlds to reject rigidly inhuman moral systems and to reassert the spiritual connectedness of societies that have become too violently mechanical and nationalistic. These are tropes, moreover, that Ginsberg sustained despite his changing poetics, which evolved as he incorporated Buddhism, improvisational composition techniques, and an increased political activism into his work.

Ginsberg's angels thus connect the queer bad beatitudes discussed in earlier chapters to Beat exaltations of poverty, transiency, and intellectual and aesthetic rebellions. Along with Kerouac and Burroughs, Ginsberg used the concept of being "Beat" to indicate how destitution and social alienation, when combined with often highly sensual and illicit erotic encounters, could enable an individual to escape a mechanical conformity to a white, patriarchal middle-class heteronormativity, egotism, and greed, and thereby attain a spiritual awareness through enhanced, non-prepackaged human intimacies. Evoking these often taboo erotic inspirations, John Tytell argues in *Naked Angels: Kerouac, Ginsberg, Burroughs* that the "Beat movement was a crystallization of a sweeping discontent with American 'virtues' of progress and power. What began with an exploration of the bowels and entrails of the city—criminality, drugs, mental hospitals—evolved into an expression of [a] visionary sensibility" as "the Beats" considered themselves to be angelic "[m]essengers of imminent apocalypse" (1991: 4, 5). Linking a "Blakean" visionary "model" to "American transcendentalism," as Tytell points out, Kerouac, Burroughs, and Ginsberg drew on Thoreau's "distrust of machines and industry" and Whitman's "egalitarian gusto" for "the raw newness and velocity of self-renewing change in America," with "[n]akedness signifying rebirth, the recovery of identity" (10, 4). For Ginsberg especially, angelic imagery prophesized valuably infernal threats to 1950s conservativism through a consciousness-expanding sensual and spiritual enlightenment of humanity, a joyously homo-erotic spiritual physicality that challenged a mechanical, clocklike reproduction of a soullessly avaricious heteronormative America.

Eroticized Angels in Kerouac and Burroughs

To appreciate a broader queer nexus of American bad beatitudes I have connected Ginsberg to Rechy and to Nugent, but an understanding of Kerouac's and Burroughs's angelic imagery explains how Ginsberg's immediate literary circle influenced his particular use of this trope across his career. Most relevantly, for instance, Ginsberg's angelic imagery evidences his circle's interest in the concepts associated with the term "Beat," which signified the condition of individuals who go through alienating, degrading, and yet joyous experiences connected to a spiritual knowledge that they seek to share, often through erotic intimacies. In *On the Road*, published in 1957 but which Ginsberg began sending to publishing houses in 1952, Kerouac connected the term "beat" to individuals being "so lonely, so sad, so tired, so quivering, so broken" that they gain the "courage" to pursue erotic connections that they might otherwise have let pass (2003: 82).[5] Kerouac links being "BEAT—the root, the soul of Beatific" to being "ragged and broken and idiotic" and yet filled with physical and spiritual "revelations" that enlightened individuals try to impart to others (195). While Kerouac showed an increasing interest in Buddhism in the 1950s, his early conceptions of being "beat" stem largely from his Catholic upbringing. Corresponding at times to Rechy's reenvisioning of Catholic tropes and Nugent's of Protestant ones, Kerouac characterizes heightened moments of physical and spiritual intensity through angelic images to evoke sublime moments that occur within and yet transcend an abject material existence. Such hybrid moments signal how a certain Beat-ness enables a spiritual enlightenment or moral uplifting so that ostensibly profane actions, such as sex outside of marriage, become sacred while ostensibly sacred actions, such as chastity and sobriety, become profane, isolating individuals from spiritual communities and substantial joys.

Significantly, Kerouac's bad beatitudes, which evoke a hybridity of unconventional sanctities and profanities, often involve an analogously multicultural, multiethnic, and racially hybrid America. Despite his anti-Semitism, increasing racism, and deep-seated homophobia, Kerouac's early work signals an appreciation for a spectrum of American citizens. In *On the Road*, for instance, when the Italian-American Sal Paradise picks up Terry, a US worker of Mexican descent, he takes her to a cheap hotel where they drink whiskey and have sex, briefly yet enjoyably merging their worn, scarred bodies. Kerouac appreciatively describes the pair as "two tired angels of some kind, hung-up forlornly ... having found the closest and most delicious thing in life together" (2003: 85). Sal Paradise, whose name implicitly evokes a Dirty Paradise, a *paradis sale*, establishes with Terry a spiritual intimacy through physical ecstasy outside of marriage as they take advantage of the interpersonal freedom provided by their seemingly hellish existence.[6] Had Sal pursued the seemingly sanctified but profanely stifling ideals of a white middle-class heteronormative American life, his and Terry's shared spiritual encounter within a more socially diverse American environment would never have come to pass.

Yet while Kerouac exalts intoxicated mixed race heterosexual intimacies out of wedlock, he hints at queer angelic communions only to deny their homoeroticism, a significant difference between his work and Ginsberg's and Burroughs's. Riding across the United States in *On the Road*, Sal and Dean Moriarty share stories and memories until they "both swayed to the rhythm and the IT of [their] final excited joy," a reified "joy" gained by revealing the "riotous angelic particulars that had been lurking in [their] souls" (2003: 209). This angelic intimacy comes as the pair gets "hot" and "excited," so much so that Dean "moaned" when he talked. Kerouac and Cassady each had same-sex encounters with other men, including with Ginsberg, but despite the erotic overtones to Sal and Dean's conversation, Kerouac relapses into a sexual conservatism and opposes any challenge to his fictional characters' conventionally heterosexual masculinity.[7] Unlike even Rechy's or Nugent's self-declared straight hustlers, who nonetheless seek hyper-masculine same-sex encounters or crave the desire of effeminate men, Kerouac links same-sex desire largely to an enervated effeminacy. He displaces any homoeroticism between Sal and Dean on to a "fag" in an "[e]ffeminate car" that offers "no pickup and no real power" in which the friends hitch a ride (208, 209, 207). Sal and Dean use the "fag" for his car without any interest in the man himself. Indeed, when Dean tries to hustle him for money, he does so without promising any actual sexual exchange, which causes the man to become "suspicious" and to keep his money (210).[8] Connecting an overt queerness with a slow, effeminate, and lonely impotence, Kerouac seeks to forestall any interpretation of Sal and Dean's mutual excitement as homoerotic by suggesting that any same-sex desire would be too degrading to allow for the powerfully fast, ecstatic knowledge sharing and spiritual connection attained in heightened moments of Beat male friendships.

Kerouac's depiction of same-sex desire was nasty but banal and so seems tame compared to Burroughs's more violent bad beatitudes in *Naked Lunch*. In the novel, which Ginsberg helped to edit and to promote to publishers from around 1954 onward, Burroughs depicts a brutal same-sex sexuality as producing agonized sublime pleasures, ones that exist both in spite of and because of a cruel response to same-sex longings.[9] A "younger" Burroughs, Ginsberg reported, "found it demeaning" to have to "be screwed in order to have an orgasm," which resulted, for Burroughs, in an eroticism shaped by a misogynist homophobia and an exciting self-loathing. The repetitious "blue movie section" in *Naked Lunch*, Ginsberg suggested, was Burroughs's attempt to deaden the humiliation of such queer acts, "to cut out all apparent thoughts, feelings, and sensory impressions" as "a way of exorcising" his sexual "obsessions" (2017: 155, 156, 157). Yet if Burroughs's repetitive variation of pornographic scenes in the novel with Johnny, Mark, and Mary work to exorcise his seemingly profane sexual desires by dulling them into unemotional routines, they also allow him to exalt anal sex by recalling its almost inextricably intermixed pleasures and pains. Burroughs describes Johnny, for instance, as being "impaled on Mark's cock," as he "screams and whimpers," orgasms, and then "slumps against Mark's body an angel on the nod," after which "Mark pats Johnny's shoulder absently." Mark's "mocking" indifference to this and other encounters isolates Johnny, treating him like a dog to pet and thus demeaning him, cruelly distancing himself from Johnny's ecstasy after their brief physical intimacy (2007: 81). The sadomasochism of Burroughs's characters stimulates an ironic or paradoxical form of angelic-ness as torture merges inextricably with elation, somewhat akin to a sacrificial Christian passion. Burroughs makes Johnny a martyr to queer sex in a world that will use him for its own selfish purposes, much as Kerouac's Sal and Dean use the "fag" with the car, much as Rechy's hustlers use their johns and his johns use their hustlers, and much as

Nugent depicts US society using queer multiracial soldiers to maintain an only ever incomplete democracy.[10]

Like Rechy and Nugent albeit with more scatological force, as if to show pleasure fighting against all odds to exist, Burroughs also describes men in acts and in locations that mix degradation and ecstasy to produce a more communal queer salvation. While Rechy describes the freedoms of the dark dirty queer bars of LA and Nugent depicts the difficult sometimes violent compromises queer men make to love each other, Burroughs emphasizes a beatific anal homoeroticism amid its connection to a repulsive excrement via his description of "[a]dolescent angels" who "sing on shithouse walls of the world" (2007: 189). Burroughs moves beyond Johnny's alienation from Mark to construct a choir of angelic outcasts in the semi-private, if not totally sequestered, realm of public toilets. In these dissolute spaces designed for transient use, these youths find the freedom to hymn together their mutual praises in relative peace. Obviously this setting is not ideal but rather than overlook it or myopically damn it, Burroughs stresses its queerly celestial elements. His abject phrasings highlight the nexus of a vital eroticism and decaying feces, the inherent irony that our primary erogenous zones are so inextricably connected to excretion. He constructs then this ironic mixture of the sacred and the profane into a queer mystery of a rebellious angelic salvation enacted by shared human pleasures in adversity.

In *Naked Lunch*, such queer angelic communities, existing in spaces that facilitate desire amid waste, usefully enable self-affirming forms of exchange that reject legal yet self-detrimental processes, such as same-sex desiring individuals pursuing heterosexual sex and heteronormative middle-class conformities. Burroughs's description of the "shithouse" "angels," for instance, corresponds to that of his "Boy Burglar, fucked in the long jail term," who "comes gibbering into the queer bar" (2007: 190). Burroughs leaves room to interpret this character as a boy who is a burglar or as a burglar who steals sexual pleasure from boys, possibly with the boys' consent albeit without society's, or as all such figures all at once. What Burroughs does make clear is that the "Boy Burglar" lives as an outlaw from legal economic and romantic exchanges. The Burglar takes conventionally unwarranted benefits from systems that try to constrain him; for instance, he finds physical pleasure in the all-male jail where queer and predominantly heterosexual men turn to each other to give and to receive sexual satisfaction. Subsequently, he seeks communion in a "queer bar," itself a criminal business within a 1950s US society that would generally have considered any such talk of love between males to be not only illegal but mentally diseased gibberish.

The Burglar, Burroughs thus indicates, exists as a mad criminal only in terms of flawed US legislation and medical diagnoses. He is not insane or immoral according to natural laws or to accurate assessments of human psychology and biology. Analogously, the sexual pleasure that he takes from and gives to other males is more vital than iniquitous according to the terms of more self-affirming methods of transaction. Refusing to partake in deadening yet legislatively sanctioned financial or romantic engagements, the Burglar finds himself "ousted from the cemetery for the nonpayment" and this ouster represents a return to life (2007: 190). The Burglar refuses to pay the emotional and physical cost for the economic and social benefits of conventional professional contexts, most of which in this period would have required the deathlike constraints for him of a facade of heteronormative behaviors. Instead, he fashions his existence on his own terms and through forbidden transactions in degraded locations that enable some privacy and, in some cases, were likely more fun than the staid decorum of graveyards.

Burroughs frames the "Boy Burglar," moreover, as a rebel not just against positive laws and conventional economic and sexual moralities but also against their allegedly divine justifications. To do so, Burroughs connects the Burglar both to Jacob's wrestling with an angelic man or a manly angel and to Satan's fall after his rebellion against God. Burroughs describes how following the Burglar's visit to the "queer bar" he ends up "wrestling with the angel hard-on all night, thrown in the homo fall of valor" (2007: 190). Reminiscent of Cullen's speaker wrestling with an angel in "The Black Christ," Burroughs revises biblical and Miltonic paradigms to symbolize how human sensuality can coerce a blessing or a liberty from a tyrannical divine force. Just as one might sympathize with Jacob or Milton's ambitious Satan, Burroughs sympathizes with his Burglar whom he associates with an individualistic pride that comes from, and despite, being damned for disobedience. For the Burglar's "fall of valor," with Burroughs's syntax suggesting both a fall from valor and a valorous fall, represents a struggle wherein to lose is also to win. It represents a spiritual win to get penetrated by or to penetrate with or even just to masturbate an angelic erection—the "hard-on" belonging to the Burglar, to another male, or to both—as this leads to physical, psychological, and spiritual blessings. Hence Burroughs's "homo fall of valor" indicates a homosexual fall enabling a certain boldness and spiritual value. As we will see, the economic, moral, and spiritual eroticism of such a "fall of valor" would echo with more explicit virtues and far less brutal resonances throughout Ginsberg's own written work, to which I now turn.

Ginsberg's Queer Beat Angels

Ginsberg was immersed in and frequently promoted writing by both Kerouac and Burroughs, but he remained intellectually and aesthetically rebellious. Aware of and yet resistant to his friends' depictions of same-sex desire, Ginsberg expands the bad beatitudes of Kerouac and Burroughs with more celebratory if not entirely uncritical depictions of same-sex desiring or gender nonconforming men. Ginsberg queers, for instance, Kerouac's interest in degradations that inspire heterosexual lovers to share knowledge through spiritualized physical intimacies, while he revises Burroughs's violent queer rebellions against capitalistic respectability to emphasize more lovingly socialistic homoerotic elations. Like Rechy and Nugent, moreover, Ginsberg connects his queer bad beatitudes to rebellions against heteronormative legal and social constraints so often bolstered by religious repressions of queerness. Of course, as I indicated earlier, in emphasizing these similarities in angelic tropes, I do not want to elide these writers' significant differences. Rechy appropriates imagery from his Hispanic Catholic childhood to celebrate angelic outlaws that form compromised yet mutually beneficial human relationships in rebellion against the religiously influenced criminalization of same-sex sex and gender nonconformity, while Nugent fashions angelic tropes with a greater emphasis on extoling multiracial, same-sex nonmonogamous partners. Pursuing an analogous yet not identical project through his angelic hipsters, Ginsberg revises Miltonic and Blakean dialectics to exalt queer sexualities as a communal means to challenge psychological and mechanically uncritical repressions of human differences. Such queer challenges, Ginsberg insists, should likewise critique the rapaciously capitalistic exploitations of a modern American industrialism.

Notably, Ginsberg's early infatuation with Cassady and Kerouac inspired him to use queer angels to consider the relative sanctities and profanities of same-sex desire in psychological contexts. In "Love Letter" (1947), dedicated to Neal Cassady, Ginsberg uses Edenic imagery to consider how absence can turn a soothing idea of a loved one into a destructive mental anguish. Recalling Satan's claim in *Paradise Lost* that the "mind is its own place, and in itself / can make a Heav'n of Hell, a Hell of Heav'n," Ginsberg describes "Eros" as an "angel of the mind" and thus susceptible to shifts in psychological perspective, since absence can turn this winged Greek divinity from a heavenly "angel" into a more hellish one. Setting Eros into Luciferian contexts, Ginsberg cautions, "Tempt Eros not" to "suck the apple of thy sad absurdity," warning the Lover not to obsess over the melancholy irony that the loved one's sweetness can make his absence bitter. Ginsberg cautions that stressing a sad, possibly temporary loss of physical proximity over a romantic if imperfect happiness can "make a Devil" of "Love" (2007: 759). In essence, the Lover can become self-destructively Luciferian as he tempts himself to focus on how an absent joy intensifies sorrow. The lover thus taints the paradisiac nature of an idealized love, frustrating himself, much as Milton's Lucifer grew discontent in Heaven and encouraged Eve to grow discontent with her state in Eden. With these Edenic references, Ginsberg alludes to how Satan's need for adulation leads to his ambitious rebellion, which causes his half-regretted alienation from God's love and his descent into Hell. Inflamed by egotism and probably lust, Ginsberg's lover vitiates the desirable state of his former existence by obsessing over his absent beloved, whose sweetness now turns sour. Still, from an inverted perspective, Lucifer does prove pragmatically heroic, as he rejects a too limiting, too self-demeaning traditional paradise. Likewise, Ginsberg's Luciferian lover emphasizes a romantic sourness as a possible preparation for rejecting an unhealthy relationship where his beloved disdains mutual commitment and respect. By dedicating this poem to Cassady, who repeatedly abandoned him, Ginsberg queers this Edenic story. He suggests that same-sex lovers could achieve unconventional forms of Edenic sanctity and peace should they have the intellectual and emotional security to pursue a less narcissistic love and to resist egotism and melancholy. If this remains unachievable, however, one might rebelliously reject an unhealthy relationship to find new forms of paradise.

Expanding his queer angelic tropes from "Love Letter," in his subsequent Kerouac-inspired "Two Sonnets" (1948), Ginsberg imagines angelic outlaws as transcending alienating capitalistic urbanities. In the first sonnet the speaker describes living in "Hell on earth" complete with "living flame" through which he glimpses "Heaven" as "[a]ngels in the air / Serenade [his] senses" (2007: 13). This "flame," Ginsberg later commented, represents not only "Hell" but also a "visionary experience," a glimpse into "paradise" (2017: 344). Ginsberg's fiery flame is thus a purgatorial one, a hell that prepares for heaven, and in the poem the speaker realizes that the angels' sensual song is the conversation of "poets, saints and fair / Characters," all intelligent artists, spiritual visionaries, or people who are simply "fair," meaning attractive or fair-minded or both, who amid this urban "inferno" have an ecstatic message to share through song and physical sensations. To obstruct this message's critique of unfair, hellishly exploitative environments, the personified city tries "burning these multitudes that climb / Her buildings" to see a better life beyond them. As such the "fame" of the messengers works outside the alienating "fame" of the marketing, commercialism, and materialistic extravagances that fuel the city's hellish growth and its quotidian existence. Ginsberg extends these critiques into the second sonnet wherein he describes an "angel in an agony of flame" who in its pain and horror predicts the self-destruction of world capitals such as New York, Chicago, London, Moscow, and Paris (2007: 13). Ginsberg presents these cities almost in a list, as if to indicate that their famously unfair celebrations of the international upper classes', corporations', or even state governments' material interests lead to an excruciating and self-defeating sameness. In these sonnets then, angelic serenades function as a sweetly sensual critique of international conformity, which threatens its angelically rebellious socioeconomic outsiders.

If the angels of "Love Letter" and "Two Sonnets" work largely in the air, Ginsberg imagines more earthly angelic eroticisms in "Psalm II" (1949). Here he constructs a progressive tripartite cosmology (an interlinked hell, earth, and heaven) to conflate sexual pleasure with a transmittable knowledge and a spiritually sensual liberation. Beginning his psalm, he imagines an external divine figure looking down before directing its gaze up through a great chain of being. A "sweet Divinity" observes "Hell, / Imprisoned joy's incognizable thought" and then looks up to a "mounted earth, that shudders to conceive," then on to "angels, borne unseen out of this world," a mixture of divinity and humanity. Ginsberg constructs an allegory wherein a captive joy remains incapable of expressing itself until an "earth" that is "mounted," both sexually and set higher in a cosmological hierarchy, exhibits a humanistic shivering toward pleasure and conceives still higher embodied spirits. Dialectically combining a worldly materiality and an unseen spirituality, Ginsberg plays with semantics, blurring the homophones "born" and "borne" to describe earth-born angels borne joyfully to a higher metaphysical plane of consciousness via a shuddering orgasm. This angelic movement upward traces the pleasures of a spiritual intellectual conception made material through a poetic representation, as "joy's incognizable thought" becomes cognizable, articulable, and even tangible when the angels "[t]ranslate the speechless stanzas of the rose," the joyful beauty liberated from underneath the earth, into the speaker's "poem," a written form to be held and read (2007: 28).

Ginsberg joins here tropes of intellectual or spiritual conception from Shakespeare's homoerotic sonnets, wherein two male lovers reproduce themselves into futurity through the intellectual flower of poetry, to Milton's own queer spiritual descriptions of sexually active angels and to inhabitants of Blake's erotic Eden. In *Paradise Lost* Raphael reveals to Adam with an angelic "[c]elestial rosy red" smile and through diverse erotic enjambments that angels "obstacle find none / Of membrane, joint or limb exclusive bars" when they "embrace / Total they mix, union of pure with pure / Desiring" (2005: 8.619, 624–8). Through his own flower imagery, Ginsberg likewise connects these tropes to Blake's rebellious spiritual eroticism manifested in poems such as "The Garden of Love" wherein the poet protests "[p]riests ... binding with briars / joys and desire" in a postlapsarian garden, an Eden overly pruned by institutional authorities rather than divine ones (1988: lns. 11–12). A spiritually ideal "Garden of Love," Blake suggests, would allow eroticism to flourish more freely. In Ginsberg's poem, with its Shakespearean, Miltonic, and Blakean resonances, a queer erotic sharing similarly signals a rebellion against infernal religious or social stigmas, not necessarily endorsed by a "sweet Divinity." This rebellion, Ginsberg suggests, can lead to an angelic joy communicable to others via art, much like the serenading "[a]ngels in the air" from "Two Sonnets" only in more earthly embodiments.

Yet while Ginsberg's speaker celebrates the rebelliousness of liberated minds and bodies, a poetic and spiritual sexuality unbound and mounting, he remains uneasy with a spirit connected to a mortal body. He worries over that "sweet dream! to be some incorruptible/Divinity, corporeal ... Suffering metamorphosis of flesh" (2007: 28). The imagined sweetness is for a static divine nature to enjoy the tension and release of a human existence, though this risks a painful corruptive aging that will disrupt an angelic love. The speaker imagines, nonetheless, that this suffering can lead to sanctity for "Holy are the Visions of the soul / The visible mind seeks out for marriage" and "[i]n flesh and flesh, imperfect spirits join / Vision upon vision," embodying holy visions in human forms, both individually and intermingling. To achieve, in other words, the holy vision of a spiritual and intellectual relationship akin to a "marriage" of two minds, "imperfect" spirits must be born into bodies themselves imperfect, bodies capable of a tangibly joyful communion but also capable of tangible sufferings from age, disease, and pain (29). The corollary to this mingling is that such imperfect flesh and its decay risk the end of any permanent spiritual ecstasy.

Eventually, though, the poet accepts imperfection and prefers a more humanlike angelic state to a too abstract divine one. Exalting a spiritualized physical erotic, the enthused speaker personalizes the angelic imagery from earlier in the poem and declares, "My name is Angel and my eyes are Fire!" even as he knows that this passionate holy vision will fade as the once vital, upward-moving Angel will become a "grey and groaning man" fated to fall. For fed up with uncertain abstractions, the speaker laments, "Am I to spend / My life in praise of the idea of God?" (Ginsberg 2007: 29). Refusing to adhere to an alienating "idea" of a God, however "sweet," the speaker actualizes this divinity in himself. He embraces the maturing decay of the body, "in each season, as the garden dies, / I die with each, until I die no more," enjoying the sensual pleasures of the unbound Blakean garden, the orgasmic little deaths that help to advance one's spiritual being prior to a physical finality when one sleeps with others no more. By embracing such temporal fleshly pleasures, physical lovers can see the very real spiritual benefits of divine myths made manifest, and subsequently rematerialized in articulable written words, in poetry, God's "myth incarnate in my flesh / Now made incarnate in Thy Psalm" (30). Evolving Blakean tropes of a cynical experience versus a naive innocence, Ginsberg's poetic visualization lauds the synthesis of a frail body and an inadequate spirit to gain a greater state of existence capable of more complete unions with others. Ginsberg takes this notion further as eroticized contexts connect lovers to each other but also to longer-lasting artistic states as angelic humans once unseen mature into productive lover-poets, translating once incognizable joys into stanzas and psalms.

When it comes to bad beatitudes, "Psalm II" presents a fairly unique because relatively nonthreatening conception of a decaying humanized God, a trope Ginsberg delineates with an explicit homoeroticism in his contemporary "Hymn" (1949). In "Hymn," as in "Psalm II," the speaker characterizes his body as marking time through decay, as a "clock of meat," while longing for "its sweet immaterial paradise," the latter contemplated "in the mind's angelical empyrean … [a] clock of light" marking perpetual celestial joys. As in "Psalm" though, such celestial joys depend upon physical embodiments, especially the human brain and mental imagery suggestive of very material male orgasms. The "clock of light," for instance, reveals "finality's joy, whence cometh / purely pearly streams of reves" and a "crownly creaminess," reminiscent of semen. The speaker imputes the sacredness inherent in such conventionally profane or obscene manifestations by disrupting cosmological distinctions between heaven and hell. He notes that "one never knew whence" this joyful "creaminess" derived. It could come "from those foul regions of the soul the ancients named Malebolge," a term Dante used to refer to an infernal "evil ditch" but which Ginsberg uses playfully to suggest the ditch of a man's buttocks or the male bulge of a man's groin. The joy might also come from a "sky called / Icecube or Avenue where the angels late fourteen … hang on and raptly gaze on us singing down," like heavenly hustlers attempting to lure the men below (2007: 44). Ginsberg's association of "Icecube" and "Avenue," meanwhile, likely refers to "ice" as a term for treating someone coldly, perhaps someone met cruising along avenues whom you touch physically while remaining emotionally and psychologically distant, or even to "ice" as slang for illicit financial exchanges.[11] Both icy references evoke pleasures that remain pointedly imperfect and temporary and yet simultaneously heavenly. This complex network of references, literary and vulgar, intentionally disrupts the value system of infernal and celestial joys and suggests that their origins are indeterminate or possibly even analogous. The confusion, Ginsberg suggests, stems from humanity's attempt to identify the "whence" of such joys. The trouble derives from classifying into subsections, such as holy or damned or spirit and body, what is actually a unified whole. Such an oppressive use of the mind, Ginsberg intimates, can itself become profane.

Ginsberg draws then on oppositions and on a Blakean synthesis of multiple binaries, such as up and down, heaven and hell, spiritual and physical, which manifest into one holy homoerotic unity. Reminiscent of Blake's declarations in his "America: A Prophecy" that "everything that lives is holy" and in "The Marriage of Heaven and Hell" that "all deities reside in the Human breast," Ginsberg laments that modern human classifications of the world still tend to mischaracterize the sacred body as profane and a profanely disembodied spirit as sacred (1988: 208; 13). In truth, Ginsberg posits, a corporealized spiritual joy comes analogously from the "foul" depths of what the "ancients," like Dante, falsely damned as an infernal hell, "Malebolge," and from the icy heights of what they falsely exalted as heaven. Blake prophesized that in a temporally and geographically new world, allegorically presented as America, such misclassifications would get reworked and that misguided priests could not so tightly bind with briars humanity's desires. Ginsberg works to fulfill this hope. Evolving Blake's dialectic theories on the marriage of heaven and hell into one holy human unity, Ginsberg's dialectic in "Hymn" ends in a homoerotic metaphorical marriage between heaven and hell. Ginsberg describes a "Diamond Seraph," whose brightness inevitably recalls the rebellious individualism of Lucifer, the brightest rebel, challenging a cold divine tyranny, and this Seraph "bares his radiant breast and asks us … to share that Love in Heaven which on Earth was so disinherited" (2007: 44). While this Love "disinherited" on "earth" is a more intense physical spirituality, such as Blake intimates in "The Garden of Love," the homoerotic angelic imagery woven throughout the poem indicates that a key facet of this Love is an erotic, indeed an orgasmic, love between men.

If writers such as Rechy and at times Cullen and Hughes characterize God, or mainstream conceptions of God, as variously indifferent to humanity or too rigidly authoritarian, Ginsberg's poetry frequently posits a divine presence as a more abstract, more morally ambivalent idea. Ginsberg imagines a "sweet Divinity" who watches and waits, as in "Psalm II," rather than one who aggressively condemns same-sex desires or who facilitates racism. Ginsberg shares with these other writers, however, a desire to reclaim the seemingly repressive angelic hierarchy of heaven for queer purposes, reformulating it in more inclusively democratic and progressive terms as a model for individuals struggling toward enlightenment. Thus in "Hymn" Ginsberg depicts his Luciferian angel, the "Diamond Seraph," as a divine emissary as he invitingly embodies the sacred spirituality of a queer love classified as profane on earth but as sacred in "Heaven."

Ginsberg's emphasis on such dialectic Blakean angels and their refining movement through time resists a static conception of heaven. Milton's, Rechy's, Cullen's, Hughes's, and Nugent's rebellious angelic outlaws all move through time, challenging religious, subcultural, and racial assumptions, but none emphasize a changing heaven so explicitly as Ginsberg's. In "Hymn" angelic bodies and minds are "clock[s]" and in his subsequent "The Terms in which I Think of Reality" (1950), Ginsberg imagines "Heaven's mystery / of changing perfection: / absolutely Eternity / changes!" Ginsberg captures the surprise of a "changing" paradise in the enjambment and the exclamation point that highlight the unexpected juxtaposition of an "Eternity" that "changes!" Reimagining a Blakean and even a Whitmanian sense of the holy democracy of the United States, Ginsberg connects his ideal of an evolving paradise to his declaration in "Terms" that "everyone's an angel," an echo of Blake's report in "America" that "everything that lives is holy" and of Whitman's "Song of Myself" wherein he insists, "Divine am I inside and out, and I make holy whatever I touch or am touched from" (Ginsberg 2007: 58; Whitman 2010: 31). Whitman in particular evokes an idealized evolution of American acceptance by enfolding individuals into an ever-enlarging sacred human collective through means of a physical intimacy, no matter how brief. Whitman's holy cruising citizens correspond to Ginsberg's egalitarian angelic-ness, inclusive of even the 1950s outcasts of communists and queers, swirling within a democratic motion. The more explicit homoerotics of Ginsberg's everyman American angels will come out more clearly in *Howl* but even in "Hymn" and "Terms" this queerness remains subtly present and merges with a more prevalent interest in progressive rather than repetitive markings of time.

Ginsberg acknowledges, of course, that this heavenly ideal is just that, an ideal, even as his tripartite structure for "Terms," with its "a," "b," and "c" sections, formally posits that this paradigm can offer a dialectical model for pragmatically perceiving a progressive reality. Part "a" of his "Terms" presents his thesis of unconventional heavenly angels ("everyone's an angel") who attempt to identify the best in "everyone," even the most marginalized of humanity. This heavenly lens leads him to his earthly antithesis in part "b" wherein he desires the "initiation / of gratifying new changes / desired in the real world," which too often fosters ungratifying repetitions. On earth "we dream" of "Heaven" to avoid the reality that the "world is a mountain / of shit" that can only be moved a few "handfuls" at a time. Consequently, in part "c," which gestures toward a synthesis, Ginsberg prods a reassessment of earth's seemingly repetitive movements from a refining heavenly perspective. Earthly movements seem static but can actually be progressive, albeit degradingly minimal. To remain hopeful, individuals must emphasize even the slightest progress otherwise an unenlightened humanity would seem little different than a "whore" who sees "her Eternity" as a progression of small financial reimbursements for her engagement with "physical love" one trick at a time. Recognizing the struggle to align Blake's and Whitman's optimism with 1950s US society, Ginsberg gestures toward a dialectic synthesis but ultimately leaves it incomplete. His "whore," like much of humanity, has "never really heard of a glad / job or joyous marriage," much less a metaphorical marriage between heaven and hell, or, worse, "thinks it isn't for her," thus unfairly excluding her from a perfection enjoyed by others (2007: 59). With this ending, Ginsberg gestures toward but never reaches a synthesis of heaven and hell on earth. He admits the difficulty of conceiving how a debasing, almost unbearably sluggish earthly progression, could lead to shared love and enlightenment while he simultaneously argues that some progressive movement, even tiny handfuls of shoveled shit, should be considered to be an angelic work in progress.

Angelic Appropriations of Industrialism: Queer Movements and Queer Mechanics

While Ginsberg's angelic poetry from the late 1940s and early 1950s queered Beat themes of shared erotic knowledge through contemplating often slow movements toward a homoerotic salvation, by 1953 he was likewise drawing on Kerouac's, Cassady's, and Burroughs's fascination with a mechanical speed. Ginsberg's bad beatitudes evolved to rebel not only against conceptions of a static heaven with stable divine authorities but against more specific geo-historical oppressors through his portrayal of the opportunities and the pitfalls of industrialism in post–Second World War US society. At the relative height of the Lavender Scare, for instance, itself exacerbated by the Red Scare and obsessions with capitalist patriarchal conformity, as the US government harassed, fired, and generally abused queer citizens, Ginsberg effectively reimagined Miltonic and Blakean angelic rebels speeding to allegedly obscene intimacies in cars or on motorcycles or by cruising in modern-day supermarkets. This speed represents less an escape from repression than men rushing to enjoy pleasurable if aging flesh and to soar out of the mire of too repetitious mechanical conventions. These industrialized settings raise moral dilemmas regarding transient commercial and sensual exchanges but the rapidity of modern encounters also jumpstarts Ginsberg's lovers along their precipitous struggle toward an erotic spiritual enlightenment. While "Love Letter" and "Psalm II" evoke this gradual erotic spiritual enlightenment in subtle terms, in works such as "The Green Automobile" (1953) and *Howl* (1955), Ginsberg's angelic tropes offer joyous descriptions of same-sex encounters as he depicts the explicit benefits of transient and even partially degrading queer ecstasies and an incipient longing for the more difficult pleasures of longer-term mutually romantic relationships.

In "The Green Automobile," for instance, Ginsberg eulogizes his intermittent and unfulfilling sexual relationship with Neal Cassady by constructing a personal poetic daydream that whisks them off on a whirlwind affair. Ginsberg chose the title, Michael Schumacher reports, because he considered "green" to be a "symbolic color of hope" and a reference to the allegedly "green robes worn by the homosexual prostitutes in ancient Rome," while the car symbolized "the transitory nature" of his intimacies with Cassady and the latter's "perpetual motion." These intimacies often consisted of a one-sided hope, with Cassady submitting to sporadic erotic encounters with Ginsberg in exchange for intellectual ones, a situation that often left Ginsberg feeling lonely and depressed, as if a sort of intellectual prostitute or beggar for love.[12] Ginsberg, Schumacher observes, "intended th[is] poem to be a personal step forward," a step through past depressions and toward his recognition that "bliss exists in the imagination," which itself can be a "way of perfecting [one's] past" (1992: 154). Indeed in Ginsberg's reimagining, the poem enhances the spiritual intensity of the friends' on-and-off again sexual relations by de-emphasizing Cassady's primary erotic preference for women. To intensify this homoerotic spiritual connection, Ginsberg merges the symbolic green car with angelic characterizations of the lovers. While the angelic imagery heightens the spiritualized sensuality between Ginsberg and the "Neal" of the poem, it also links this personal fantasy to

Ginsberg's more abstract earlier interests in physical and spiritual movements away from seemingly useless repetitions and toward a progressive, if here much more fast-paced, journey to enlightenment.

In "The Green Automobile," Ginsberg uses a car and angelic characterizations to imagine a liberating same-sex eroticism that counters the constraints of a domestic heterosexuality. Ginsberg begins his disruptive fantasy by bringing Neal a green car, which Neal takes control of to flee the "inside" of his home where "his wife and three / children sprawl naked / on the living room floor." Fleeing as if from a minimum security prison, Neal bolts through "his manly gate," a symbol of his adult male privilege, to escape a coarse marital fecundity that threatens to wall him in and ground him down. Unlike his floor-bound wife and children, Neal can determine his own fast-paced coming and going. Rebelling against heteronormative familial obligations, he rushes with "heroic beer" to Ginsberg's car to begin their intoxicating "pilgrimage" to mountains and forests, "laughing in each other's arms, / delight surpassing the highest Rockies," a rarefied air wherein they meet other "angels of anxiety," likely other men risking taboo and consequently anxious pursuits of pleasure (2007: 91). The moveable space of the car provides the lovers with a semi-private setting within which they can enjoy the forbidden euphoria inspired by each other's bodies and within which they can rise with dangerous speeds from the constraining security of home to new metaphysical peaks of existence. As such, the car facilitates an epic spiritual narrative reminiscent of those by Milton and Blake only with the addition of an intense same-sex eroticism as an intrinsic part of the desire to seek enlightenment beyond one's home and beyond the institutional securities of religious, social, and legal conformity.

Noticeably, Ginsberg uses angelic terms to elevate these lovers as they speed off iconoclastically, rebelling against heteronormative intellectual and psychological tyrannies to enjoy the freedom of perspectives that value same-sex intimacies. As they travel a "cloudy highway" joining other "angels," Ginsberg and Neal eventually find an "unnatural radiance" that ends up "illuminating" their surroundings with an unearthly spiritual clarity. This angelic vision enables a more comprehensive, progressive view of a man maturing in "eternity," similar to that evoked in "Terms," as these male lovers see the advent of "another spring," a new emotionally fecund advance that overwhelms them with "love" (2007: 91). By achieving a passionate intimacy, these men observe "together / the beauty of souls / hidden like diamonds / in the clock of the world" (92). In essence, their taboo eroticism facilitates a velocity through higher landscapes. This metaphorical height allows them to see the transcendent divine value that can evolve, often out of sight, from within the manure or clocklike repetitions of their daily environment, as carbon under pressure can crystallize over time into diamonds.

In the poem, however, Ginsberg consistently recalls that this angelic flight through marginalized spaces is a transitory if helpful fantasy of a problematic personal past. He delves into his former disheartening relationship with Cassady, particularly their time in Denver when Cassady mostly avoided him, to reimagine it as a long-lasting optimistic ideal of a spiritually physical same-sex love.[13] Ginsberg revisits this humiliating time, like so many other men recall grimy bars, theaters, or parks, to find the beauty in the debased. To heighten this effect, Ginsberg imagines the lovers driving from the mountains to Denver where they visit "flophouse jazzjoint jail" and "whorehouse," a series of down-and-out, often sensualized venues that encourage them to take pleasure in what they can and where they can for a minimal exchange of money and time. Following visits to such marginalized places where nonnormative pleasures have room to exist, Ginsberg imagines founding a "miraculous college of the body / up on [a] bus terminal roof," a divinely, erotically, and thoughtfully charged investigation into the pleasure that can exist in fantastical breaks from life's journey and that have long-lasting, uplifting effects in the real world. For these moments, Ginsberg argues, if partly fantasy are nonetheless "more real than the engine / on a track in the desert" and "purer than [the] Greyhound" buses that pause at the terminal beneath the lovers (2007: 92). In these scenes Ginsberg focuses on flashes of a spiritual physicality that generate long-lasting memories that perfect one's lived reality. He and Neal "share an archangelic cigarette," an ephemeral phallic stimulation of a sacredly profane *spiritus* or breath, after which they "kneel" with "naked breasts" and "renew" an old "solitary vow," thus merging physically erotic sensations with recapitulations of past emotional, quasi-marital connections (93). These poetic moments, built on Ginsberg's own imperfect sexual and emotional past encounters with the flesh-and-blood Cassady, transform themselves into a poetic vision of transitory enlightenment, whereby imagination triumphs over actuality to bring life to Ginsberg's conception of an intense romance with another man.[14]

This angelic imagination likewise inspires Ginsberg's consideration of how his and Neal's erotic journey will eventually influence the lived experiences of a wider public. "How many Saturday nights," Ginsberg wonders toward the poem's end, "will be / made drunken by this legend? / How will young Denver come to mourn/her forgotten sexual angel?" (2007: 93). In a linked series of events, Ginsberg's fleeting moments with Cassady inspire the erotic visions of the poem, which in turn Ginsberg foresees as lubricating the weekend adventures of young readers who will mourn the original inspirational model, Cassady himself, whom they never quite knew and so who becomes "forgotten" over time in favor of his intoxicatingly recalled angelic legend. The angelic legend lives on of not just Neal but of Ginsberg too, as the poem enshrines the pair as "real heroes" who have become "angels of the world's desire," both in terms of loved objects and messengers of other's desires. The pair forms therefore "an ageless monument to love / in the imagination," including specifically the queer desire between these two men. Although the poem itself is an admitted fantasy, "a present / from my [the poet's] imagination," this almost Shakespearean gift of an eternal now and an eternal love, which in actuality fell far short of Ginsberg's fantasy, is one designed to inspire readers to acknowledge the valuable, even sacred spirituality of their own aging flesh and to pursue their own taboo queer pleasures in alienated Beat environments (94).

Roughly fifteen years later, however, after Cassady's death, Ginsberg had a bit more difficulty eulogizing Neal in erotically angelic terms as age, disillusionment, and corporeal decay disrupted his desire. Meditating on an automotive accident he had in 1968, Ginsberg uses "Car Crash" (1968–9) to recall his concerns with his damaged and aging body, which he tries to rejuvenate through masturbatory memories of old lovers. Unlike in "The Green Automobile" though, an obvious predecessor to this poem about an out-of-control car, the initial solace of erotic recollections falls flat, not only from general physical decay but also from his friends' and lovers' inability to outrace their personal demons. Ginsberg laments Peter Orlovsky's mad anguish, Jack Kerouac's numbing drunkenness, and Neal's death, "almost a year turned to ash, angel / in his own midnight without a phonecall" (2003: 518). Ginsberg himself has now only his memory of an ideal memory, a constantly displaced construct, for Neal's angelic radiance has gone dark and is uncommunicative. In "Rain-wet" (1969) Ginsberg will call such palimpsests, memories of memories, "nameless angels of half-life" after referring to a masturbatory nighttime fantasy of Neal (537). Similarly, in "Over Denver Again" (1969), which follows "Car Crash" in Ginsberg's *Collected Poems*, his speaker refers to a queer courier's "alleyway," suggesting another cryptic, backdoor communication regarding the variations of human love, including implicitly anal sex, which angelic queer partners once manifested on earth. Any message though, Ginsberg prophesizes, will likely disappear "when the Earth Angel's dead," a tragedy stemming from Neal's own fading angelic trace, his half-life, which echoes Orlovsky's mental instability and Kerouac's alcoholic aggression, with the result that a "dead material planet'll revolve robotlike" (519). Having lost or abandoned the beauty of nonnormative loves and desires, the spirituality of humanity's diverse psychologies and physiologies, the world becomes flatly mechanical. The speedy, liberating opportunities of the car turn in on themselves and become robotlike, angels to mechanical failures, having abandoned a loving humanity.

Even before the late 1960s, though, Ginsberg had grown concerned with avoiding a repetitious, robotic existence and with pursuing a spiritual evolution attained through same-sex sex, which could sanctify even an imperfect body. As he wrote in "Song" (1954), be passionate or coolly calm, "obsessed with angels / or machines," with intoxicatingly imprudent lovers or with men who go coldly through daily motions, the last hope is for "love" and this love, he argues, requires a "return / to the body" (2007: 120). Despite any initial desire to flee the body's imperfections and disappointments, one's spiritual and earthbound mechanical body should merge, Ginsberg argues, when one loves oneself comprehensively, as this allows one to connect to someone else spiritually, emotionally, and physically. This love opens the opportunity for two bodies, however blemished or flawed, to come together to share the responsibility of bearing the burden of existing within the "world," of being one link in a communal chain (119). The relief of finding someone with whom to share the responsibility of existing in a larger, too often hostile community manifests itself in physical terms, as one's body and soul remain happy and joyous. The joy of physical intimacies brings together the angelic and the animalistic, instinctive mechanics of humanity so that two people, including two men having sex, can lead to a soulful enlightenment. This enlightenment raises humanity above a cold reactionary existence and eases the burdens of living on one's own in "solitude" and "dissatisfaction" amid others who depend on you and to whom you should feel a responsibility, however indirectly (119).

Ginsberg's insistence that a spiritually aware humanizing enlightenment can fight the conservative mechanistic elements of US society comes across most complexly in *Howl*. Blending both abstract and highly personalized circumstances, such as his romanticization of Neal, Ginsberg uses *Howl* to insist that nominally obscene encounters can facilitate knowledge sharing that might improve a conservative US culture by unfettering sexual, spiritual, and more socialist economic pursuits.[15] Illicit erotic encounters, he suggests, can stimulate analogously illicit yet worthwhile cosmopolitan perspectives, more worldly bad beatitudes. These intellectual and socially oriented bad beatitudes challenge an inhumanely industrialized, rapaciously capitalistic society that adheres too rigidly to a Christian Anglo-Saxon nationalism and thereby dulls human joys and alienates a large portion of the United States' undervalued working population.

In *Howl*, Ginsberg quickly associates intellectual rebels against social constraints with a transcendent angelic imagery. He connects his famous preludial line "I saw the best minds of my generation destroyed by madness" with the appositive "angelheaded hipsters" and these brilliant if ostensibly insane angelic hipsters provide the antecedent for the reiterated "who" that forms the base for the anaphoric structure of the first section. Initially, this insistent recollection positions the "angelheaded hipsters" as messengers of sacred knowledge designed to warn against the self-destructiveness of a world gone wrong (2007: 134). Like modern-day Cassandras or like Burroughs and Kerouac, such prophets inevitably seem mad and dangerous. Considering themselves to be "[m]essengers of imminent apocalypse," as John Tytell observes, "the Beats believed that they were the angels of holocaust," powerful heralds of a destruction that could also be "cleansing and purgative," as "Ginsberg's and Kerouac's pathway to beatitude stemmed from Burroughs's nightmare of devastation" (1991: 5, 14, 132). Drawing on these real-life inspirations, Ginsberg depicts his "angelheaded hipsters burning for the ancient heavenly connection to the starry dynamo in the machinery of night" as they try to rip away a consciousness locked in step with the mechanical neo-Miltonian "Moloch whose soul is electricity and banks" as detailed in the poem's second section (2007: 134, 139).[16] Such psychic and physical breaks from the norms of modern work, within factories, bureaucratic corporations, or other profit-driven commercial endeavors, allow these hipsters to reconnect their minds to an enlightening and spiritualizing dynamism. The hipsters' intellectual realignment reconciles progressive human connections with a larger celestial spiritual consciousness, one less individualistically avaricious and more cognizant of social allegiances that should spread across temporal, spatial, political, and socioeconomic boundaries.

This angelic imagery reflects, of course, not just spiritual Beat intellectuals and their industrial and economic critiques but also Ginsberg's praise for same-sex desiring men who had to transcend, however cautiously or fearfully, rote conservative repressions. As *Howl* continues, Ginsberg diverges from Kerouac's reluctant and Burroughs's violent homoeroticism to exalt in same-sex intimacies. Using the queer connotations of a symbolic angelic nature, Ginsberg characterizes how same-sex sexual encounters might exuberantly facilitate cross-cultural, cross-class, and cosmopolitan associations for various queer communities. Ginsberg's "angelheaded hipsters," for instance, eagerly let "themselves be fucked in the ass by saintly motorcyclists," as they "screamed with joy" and "blew and were blown by those human seraphim, the sailors," who offer "caresses of Atlantic and Caribbean love" (2007: 134, 136). Angelic hipsters, spiritualized and butch-er counterparts to the oft-derided "fairy" figure, join in mutual erotic encounters with same-sex desiring bikers, early manifestations of the queer hyper-masculinity soon to be popularized by Bob Mizer and Tom of Finland, and sailors, who were already forming a part of a manly queer subcultural lore.[17] In coming together, these figures achieve a level of sanctity because their very outlaw behaviors enable them to find authentic, joyful connections. Ginsberg's intermingling of his hipsters, based primarily on college-educated white men, with bikers and sailors, at this point representatives of working-class "trade" who desired same-sex sex but did not necessarily identify as queer, indicates cross-class and possibly even cross-racial encounters between men from across nations bordering the Atlantic ocean and the Caribbean who find erotic release within the United States.[18]

Ginsberg spiritualizes these cosmopolitan socio-sexual pleasures to challenge unenlightened understandings of same-sex sex as painful and degrading. An "American audience would expect," Ginsberg later noted, someone to describe anal sex with the word "pain," but in *Howl* he wrote "'and screamed with joy'— which is really true, absolutely, one hundred per cent" (2001: 313). Ninety-eight per cent is more likely but by indulging in hyperbole Ginsberg explicitly rejects a mechanical or robot-like adherence to American Judeo-Christian homophobia. Rather, he again reaffirms all human nature as ecstatically "holy," as clarified in his "Footnote to Howl," by insisting that these diversely queer figures can find true joy through shared same-sex erotic acts (2007: 142). These representations become psychologically and spiritually beneficial because they attempt, at least, to resist the intellectual, cultural, racial, and spiritual divisions that divided US society in the 1950s up to today.

Most pointedly perhaps, by flouting stultifying norms, stereotypes separating male intellectuals from bad bikers, as well as class and racial divisions, these queer angelic outlaws defy the constraints of an egotistically avaricious American culture. As Ben Lee has suggested, Ginsberg "attacks white-collar culture" in particular as "he seeds his Beat poems with heroic images of the lumpen proletariat: musicians, bums, junkies, and other 'angels' of Skid Row," which in *Howl* helps Ginsberg "to merge his own generation of angel-headed hipsters with his parents' generation of dedicated socialists and impassioned communists" (2004: 376, 382). Indeed, Ginsberg's angelic outlaws symbolically seed rebellions against miserly, metaphorically deadly forms of capitalism and religious repressions as they go "scattering their semen freely" in free spaces, such as "public parks" and unguarded "cemeteries" (2007: 136). These free dispersals subvert middle-class moral goals that require an expanding, profit-driven income to support American versions of cross-sex marriage, parenthood, and luxury commodities. Ginsberg's *Howl* thus updates Blake's critique of an unnatural religious sexual shame and capitalistic enclosures in "The Garden of Love," his symbolic garden enclosed by priests and turned into a graveyard, and Burroughs's quasi-admiration for his "Boy Burglar," who cruising through a "jail" and a "cemetery" evades the morbid socioeconomic, legal, and religious constraints of twentieth-century America. Ginsberg himself cultivates a queer, relatively carefree sharing that just as rebelliously seeks taboo pleasures in marginalized spaces, albeit not a collectivity as explicitly political or ideologically orthodox as that envisioned by his parents.

Still, Ginsberg's collectivity allows for the plantings of improved if notably imperfect forms of social exchange that reject the preeminence of commercially exploitative relationships in American culture. Ginsberg's enlightened erotic sharing of space, bodies, and seed, the latter representing fruit or renewable capital for a progressive social future, defies what he presents as heteronormative, excessively profit-driven capitalistic American "fate[s]." Queer angelheaded hipsters and their sex partners defy the three modern instances of "fate," including "the one eyed shrew of the heterosexual dollar the one eyed shrew that winks out of the womb and the one eyed shrew that does nothing but ... snip the intellectual golden threads of the craftsman's loom" (2007: 136). Ginsberg's angelic angels value the renewable intellectual gold of nonmonetized sensual enlightenments and of worker-determined, nonindustrial productions. As such, they craft new visions through creatively lauding sex without childbearing, with no child winking from a womb, and recreation as a form of procreation in the realms of consciousness and art. Pursuing these values allows queer angelic men to refashion their own world and communities, despite pushback from family, friends, employers, social institutions, and even more conservative assimilationist queer men. Such a resistance overtly challenges, for instance, the crude "nitroglycerine" or explosive "shrieks of the fairies of advertising," queer men who self-injuriously validate desires for shrewish, self-interested wealth through puffing up an emotionally empty materialism (137). If radical in that they refuse to or cannot silence their effeminacy under the constraints of a patriarchal masculinity, these fairies, not quite angelic, adhere to for-profit principles that profanely exaggerate the consolations of a material acquisitiveness. In abstraction such a queer US conservativism signals "Cocksucker[s] in Moloch," the tense, hysterical avariciousness of queer men who sacrifice their emotional and psychological desires and the pleasures of a broader sociability for assimilative financial goals that will launch them into the repressively staid realms of the American middle and upper classes (139). How much more beneficial, Ginsberg suggests, to struggle against conformist standards of success and to aim for a more socially unifying, more honest, and thus more enlightened eroticized queer connectivity?

Ginsberg's erotic connective vision is of course itself hierarchical and fragmented but he implies that it remains effectively seditious. In *Howl*, as in "The Green Automobile," he acknowledges that in a flawed world enlightenment and exaltation will be partial, temporary, and rife with madness and divisions caused by unequal and irrational distributions of power. Certain parks, streets, bars, and cemeteries offer the freedom for erotic cross-cultural connections but only because they are socially peripheral and their denizens are without the desire for or the means to warrant policing in those spaces, save for unwanted and sadistic raids. Equivalently, after their sexual encounters hipsters, motorcyclists, sailors, and other same-sex-seeking men frequently take advantage of individual freedoms to drift off to their more familiar spheres of unequal influence. Any commingling screams of joy thus become intense enlightenments cut short. Still, some angelic outlaws remain covertly subversive. If they disappear from queer spaces to avoid arrest or threats of blackmail from authorities or because transient lovers flee, many reappear as agitators against their exploiters and oppressors. Ginsberg's angelic outlaws reappear "investigating the FBI ... with big pacifist eyes sexy in their dark skin," one of Ginsberg's rare poetic nods to a multiracial queer community, or "protesting ... Capitalism," passing out "Supercommunist pamphlets," and even fighting back against an unjust and financially mismanaged police state as they "bit detectives" and "shrieked with delight in policecars" having committed "no crime but their own wild cooking pederasty and intoxication" (2007: 135). Connecting economically wasteful and immoral surveillance of queer, pacifist, and anti-capitalist dissidents, Ginsberg goes so far as to suggest a "sex[iness]" and even an uncomfortably manic "delight" in protesting and in being caught protesting such immorally oppressive abuses of institutional power. If, moreover, these angelic protests risk humiliation, such as a reactionary confinement by the police state, they nonetheless help to redefine publicly, through pamphlets, visual images, and even a mordant physical assertiveness, a new queer outlaw American morality.

Concomitantly, Ginsberg uses his queer angelic hipsters to subvert more myopically conservative versions of American Christianity, which regularly demonize queer sex, by emphasizing the plurality of religious contexts across the United States, thus implicitly undermining any one national spiritual truth. Like Beat challenges to erotic repressions in *Howl* such angelic religious subversions work only imperfectly in the poem as they manifest through hipsters' engagements with dirty, transient, and disaffected spaces that offer discretely labelled and therefore misleadingly fragmented glimpses of a universal whole. Yet Ginsberg's insistence on these very fragmentations distances any one religion from a central authoritative position. He describes for instance how his intellectual heroes "bared their brains to heaven under the El and saw Mohammedan angels staggering on tenement roofs," "hallucinat[ed] Arkansas and a Blake-like tragedy," "vanished into nowhere Zen New Jersey," and "studied Plotinus Poe St. John of the Cross telepathy and bop kabbalah because the cosmos instinctively vibrated at their feet in Kansas" (2007: 134, 135). Taking advantage of marginalized urban spaces, such as under elevated trains or in low-rent housing, and of more provincial, far-flung American locations, such as Arkansas, Kansas, and "nowhere" New Jersey, Ginsberg's angelic outlaws seek new transcendental or spiritual models by embracing a range of Muslim, Buddhist, Catholic, Jewish, and even literary mysticisms.[19] These Beat philosophical studies might range from detailed to superficial, as it is hard to concentrate under an El, but Ginsberg suggests how even encounters with the energetically popular or "bop" varieties of diverse religious thoughts can offer staggering visions that challenge the dominant conservative Protestantism of America, which by this point was almost mechanically queerphobic and vocally capitalistic.[20]

To get beyond such a mechanically reiterative conservativism, Ginsberg emphatically connects diverse spiritual meditations regarding oneself and one's environment with a "Blake-like tragedy," a painful but progressive synthesis of innocence and experience, faith and cynicism, and heaven and hell. This tragic synthesis ultimately redefines the terms "sacred and profane," "good and bad," and "moral and immoral" through ideological destructions that lead to freer communications, a more practical use of human-made goods, and a rejection of violent institutions. These enlightening reevaluations stem, Ginsberg suggests, from an awesome terror and ecstasy that inspires conventionally profane but actually sacred thoughts and acts. From "publishing obscene odes on the windows of the skull" (just as Ginsberg wrote obscene phrases on his dorm windows while at Columbia) to "burning ... money in wastebaskets," Ginsberg lauds resistances against censorship and against over-valuations of symbolic paper.[21] At an extreme, it remains more useful to burn money in trashcans to provide heat to cold individuals than to allow rich individuals to hoard it away. These reevaluations of innocence and experience or creativity and destructiveness, Ginsberg submits, challenge so many allegedly authoritative "scholars of war," officials of institutions who fight for too often particularized visions of nationality, class, or tradition that splinter what could otherwise be a more peaceful because more comprehensively beneficial society (2007: 134). Ginsberg thus ends *Howl* on an optimistic if problematic Blake-ean note by insisting on the value of such a comprehensiveness, on the bridging or merging between a fractured world and a celestial ideal, by declaring an omnipresent value: "Everything is holy! everybody's holy ... Everyman's an angel!" Even evil once presented as good, such as censorship, sexual repressions, or support of dehumanizing and financially exploitative forms of industrialism, can be turned to good if one uses it to recognize and to empower the "Angel in Moloch!" (142). While this certainly cannot erase past evils, and it is unhelpful to consider the likes of Adolf Hitler or American slaveholders as "holy," a sense of the sanctity of humanity, its angelic-ness representing a combination of humanity's animalistic and divine natures, should broaden our supportive approach to a variety of nonviolent behaviors, such as same-sex intimacy and socialism, which could prove useful were they not portrayed as automatically damnable and obscene.

Queer Angels and Holy Global Consumerisms

To think through the problematically dialectic holiness imagined in *Howl*, Ginsberg often imagines socialist queer consumerisms in order to assess the angelic paths that he hoped the United States would take both in national and in international arenas. Consistently linking erotic to commercial exchanges, Ginsberg frequently aligned an angelic queer consumerism with relatively nonexploitative methods of sharing, such as men "scattering their semen freely," rather than an overvalued materialism, such as that advocated by shrieking "fairies of advertising." A continuous concern for Ginsberg is the spiritual danger of inflating the value of materialistic success, self-centered consumerist desires, and economic exploitation in the United States' domestic and international relations. As Allan Johnston has noted, in his early poetry Ginsberg's "consciousness teeters between a desire for spiritual realization and a sense of entrapment in a world dominated by a seductive consumerist ethos." In "A Supermarket in California" (1955), Johnston argues, Ginsberg works to transcend this ethos and "to achieve vision through commodities," aestheticizing them to imagine their connection to people (2005: 117). In "A Supermarket," as in *Howl*, I would add, Ginsberg envisions the connections between commodities, people, and spirituality to establish a queer eroticism as one useful spur to an enlightened consciousness, an angelic-ness that challenges a cold capitalist indifference by imagining the just exchanges possible for erotic relations as well as for America's relations with an international community.

Ginsberg begins this enlightening process in "A Supermarket" by recalling Walt Whitman as a queer predecessor who celebrated a diverse American community, heterogeneous and yet interdependent, through homoerotic tropes. Updating a Whitmanic line of thinking, Ginsberg imagines entering a "neon fruit supermarket" while "dreaming" of a fruitful American plethora. Ginsberg evokes here a complex conflation of flashy capitalist advertising via neon signs and the often inequitable commodification of goods imported at low costs from abroad to capitalize on Americans' basic needs, such as to eat and to enjoy one's senses. Ginsberg resists exploitative commodification by focusing on the relatively natural, non-neon variety of produce in the market, which he associates with the multitude of sexual desires in a multiethnic United States. He sees a variety of fruits and vegetables all paired with familiar heteronormative families, as well as with Federico García Lorca, the famous Spanish poet frequently associated with a subtle homoeroticism and socialism. Lorca's individual Spanish presence subverts the seeming omnipresence of a state-sponsored Anglo-Saxon American capitalism and the ostensible naturalness of heteronormative familial roles. Ginsberg evokes the force of this capitalistic heteronormativity through the "store detective" who follows him in the poem (2007: 144). Frank Kearful suggests that Ginsberg imagines the detective as following him "less as a suspected shoplifter than as a suspected fruit trailing another," or queer Ginsberg trailing queer Lorca (2013: 94). As such the detective functions as a state-sanctioned persecutor of queer desire as much as a servant of capitalist commercialism. The detective also indicates then how Ginsberg, Whitman, and Lorca try to elude conventional forms of exchange and attainments of pleasure, which often manifest themselves in capitalistic endeavors intended to support a husband or a wife and children. Lorca's presence, in conjunction with Whitman's and Ginsberg's own, emphasizes a form of creative and frequently noncommodified re-production, primarily a fruitful queer poetry, and lineages outside of conventional familial ones.

Expanding Lorca's resonances, Ginsberg also imagines Whitman combining a spiritualized erotic cruising with shopping for food, juxtaposing both searches to emphasize spiritually enlightened processes of satisfying human needs in an ethical fashion. Ginsberg imagines, in other words, a bridge-like angelic state of obtaining human sustenance as a means to support a transcendental community via a queerly, in the senses of unconventionally and erotically, fair means. In "A Supermarket" Ginsberg's Whitman walks "poking among the meats in the refrigerator and eyeing the grocery boys." Same-sex eroticism mingles with consumerism as Whitman looks for meat to eat and human flesh for sensual pleasure. But this is a queer consumerism that Whitman wants to distance from exploitation. His question, "[w]hat price bananas?" serves as a potentially crude proposition for prostitution, bananas representing variously fruit and phalli available for purchase, just as much as it signals his refusal to be exploited by being overcharged for food or same-sex sex (2007: 144).[22] Whitman also, however, does not want to gain sex simply because he can pay to touch a boy who needs money nor does he want to purchase cheap fruit produced by near-slave labor for the benefit of imperialists. As George Monteiro has noted, "there has been a human price paid for the benefit of the United Fruit Company" and Ginsberg's Whitman wants to know what this price was (2006: n.p).[23] Ginsberg mitigates economic exploitation, to the degree that he can, by presenting Whitman as an ethical shopper and cruiser, as he asks individual grocery clerks, "[w]ho killed the pork chops? ... Are you my Angel?"[24] Refusing to mystify entirely the processes of production, he questions how the pork came to be for sale in this store, just as he wants to clarify his expectations for any potential commercialized sexual exchange to avoid it becoming mutually demeaning. Perhaps neither of these situations are perfect, paying to eat dead flesh or paying for sex with live flesh, but there are better and worse ways of pursuing these goals. Whitman does not want to eat sadistically killed animals and, knowing that he is an "old grubber," he seeks encounters with a young man who wants to be his "Angel," who will appreciate his mind, personality, and the little money that he can offer, and who will gladly accept his advances by appreciating the spiritual intimacy of physicality (2007: 144). Rather than a participant in an all-around humiliating erotic encounter, Ginsberg's Whitman wants his "Angel" to represent an in-between figure who manifests a spark of divinity on earth in human form and who will agree to mutually if not homogenously beneficial and uplifting exchanges, functioning analogously to the Professor's ideal of angelic interviews in Rechy's *City of Night*.

Despite this seeming plethora of culinary and erotic opportunities, the poem ends on a curiously ascetic note, one that stresses the ethical quandaries of even passive forms of consumption in twentieth-century US culture. Dissatisfied with his options, Ginsberg's Whitman chooses only imagined pleasures as he refuses, for this evening at least, to buy into an American system that encourages a generally unethical commodified exchange of pleasures. Not finding properly produced food or a suitably angelic sex partner or unable to afford the ethical options on offer, Whitman, now joined in the poem by Ginsberg, obtains primarily psychological and aesthetic pleasures. Ginsberg imagines strolling through the store with Whitman as only in their "solitary fancy," in their imagination, do they indulge their desires, "never passing the cashier" to buy and physically taste what they want (2007: 144). As Rachel Bowlby points out, Ginsberg indulges in the "fantasy space" of the grocery store without having to pass the "barrier" of the checkout line that ends the free-for-all dream of choice and plentitude (2002: 197). From one perspective then, Whitman and Ginsberg avoid financially supporting a system that they fear takes advantage of consumers and exploits agricultural workers and low-level grocery clerks. Yet from another, the poets gain almost unchecked stimulus for erotic fantasies and for their art by taking advantage of processes that have provided it to them, such as the supermarket, which indirectly pays the farmers and directly pays the clerks whom the men ogle for free. Perhaps the taxes the poets pay to support roads and schools, which the store relies on to receive and send off goods, or perhaps the resultant poetry Whitman and Ginsberg produce provides an adequate intellectual, psychological, or even spiritual social recompense for their inspirations, but this remains uncertain. The economic market is too complex, even within the bounds of this poem, to determine completely and assuredly an entirely ethical course of action and so almost everyone implicated within it, the store owners, the grocery clerks, the parents who need to feed their children, and the poets, remains stuck with only ethically imperfect actions. This dilemma leads Ginsberg to imagine himself and Whitman as leaving the store to "stroll dreaming of the lost America of love," an America "lost" not so much to the past as to missed opportunities to structure an economic system upon a social "love" of humanity rather than upon an undue corporate and individualistic greed (2007: 144).

Widening his lens from that of "A Supermarket in California" to "America" (1956), Ginsberg makes an almost instant leap from personal to public and from national to international socioeconomic exploitations. Stressing destructively unequal exchanges, Ginsberg announces, "America I've given you all and now I'm nothing ... America when will we end the human war?" (2007: 154). Using somewhat manically juxtaposed jumps among personal, national, and global abuses by the United Stated, Ginsberg insists simultaneously on his personal victimization, having gained little (so far) if not "nothing" in return for being a queer American poet, and on his guilt from being part of an American "we" that has brutalized its fellow citizens and acted brutally in global contexts. Moving in wide swathes that highlight diverse and often ghettoized US populations, he references visiting New York's "Chinatown," serving Sino-American citizens, insists "I am the Scottsboro boys," and recalls the Russian Jewish "Communist" meetings that his mother took him to as a child (154, 155). Attempting to connect personal, national, and global circumstances, while acknowledging differences within and without national borders, Ginsberg works to balance identifying with and admitting to a wide range of victimizations and culpabilities.

Of course, such generalized attempts at empathy and identifications inevitably run into problematic cultural appropriations and failures to distinguish adequately between forms of oppression. Working with Bob Kaufman's poetry, Maria Damon has pointed out that "white male Beats, envious of what they saw as alternative embodiments" to the "stultifying options" of middle-class life; grew enamored of "Blacks, women, migrant workers, and so on; and figured them as angels, ghosts, or shadows" (2015: 170). Yet, she argues, "for all its attempts to voice" the "suffering" of minority US denizens as a sacred experience within an infernal world, "the Beat movement succeeded primarily in romanticizing it as a literary and lived gesture that merely exacerbated the untenability of the yoking of Heaven and Hell" (173). Indeed, in an undoubtedly over idealistic fashion, Ginsberg tries to connect the individual to a large-scale American diversity, echoing previous Whitmanic and even Blakean romantic unifications of a miscellaneous, often contradictory America, both sacred and profane. "It occurs to me that I am America," Ginsberg reports, attempting to personalize and to link together American resistances to anti-Semitism, to homophobia, to racism, and to an anti-immigrant white heteronormative nationalism (2007: 155). Ginsberg hopes that this linkage might collectively overpower personal and national reactionary tendencies. Yet he is certainly not, as he claims, one of the Scottsboro boys and his enlightened consciousness stemming from his queer Jewish Russian quasi-communist background can go only so far to understanding their position when he is not himself stuck in prison, a victim of a systematic racism that prevents him from obtaining fair trials, jobs, housing, or widely influential venues for publicizing radical views. As such, this particular attempt to unite, in himself, the heavenly and hellish goals of US society comes off as too overconfident and ineffective.

As the above indicates, such sympathetic attempts at establishing a US connectivity and collective agency have clear limitations, including risks of collaborating with reactionary oppressors. In Chapter 1 I discussed Rechy's critique of subversive outlaws who appropriate the tactics of oppressive forces but in doing so risk colluding with them. Ginsberg's attempts at a national connectivity risk just such a collusion as he critically ventriloquizes more conservative, nationalistic, and often racist Cold War US fears that "Asia is rising" and that militaristically aggressive "bad Russians" are threatening a general American prosperity, albeit one certainly not enjoyed by the Scottsboro men or their families (2007: 155). Following Whitman's famous American lyric, "Do I contradict myself? / Very well then .... I contradict myself; / I am large .... I contain multitudes," Ginsberg positions himself within these varying and often oppositional American camps as a means to redirect them from inside the overarching category of US citizenry, which links diverse races, sexualities, genders, etc., together (2010: 69). In other words, Ginsberg claims the position of these xenophobic and bigoted voices to bring himself into their overarching American "we" so that he can more effectively ask, "when will we end the human war," a rhetorical tactic that simultaneously admits his partial culpability for the human war as a US citizen but that attempts as such a citizen to reinforce the intrinsic heterogeneity of the United States against the illusion of its white Anglo-Saxon Protestant supremacists (2007: 154). Unfortunately, such strategies, however well intentioned, inherently repeat, with a too ambiguous irony or satire, and so normalize the queerphobia, racism, and xenophobia of a Caucasian Protestant heterosexual, not to mention exploitatively capitalist, civic elite.

Ginsberg's strategy of critique from within also overemphasizes the efficacy of dissenting constituent voices. Ginsberg subtly admits this when he observes, "I am talking to myself again," a recognition that reflects his desire to talk to America and that acknowledges that he is only one part of America, a part unheard or ignored by most of the voting public, one individual against many (2007: 155). Even as a part of America, Ginsberg's political and economic influence thus remains severely limited. He is one angel in a choir. He himself has to ask for and cannot individually enact an "end" to the US participation in an imperialistic, racist, and sexually repressive "human war" and he could not as an American representative come even close to freeing the actual Scottsboro boys.

Yet in spite of these significant pitfalls to wide-ranging poetic sympathies, Ginsberg insists on the salutary potentials of a queer erotic initiative that could at least help to correct social and economic inequalities in the United States' global and more local environment. "America," he asks, "when will you be angelic? / When will you take off your clothes? ... when will you send your eggs to India" (2007: 154). Ginsberg scaffolds a litany of questions, alluding diversely to spirituality, nudity, hunger, and trade to build to his belief that an angelically queer, honest, and unrepressed eroticism can support communal sympathies and a reconsideration of the processes of commercial exchange. An erotic openness, Ginsberg hopes, would do away with the covers and symbols that cloak greed in respectability and that distract from more beneficial forms of engagement. Rather than veil immediate human needs with the symbolic financial language of international trade, for instance, the United States should send its surplus of life-giving food, such as eggs, to those nations that need it, such as India, which have stewarded for the world such spiritual treasures as Buddhist teachings. Money functions similarly to clothing as it offers one more repressive intermediary, an abstract symbol, which distracts from diverse forms of actual needs, such as hunger, and of necessary productions, such as food. Disregarding the symbolic functions of clothes and money, moreover, could allow a recognition of individual human beauties that in and of themselves often warrant the support of an international community to fulfill their potential.

Personally, Ginsberg hopes that with less focus on money, one might discern his own charms as evidence of his human worth, which warrants society offering him sustenance in exchange for his valuably angelic continued existence. "When can I go into the supermarket and buy what I need with my good looks?" Ginsberg wonders. This need not be a degrading prostitution but a new form of exchange that works even in local supermarkets, just as Whitman's poetic production might have earned him food and sex in "A Supermarket." This emphasis on myriad values, from beauty to a spiritual eroticism to poetry, that individuals can offer a society in exchange for goods and intimacies offers a socialist, humanist challenge to the ideological and practical "machinery" of an international and national capitalism (2007: 154). Refusing "to join the Army or turn lathes in precision parts factories," Ginsberg uses his openly declared same-sex desires, which in the 1950s would officially hinder him from joining the Army, to imagine himself working to put the United States' national and international strengths to more life-enhancing labors, "America I'm putting my queer shoulder to the wheel" (156). In this case, Ginsberg imagines an angelic queerness as motivating a forward-thinking progress that could inspire a more inclusive and mutually beneficial American identity, an angelic America. Obviously in setting up such new international and national forms of exchanges the revolutionary devil would be in the details, but even the poetic fantasy serves as a radical bad beatitude.

Reactionary Angels: The Tempting Traps of Violence and Quietism

A prolific evolving poet, Ginsberg gradually developed his style, themes, and symbolic tropes beyond his 1950s triumphs. "During a 1963 trip to Israel, India, and Japan," Lewis Hyde remarks, "Ginsberg slowly abandoned his gods and their adjunct devils and angels" (1984: 6). From 1963 onward, as Tony Trigilio has noted, Ginsberg advanced his "Buddhist poetics" in particular (2007: 79). Although Ginsberg's politics and poetics took new directions as he aged and as he learned more about civil rights and anti-war movements, queer angelic outlaws remained a consistent if ripening facet of his poetic language. While Ginsberg's angelic imagery in the 1950s can be traced along trajectories similar to those established in *Howl*, "A Supermarket," and "America," in his later poetry Ginsberg depicted more confrontational, almost reactionary angels. With more egotistic and self-protective agendas than in "America," these latter angels borrow the repressive tactics of their enemies and end up much more deeply in "collaboration," to borrow Rechy's term from his critique of queer outlaws, with the very authoritarian ideologies that they had hoped to subvert. Ginsberg thus uses these angelic figures to critique how liberal intentions can so quickly turn against themselves.

In "Violence" (1968), for instance, Ginsberg laments a general hostility accepted by outlaw leftists or countercultural figures who reiterate cruelty and a ruthless rhetoric in a self-injurious fashion. He moves from describing a knife being stuck in a slumming overfed, well-dressed gay man's jacket, presumably into his stomach or back, to the murder of Robert "Bobby" Hutton by Oakland police after the Black Panthers protested California's Mulford Act, which hindered the group's ability to protect black neighborhoods by patrolling with loaded guns. In both cases, Ginsberg despises the deaths but suggests that an exploitative homoeroticism, signaled by the slumming cruiser, and a defensive threat of violence leads to more tragic destructions of already disenfranchised individuals. Ginsberg further links these incidents to diverse protests in 1966 and 1968 when beautiful "[l]onghaired angels / armed with gasmasks & Acid" protested curfews, censorship, economic inequalities, and other forms of discrimination in Paris, Harlem, Los Angeles, Chicago, and elsewhere (2007: 511). While supportive of these protests, Ginsberg grieves that these angelic youthful hippies have "armed" themselves with seemingly defensive gestures, such as gas masks and LSD, the latter to be used not for enlightenment or for fun but to slip nonconsensually to a general population. In this fashion, Ginsberg suggests, these countercultural angels in effect fortify the violent ideology of their opponents.

Ginsberg laments here how subversive physical and spiritual stimuli, such as youthful beauty or certain intoxicants, can get perverted for profane purposes. He was intensely interested in LSD as a path to enlightenment but in the summer of 1968 the drug had also become a weapon when the Yippies threatened to taint Chicago's water supply with it during that year's Democratic National Convention.[25] Such concerns about the perverse uses of LSD were likely on Ginsberg's mind in "Violence" as he next references the "Angry Democrats" who were to "gather in Chicago / fantasizing armies running / thru Sewers sprayed with Mace." Ginsberg quickly then connects more militaristic, politically rebellious angels with "chic fairy gangsters" in Mexico City who "with bloody hands/hustle after midnight to cut my throat from its beard" (2010: 511). These "chic fairy gangsters" are queer angels *manqué*, men who compromise their spiritual potential by pursuing an economically problematic materialism. This materialism leads them to destroy on a metaphorical level (to de-beard) those bearded bearish queer men who disregard the standards set by those urbane "fairies of advertising" critiqued in *Howl*. On a less metaphorical level, Ginsberg imagines the gangster-ish extremes to which some fairies might go to get money to obtain their fashionable luxuries, including murderous robberies. Throughout the poem, he laments what he perceives as the self-destructive behavior of worldwide angelic rebels who appropriate the violent strategies of the conservative tyrannical authorities who claim to represent a moral majority.

Ginsberg likewise critiqued socioeconomically privileged angelic progressives who collaborated indirectly with tyrannical authorities by remaining aloof in their own heavenly havens. In "Going to Chicago" (1968), Ginsberg recounts flying toward the protests of the Democratic National Convention as he hears in his own blood the "Angel King's voice," the voice of an incorporeal young man representative of Ginsberg's own naive idealism, promising him peace. This sophomoric disembodied ideal forgets its own place amid bleeding suffering bodies. Ginsberg stresses this irony when he describes the "Angel King" singing about his own glory while crowds in Chicago lament and cry out "over Meat and Metal microphone" (2007: 514). The narcissistic teenage Angel exults in his own splendor as uncritically reactive human forces and unfeeling metallic, robotic-like projections of government voices aggressively repress and arrest protestors' bodies and spirits.

Subsequently in "Thoughts Sitting Breathing" (1973) Ginsberg lambasts the effectiveness of passive would-be activists who seclude themselves far from any crowd. What is the use of protestors, he asks, who calmly remain sitting as they claim to "storm Heaven with [their] mental guns?" Ginsberg decries the violent rhetoric that pervades pacifist forms of protest conceived of as mental or spiritual warfare, a perverse echo of physical warfare. He also exhibits frustration with passive protestors, including at times himself, who simply meditate, safely far off from strife. These individuals are perhaps not so different from those who sing protest songs in affluent and relatively secure enclaves, enjoying the sweetly commercialized, false consolations of sugar-fueled or drug-fueled satisfactions. As such, he advises mockingly, "[L]et Angels alone to play their guitars in Hollywood and drink their Coke-snuff in mountainside bathroom peace" (2007: 597). If these angels believe that they are mentally storming Heaven, the siege remains only in their mind. Ginsberg relates such mental flights to a Hollywood-esque cinematic escapism and the consumption of "Coke-snuff," signaling equally the imperialistic violence of US shoppers' desire for caffeinated sugar-fixes and the analogously unhealthy high of snorted cocaine. This sort of protest allows relatively fortunate American citizens to consume immorally acquired produce, which they can then defecate, metaphorically and in reality, on the rest of the world, afterward washing their hands of any nastiness in "peace" in a beautiful "bathroom." This passivity seems ineffective against the active violence of sad sufferers showing off actual and metaphorical weapons, such as the pro-Vietnam-war and socially infamous Hell's Angels, Richard Nixon, and "Wall Street brokers smoking in rage over dwindling oil supplies" (599). By not more actively countering these forces, passive privileged would-be progressive angels unwittingly aid a political and financial elite. They utilize similarly violent ideologies and shore up brutally repressive global American institutional policies by shopping for the products of imperialism while sanctimoniously singing songs of peace.

All of these witting and unwitting collaborators with an American tyranny provide a tragic foil to Ginsberg's portrayal of more helpless angels across the world. In "September on Jessore Road" (1971), for instance, Ginsberg describes hungry and abused refugees walking from Kolkata, India, to Jessore, Bangladesh, as "[s]tarving black angels in human disguise" who wait for an "American Angel machine" to drop provisions for them (2007: 579, 581). Ginsberg's next line, however, imagines Ambassador Ellsworth Bunker's helicopters shooting down young people playing suggesting that what will likely come from the United States through sun-filled skies will be planes dropping bombs and bullets as the Moloch-like superpower uses mechanically attained heights to distance its pilots from the sacred nonviolent life of the local civilians killed on the ground. Foregoing a merciful assistance, the "American Angel" machines become the oppressive force of a tyrannous celestial authority. Mechanically, robotically, these forces follow orders without acknowledging the clear individual circumstances of the cruelly condemned beings below them who are trying to travel to a better life. Ginsberg's "Angel Machine[s]" thus work analogously to Miss Destiny's vision of a divine Evil Angel who passes an automatic inhuman judgment on her angelic community of drag queens, hustlers, and scores. Ginsberg's "Angel Machine[s]" also echo neo-Miltonic or Blakean depictions of a divine tyranny over rebel angels and angelic humans who incur a celestial wrath for participating in subversive socioeconomic or sexual politics or who simply search for a better earthly life.

Ginsberg's angelic characters in "September" are of course not necessarily interested in same-sex sex or gender nonconformity, and if they are, these are not their dominant traits here. Still, these figures ought to be read alongside the queer connotations that Ginsberg generally associates with his extensive angelic imagery. In his poetry Ginsberg repeatedly uses interlinked queer perspectives—from queer eroticisms to queer socioeconomic exchanges to queer sympathies for marginalized individuals—to advocate for humanitarian consideration for individuals conventionally mislabeled as inherently abject. He uses angelic imagery to emphasize the spiritual potential for human minds and bodies no matter how downtrodden, marginalized, or misguidedly violent, even if his rhetoric remains a bit too optimistic regarding this latter category. The more radical of these characters are Ginsberg's Beat angels and they fashion his particular version of a bad beatitude. If Ginsberg's own same sex inclinations use an erotic energy to reevaluate the allegedly illegal, immoral, sick, and profane connotations of those who pursue homoerotic activities, it is to his credit that he uses this consciousness-expanding queer perspective to insist on the spiritual value of unfairly or unjustly oppressed individuals with whom he has no apparent erotic affinity. Aesthetically and socially, Ginsberg's larger interest late in his career was to use his conscious expanding techniques to move beyond erotic sympathies to facilitate an active spiritual affinity for horrifically oppressed outcasts across the world. Rather than engage in the passivity of either allegedly progressive but actually narcissistic values of Coked-out angelic protestors or an allegedly divine but actually repressive American spiritual violence, Ginsberg encourages sympathy for global populations whom American citizens should keep in mind when they work to influence the United States' political processes, as Ginsberg himself did through his poetry, public appearances, interviews, and political protests. As a rule, Ginsberg himself was no apathetic angel.

Conclusion

While I have emphasized how Ginsberg, more explicitly than Rechy or Nugent, connects queer bad beatitudes to socioeconomic critiques of a Christian capitalist and industrial America, I want to end this chapter by gesturing to how Ginsberg's rhetoric shifted, if only slightly, with the advent of HIV/AIDS in the 1980s and 1990s. Thinking about HIV/AIDS clearly occupied Ginsberg's private sex life, but in his public life he mostly linked the subject to more general thoughts about living peacefully and avoiding unnecessary suffering. In an 1987 interview, for instance, he noted his own "safe sex" strategies and that he himself had not "met too many people that've had direct AIDS horror show," though he had, he notes, "raised money" for people suffering from AIDS (2017: 185). In the documentary *Silence=Death* (1990), Ginsberg states, perhaps too abstractly, "the planet itself has AIDS" and he associates the HIV virus with humanity's unsafe actions with its environment (Praunheim 1991). In a 1994 interview, roughly three years before his own death, he was still referring abstractly and only very briefly and impersonally to AIDS, "[t]he patient has AIDS. How do you live with that? ... [By] trying not to create more suffering than already exists" (2019: 167). In his few poetic references to the virus, he likewise focuses on his hopes for his own continued health, as in "Sphincter" (1986) where the risk of "AIDS" briefly passes as a possible concern alongside more certain physical decays that stem from old age, and in "Grandma Earth's Song" (1988) where "old presidents get AIDS" as one of a litany of problems in a self-destructing world (2007: 950, 973). In "Research" (1992), Ginsberg critiques myopic, predetermined investigative agendas that pervert notions of sin, nature, and moral retributions, as he satirizes language of the religious right suggesting that "AIDS" has been shown to be "a plague sent to punish gay Angelmakers" (1026). Ginsberg evokes the horror here of describing AIDS in spiritual terms as a punishment for men whom he posits as fashioning, perhaps even unbeknownst to themselves, taboo forms of lust, love, and sensuality into new spiritual heights. This line is a brief but striking evolution of Ginsberg's queer angelic bad beatitudes, though he does not follow this connection of AIDS and a queer angelic-ness any further. Numerous other queer authors, however, were substantially more interested in such connections as they explored HIV/AIDS, queer angelic-ness amid sickness, and the continuing aftermath of a spiritual sensuality born out of degradation, and it is to these authors that I turn in the next chapter.

4

Angels amid Affliction: Angelic Immigrants and an Expansive Americanism in the Era of HIV/AIDS

Rechy, Nugent, and Ginsberg all developed angelic outlaws to value men who rebelled against conventional religious, legal, social, and even medical repressions of same-sex desire and gender nonconformity. Forced to travel between mainstream and marginalized social and geographical spaces, these men function as bridge figures as they span diverse realms and diverse states-of-being. Moving from standard conceptions of American masculinity, including military life, to bars, backrooms, and alleys, all characterized as variations of heaven and hell, these queer angelic outlaws reevaluate their identifications as simultaneously moral and immoral, spiritual and corporeal, and sick and healthy. In doing so, they illustrate the tyranny and terrors of nominally sanctified, heavenly arenas as well as the ecstatic liberties and virtues that exist within coerced yet often embraced hellish degradations, which I have been calling bad beatitudes. The rhetoric of these bad beatitudes shifted notably, however, during the 1980s and 1990s due to HIV/AIDS. Struggling to make sense of an often senseless influx of pain and death, authors frequently infused eroticized human bodies with spiritual graces alongside and even at times because of their sickness. They insisted on the spiritual and physical value of sick queer individuals or the caretakers of sick queer friends and lovers by imagining them as angelic outlaws. Rather than naively celebrating or romanticizing illness, these authors use angelic tropes to acknowledge the physical, mental, and spiritual fortitude and the communal ties that developed through fighting the disease, fighting unhelpful authority figures, and fighting a larger, often uncaring American society.

These angelic bad beatitudes offered a valued, cross-genre phenomenon after the advent of AIDS. Angelic outlaw tropes appear in verse in Essex Hemphill's *Conditions* (1986), Assotto Saint's *Stations* (1989) and *Wishing for Wings* (1994), and Timothy Liu's *Vox Angelica* (1992); on the stage and on the page in Tony Kushner's *Angels in America* (1991–2), James Carroll Pickett's *Queen of Angels* (1992), Bill Russell and Janet Hood's *Elegies for Angels, Punks and Raging Queens* (1996), as well as in Jonathan Larson's *Rent* (1996) through the trans outlaw Angel; and in novels such as James McCourt's *Time Remaining* (1993), Allan Gurganus's *Plays Well with Others* (1997), and most recently, Rabih Alameddine's *Angel of History* (2016). As queer writers worked to grasp what little solace, recompense, or control they could over a newly hellish world, they frequently turned to angelic outlaws and to bad beatitudes to appreciate and to lament the metaphorical and literal suffering that so quickly became embedded with writing about HIV/AIDS.

Sickness, death, and tragedy, of course, as well as the consolations connected to these calamities, have long been recurrent tropes of queer literature and culture, and so they understandably form the background for writing about HIV/AIDS. "One does not have to subscribe to the myth of the tragic queer," as Gregory Woods argues, "to recognise that the theme of mortal danger—along with *carpe diem*, its corollary—has recurred throughout the history of ['gay'] literature," such that in "the literature of AIDS we return, as it were, to our roots" (1998: 370). Woods is certainly right, and it is worth considering that the themes of "mortal danger" and an optimistic "*carpe diem*" often functioned not just as corollaries but also as a hybrid trope. These literary roots established a mixed foundation of fear and consolation in queer literature, a desire to undergo humiliations and mortifications in order to obtain queer romantic and erotic connections. Such queer consolations, as the previous chapters illustrate, often rely upon hybrid tensions of pain and pleasure as well as spirituality and sensuality, and authors examining HIV/AIDS reimagined these well-established volatile mixtures. Tensions among spiritually physical pains and pleasures were, as I have argued, rarely clear-cut, and in HIV/AIDS writing as well, most authors avoided the artlessness of presenting illness itself as ipso facto spiritual as once strong bodies decay throughout a narrative. Rather, playwrights, poets, and novelists in particular, as Steven Kruger observes, often worked to "question, rewrite, and subvert the narrative structures" of AIDS literature by depicting the physical decline of people with AIDS and the spread of the virus in ways that intervened "against the implicit and explicit homophobia of those structures" (2013: 4). Often, such literary interventions reject any intrinsic sense of HIV/AIDS as a divine or a moral punishment that stems chronologically and consequentially from allegedly depraved acts in and of themselves.[1] Rather, by celebrating queer angelic outlaws amid the physical decline of individuals and the broader epidemic, writers often insist on the continued spiritually and physically erotic value of the queer American experience in the midst of and even because of a health crisis that was linked to, albeit not intrinsic to, same-sex sex.

As if to follow suit, critical responses to such spiritual and physical tensions in queer culture often themselves worked in opposition. From an optimistic perspective, early critics such as Toby Johnson lauded the spiritualization of sex amid sickness. Johnson contended that "the rise of a gay counterculture in the 1970s in the dominant Western society and its battle with the tragedy of AIDS in the 1980s play an integral—and even leading—role in the development of new paradigms of human nature, especially in the area of spirituality" (1993: 131). Johnson argues that this "paradigm shift in the experience of sexuality—which is the spiritual message of gay love—is that we can and should love creation, emotionally and physically, for its own sake" (138). Critics such as Susan Sontag, however, were more skeptical of any spiritual interpretations of a horrific biological trauma. Emphasizing apocalyptic tropes, Sontag argued that early calls for sexual restraint in the 1980s indicated "a broad tendency in our culture, an end-of-an-era feeling, that AIDS is reinforcing; an exhaustion, for many, of purely secular ideals—ideals that seemed to encourage libertinism or at least not provide any coherent inhibition against it—in which the response to AIDS finds its place" (1989: 78). Sontag sees in this rejection of secularism a dangerously restrictive return to more familiar and more repressive spiritual and moral erotic and romantic norms. More recently, Tim Dean has noted that as HIV has become less apocalyptic, at least in the United States with the advent of life-prolonging drugs, some small queer subcultures actively seek a transcendental, sometimes spiritual connection through condomless sex, whereby heightened risks of contracting HIV through group sex sparks particularly intense intimacies, which participants "often characterize as sacred, rather than profane" (2009: 46). If Johnson's lauding of new queer spiritual sexualities rings a bit too optimistic, Sontag's general opposition of spirituality to secular sexual freedoms, including promiscuity, frequently collapses in the spiritual erotics of queer culture of the 1990s and early 2000s, particularly in queer literature with angelic outlaws. Dean's description of the spiritual rhetoric used by men who pursue dangerous sex to obtain new forms of intimacy perhaps comes closest to the literary bad beatitudes I discuss below, with the vitally key exception that most writers mourn the trauma of seroconverting rather than celebrate it, even as they spiritualize the pleasures inherent in sex that is no longer ever truly "safe."

Considering issues like spiritualization and safety, it would be nice, I think, to argue that this angelic outlaw literature presents a queer spiritual eroticism as stressing present and future strengths against adversity or as accentuating emotional, psychological, and spiritual health despite physical infection or illness due to HIV/AIDS, but such claims would be overly simplistic. Rather, angelic queer characters predominantly emphasize spirituality as achieved through the route of psychologically disturbing and physically dangerous sex in the age of AIDS. They present queer behaviors and spaces that have been circumstantially merged with danger, disease, and sometimes death with a spiritual value not just beyond but often actively inclusive of and immersed in dangerous physical pleasures and psychological intimacies. Angelic images, in particular, acknowledge the sheer intensity of pursuing the sensually sacred within the conventionally profane as a sexually transmitted virus debilitated transgressive yet beautiful queer bodies and minds. While these bad beatitudes have obvious correlations with those explored in earlier chapters, authors notably evolve these tropes as they filter this spiritual value so extensively and so carefully through the alembic of memory, imagining the delicate balancing act of recalling past and present pains and pleasures amid the massively disruptive contemporary trauma of HIV/AIDS. This final chapter explores then how writers such as Hemphill, McCourt, Gurganus, and particularly Alameddine investigate how one can remember certain painful pleasures, during sex and after, so as not to allow past traumas to overwhelm one's all too qualified joys in the present and future.

To begin, I argue that Hemphill and writers of his generation formulate a spiritual erotic value to think through how struggles with HIV/AIDS interconnect both with reactions against the pathologization of queer bodies and with chronic struggles against racial, gendered, and socioeconomic hierarchies in US contexts. After introducing the importance of memory to queer bad beatitudes through writers who worked in the 1980s and early 1990s, I turn to Alameddine's *Angel of History*, which extends this critique of ambivalent memory into the twenty-first century. Alameddine's engagement with HIV/AIDS evokes memories of repression, shame, and the destruction of queer pleasurably erotic bodies to illustrate how and why queer individuals must struggle to prevent these memories from overtaking their joy in the present and in an imagined future. For Alameddine, forgetting past pleasures, often experienced in demeaning contexts, in order to avoid recalling a simultaneous degradation, risks a mind-numbing apathy. A more balanced remembering, however, risks a melancholic ambivalence toward the past, present, and future rather than an enjoyment of tension between the sacred in the profane and the profane in the sacred. At stake in such permutations of memory, moreover, Alameddine insists, are conceptions of citizenship in both the national population and more localized queer communities, as queer people living with or alongside those with HIV/AIDS get caught in battles over recalling or remembering who has what rights within any body politic. Mainstream responses to HIV/AIDS in the United States, Alameddine suggests, too often fashioned queer individuals as analogous to unwanted immigrants, alienating both groups from institutional and legal socioeconomic protections even while encouraging them to reimagine hybrid, never monolithic national and subcultural identities. Overall then, Alameddine's novel presents a particularly ambivalent and melancholic conclusion to this study. For more than any other author considered, Alameddine characterizes his Luciferian queer immigrant protagonist Jacob as wrestling with not just hierarchical repressions but also the painful pleasures enjoyed by so many angelic American outlaws before him. While I will resist this melancholy in my conclusion, Alameddine presents a powerful engagement with and a unique resistance to angelic bad beatitudes.

Recollections and Revolt: Memories in Angelic AIDS Literature

Queer angelic imagery in the early HIV/AIDS era evoked new tensions between conceptions of pain and pleasure, health and sickness, as well as salvation and damnation. These often unreconcilable themes, each struggling for dominance, manifested the greatest ambivalence when it came to personal memories of before and after the arrival of AIDS. This ambivalence, as numerous authors evidence, became particularly acute in memories linked to celebrations of and revolts against nationalistic American ideals. Randy Shilts, for instance, begins his 1987 chronicle of the AIDS crisis, *And the Band Played On*, with a description of New York City on July 4, 1976, as people from around the world poured in, some of them perhaps already carrying HIV, to admire the United States' bicentennial festivities and to enjoy its growing tolerance for queer communities, which a homophobic backlash energized by the epidemic would soon threaten anew. Explicitly paralleling national chronologies with personal ones, Shilts describes how HIV/AIDS would soon "cleave lives in two," such that "[b]efore" the virus "meant innocence and excess, idealism and hubris," and "after" meant "death" (1987: 12). Shilts carefully emphasizes, of course, how naively dividing recent queer memories into a prelapsarian "before" and a postlapsarian "after" reveals a porousness akin to that of national boundaries and the faultiness of hypernationalistic histories, as the "before" era was itself fraught with sexual diseases and repressions, even in the more tolerant 1960s and 1970s, and the "after" would revolt against repression and death by forming vital new communities and identities.

If at times biased and idiosyncratic, Shilts's narrative provides a fine frame for understanding how fiction too worked to reassess such national and personal queer histories in the AIDS-era in almost apocalyptic terms. Monica Pearl observes that after offering a presentist grappling with daily life with AIDS in the 1980s, around 1994 AIDS fiction became more pointedly "retrospective," providing a "grand sweep of historical events and trends culminating in the losses incurred from AIDS" (2013: 5). In such retrospective writing, poets, playwrights, and novelists frequently ask queer Americans to reassess their relationships to a repressive state in which they have long been simultaneously denizens and exiles slipping in and out of a sick body politic. Such broad questioning inevitably critiques how more personal memories of pleasures and hardships affect perceptions of an ostensibly new present. Angelic outlaws in AIDS literature inherently foreground such reassessments on an epic level, connecting past and present national alienations of minority denizens, whether due to sexuality or race or both, in specifically spiritual and erotic contexts. As we will see, the more angelic characters remember their past lives, rejoicing in erotic pleasures despite their now known dangers, the more likely they are to stage a Luciferian revolt against repressively hierarchical powers in their present with the hope for a better future.

Pearl convincingly places a "sweep[ing]" "retrospective" turn of AIDS literature in the mid-1990s, but angelic revolts against psychological, social, and religious powers were using memory as an insurrectionary tactic even in the mid-1980s. In *Conditions* (1986), to cite one example, Hemphill's poetry recalls the literary rebellions of queer black men in the United States, such as those discussed in Chapter 2, as he evolves his own bad beatitudes in the age of AIDS.[2] For Hemphill, the tensions of necessary sex (including love, lust, and multifarious dangerous emotional encounters) amid historically continuous racial and homophobic violence offer a path to transcendence, as a fall from conventional religious and social grace offers a leap into a spiritual erotic embrace. In "XIV" for instance, Hemphill reimagines psychological and physical positions and their spiritually erotic value. With his speaker elevating himself for pleasures through sex, he raises "his legs" while "fucking fallen angels" and then, reversing positions, he tells his partner to lift his "legs" as the speaker himself becomes an "angel, / falling" (2000: 176). Top becoming bottom and bottom becoming top presents a balanced strain, mingling active and passive, where falling into love, lust, and a conventionally degrading emasculation, comes with rising pleasures of release and spiritual connection. To emphasize the significance of this still revolutionary way of thinking about sex, Hemphill characterizes it as a Luciferian revolt against remembered social, religious, and gender norms for men. While this angelic rhetoric thus recalls that of earlier queer writers, Hemphill's eroticized spiritual heights occur with new fears, as indicated by the earlier poem "Now We Think": "Now we think / as we fuck" how an orgasm could be both pleasurable and fatal should a "lethal leak" in a condom accidentally allow for the transmission of HIV, in the early 1980s a likely death sentence (169). Despite the risk of AIDS though, even with prophylactics, exciting and socially connective sex continues much as it had among older queer men dealing with fears pertaining to class, economics, and a generalized and institutional racism and homophobia. Angelic imagery likewise continues to critique hierarchical oppressions and to fashion a revolt against threats to queer communities on an epic level. Queer sex maintains for Hemphill its physical, psychological, emotion, and spiritual values despite the risk of HIV/AIDS. In fact, with the threat the virus presents to queer men having sex, the sheer willingness to continue having even hopefully "safe" sex can make the act a still greater commitment to self and to community advancement.

In later works too, such as McCourt's *Time Remaining* (1993) and Gurganus's *Plays Well with Others* (1997), recollections of failed romantic ideals and of friends lost to AIDS, set against a historical background of remembered queer repressions, enact pointedly physical and spiritual angelic rebellions. In these works, the very recounting of past painful pleasures fights any present-day apathy or the forgetting of past joys, while offering qualified consolations in lives lived despite loss. Few people want to appreciate memories or their own lives more because others have died, but finding joy through pain, McCourt and Gurganus suggest, is better than a suicidal rage or nihilism. In *Time Remaining*, for instance, Odette, a trans ballerina and former soldier, recalls spreading the ashes of the "Eleven against Heaven," a group of her close Luciferian friends who died of AIDS, as she luxuriates in detailing their wild sexual and gender transgressions throughout the United States and Europe. Similarly, in *Plays Well with Others*, Allan Gurganus imagines the spread of AIDS in New York during his description of a scene on July 4, 1984, when his characters gather to present new artistic works on the theme of "Heaven," including a musical piece imagining "Paradise Lost then Corrected!" and Hartley Mims's story "Toward a More Precise Identification of the Newer Angels" (1999: 152, 156, 150). As the progressive ideals of the American political left fall prey to a renewed conservative nationalism in the 1980s, the novel ends with a copy of Hartley's fantasy of an eroticized heaven. In Hartley's retrospection, which takes place "After After" or after the first aftermath of AIDS deaths, his own "Corrected" version of *Paradise Lost* now welcomes as "Newer Angels" his dead gay friends, whom the American religious right would so easily condemn to hell (24). Both Odette and Hartley offer painfully pleasurable memories of dead friends so as to rebel themselves, in a neo-Miltonic fashion, against conservative ideologies that would force the hard-won joys of gay experience back into the closet of cultural consciousness and, perhaps as nefariously, back into the realm of spiritual condemnation. Instead, McCourt and Gurganus have their living characters rejoice in a spiritual erotic sensuality that remains desirable even with its new associated dangers, perhaps even more desirable now in that celebrating such sex serves as a refusal to return to an equation of queer sex with shame.

Hemphill, McCourt, and Gurganus provide a relevant literary background for more recent depictions of AIDS-influenced bad beatitudes, such as Alameddine's *Angel of History*. Alameddine, however, shows a particular interest in remembering the past so as to strategically forget it, to process it, and to let it go. Set in twenty-first-century San Francisco, but steeped in memories of the 1980s and 1990s, his novel considers how to achieve a balance of "before" and "after" in order to be able to enjoy the present. Jacob, Alameddine's middle-aged Yemen-born minor poet protagonist, lost his closest friends in the epidemic, and to deal with his present, his own "After After" to borrow Gurganus's phrase, he tries to forget his consistent cultural displacements by falling into an insipid perfunctory existence. Having undertaken rituals of alienation, shame, endurance, and survival through intense sexual masochism in the pre- and early AIDS era, Jacob's subsequent loss of his social circle finally overwhelms him. Remaining uninfected but not unscathed, he mutes his accumulated anger by submerging his intense codependent yet unreconcilable early pains and pleasures into his subconscious. This strategy dulls the horrors of his past, but it also mires him unhealthily within it, enabling him to blame AIDS for the demise of his relationships with his friends and particularly with his unfaithful lover, Doc. Keeping his memories of these dead men at a safely memorialized, elegiac distance, Jacob nurtures a half-forgetful, unhealthy romantic apathy in his present.

Increasingly lonely, however, Jacob slowly returns to his memories, which erode his self-detrimental indifference to his contemporary environment. As this happens, Jacob recognizes how his own and others' contemporary indifference to queer suffering colludes with mainstream repressions of nonhomonormative queer lives. His anger at this collusion spurs him to reconnect his history to his present, essentially reimagining his role as a queer cosmopolitan American. While Rechy, Nugent, Hemphill, and others, as I have discussed, have noted the alienation of queer angelic outlaws of color in US society, Alameddine expands this perspective by focusing on a queer immigrant of color (queer immigrants being almost ipso facto outlaws in the United States prior to 1990) struggling to merge his diverse cultural histories.[3] Fortunately, Alameddine's Angel of History is Satan, the archetypal cosmopolitan or really cosmic immigrant, and as Satan contextualizes the tyrannical peace of heaven and the liberating chaos of hell, he encourages Jacob to contextualize his memories of the dead alongside memories of homophobia, exile, racism, romantic betrayals, and AIDS.[4] This encouragement allows Jacob to engage his history more productively and to appreciate the richness of his imperfect present and future. Jacob, Satan suggests, should benefit from his own dislocations and reject any peace that requires a demeaning masochistic submission to an idealized normative hierarchy.

Notably, Alameddine leaves it ambiguous as to whether this neo-Miltonic Satan represents an actual figure or simply a rebellious portion of Jacob's psyche. Jacob, for instance, repeatedly refers to himself as having been "hurled headlong flaming from th'ethereal sky" (2016: 35, 227, 294, a direct echo of Milton's *Paradise Lost* 1.45) and he visits a psychiatric clinic to stop Satan's voice. Yet whether a manifestation of Jacob's psychomachia or the Archfiend himself, Satan's effect remains the same: he offers a perspective with which Jacob wrestles, not wanting the pain of remembering past pleasures amid alienations or the struggle of reconsidering his own role as an American. As Satan gradually dominates, he forces Jacob to rebel against his apathy if not precisely his melancholic longing for an unfulfilled romance with the dead Doc or his entrenched conception of an America equating to the white, middle-class professional culture that Doc represents. As such, Jacob's continued resistance to Satan indicates how even fruitful engagements with bad beatitudes can be so psychologically fraught that they lead to only ever qualified cultural revolts. More than any other writer discussed in this study, Alameddine allows his Luciferian protagonist to explore the deadening relief of wallowing in a failed rebellion.

Forgetting to Remember: AIDS-Inspired Apathy

To emphasize a balance of remembering and forgetting and to obtain thereby a satisfying present, Alameddine begins *Angel* with Satan fighting Jacob's isolating and stagnant apathy. Satan confronts Jacob's mixed eagerness and reluctance to forget loved ones who died from AIDS, an ambivalent psychological state that prevents Jacob from happily recalling his friends and thus desiring to seek new ones. Reassessing Jacob's depression, Satan looks around his apartment and insists on the existence of "dignity" even amid "decay" (2016: 1). Satan promotes a multifaceted state-of-being wherein physical and emotional decline merges with self-respect for persevering, a solacing honor at keeping oneself moving and remembering past successes that the inevitable aches of aging, including mourning and regret, should enhance. Jacob, Satan suggests, should value his own achievements and experiences even as they fade away. Jacob's life has, to be sure, decayed. He has gotten older, he has lost his social circle, and he now has "problems" with his poetry, a sort of aesthetic impotence, but he refuses to acknowledge the "dignity" of his situation, of the psychological, emotional, and social distinctions available to older individuals who have had varied engagements with different arts, languages, cultures, time periods, and people (102). He has taken to eating by himself at night, isolated, where he dulls his mind by gazing at "blank" spaces in his apartment (1). Other space hold "photos" of Jacob's dead friends, "young men" who it turns out died of AIDS years before, but Jacob ignores these images (4). If Rechy's Professor and Skipper rely too much on old photographs to determine their self-worth and dignity, Jacob relies on them too little. Unable to throw the photographs out, he ignores them and thereby fails to use them to recall some happiness into his present and to inspire him to find new friends. Attempting to counter this stagnancy, Satan urges Jacob to engage the consoling catharsis of acknowledging painful repressions so that he can see the dignity in his own life, such as the friendship he is capable of enjoying, to use this joy in his current life, and to move forward.

To challenge this depressing forgetfulness, Satan coaxes repressed memories into Jacob's consciousness by interviewing spiritual figures who have supported him since his childhood. Like Satan, these spiritual beings serve as much as manifestations of Jacob's psyche as independent characters, particularly the Fourteen Holy Helpers, a grouping of marginalized Middle Eastern saints. Satan's interviews consequently function analogously to Catholic confessions, to psychological case histories, and to self-explorations, so far as they promote understanding and cathartic healing, whether of a spiritual, emotional, or physical sort. Satan's turn to the Fourteen Holy Helpers proves particularly useful as they signal the tenacity of certain marginalized yet emotionally and psychologically affirming memories and histories. Jacob learns of these "Eastern saints," for instance, in a French Catholic school in Lebanon from Sœur Salwa, an Arabic name meaning "solace" or "comfort" (2016: 82; Wehr 1979: 498). Speaking to the Arab students in their own language, Sœur Salwa defied the "French mother superior" by refusing to allow her and other "Western Catholic nuns" to hide Christ's "true Word" from their students, which she achieves in part by reminding the latter that some Arabs had been followers of Christ and Christianity before there had been French people at all, much less French Catholics (2016: 81, 82, 83). Herself an outlaw fighting Western European claims of spiritual originality and authenticity, Salwa offers solace to her demeaned Arab students by reminding them of how Christ and his saints transmitted their message to Arab people prior to the Western Europeans, who twisted Christianity to bolster their own national colonialism. The French mother superior eventually fires Salwa from the school, reasserting French political and socioeconomic power, but Jacob remembers her descriptions of how the Holy Helpers continued to nurture their followers despite the Italian-based pope having degraded the "Eastern saints" by taking their holy celebrations off of the most expansive version of the liturgical Catholic calendar (82). Like Salwa, the downgraded yet persistent Holy Helpers exemplify for Jacob the successful defiance of an official degradation and they thereby offer him some comfort, even in America. Thus, as Satan insists, the interviews with these saints are to succor Jacob who sees these blessed figures as memorials of past cultures, past faiths, past mentors, past lovers, and past friends, and so they in particular, with their superabundance of significations, can "help him remember" his own past, which remains vital to his attaining a more satisfactory future (5). By churning up the fertile ground of Jacob's memories, Satan hopes that Jacob will recall and acknowledge the dignifying and lasting fruit of his own losses.

Recalling repressed memories, however, can be overwhelming and Alameddine acknowledges that framing recollections strategically can be useful. To survive in a relationship, in a nation, and especially in a complex society, which all inevitably manifest degrees of past betrayals, deceits, and offenses, individuals must de-emphasize some resentments within personal and public histories to live happily in the present and into the future.[5] Individuals must nonetheless recall injuries and grievances to stimulate and to justify counteracting revolts.

Correspondingly, to focus only on anger and loss would lead to depression and torment and be no less unhealthy than over-idealizing the past. Jacob clearly intuits the need for balanced recollections even as he fails to achieve them, as he keeps his photographs but unhelpfully ignores them. Jacob's struggle with this balance intensifies as the psychological and spiritual pressure of Satan's interviews builds, prodding Jacob's memories. Barriers dissolve in Jacob's mind as he reluctantly recalls scenes from his childhood and his early adult life with Doc. Rather than seeking better balances of good and bad, however, Jacob initially defangs these memories. He tells them, for instance, not to the combative Satan or to new friends but to a reimagined version of Doc, who finally listens without talking back. Purposefully downplaying Doc's emotional coldness prior to his death, Jacob vainly tries to rekindle their closeness by narrating to him memories of Yemen, Egypt, Lebanon, and his early days in the United States. He rationalizes directing these recollections to his once aloof, now dead lover by articulating a "need" to share his story combined with a "concomitant desire to forget" it, to "inter it" within some ostensibly indifferent capsule (2016: 17). Jacob admits his desire to preserve the past, to finding some comfort in its existence, so long as he need not interrogate it. As Jacob resists any balanced or critical recollections, this version of Doc provides a perfect frame or repository for his selective memories, one that cannot refuse his offerings, much less challenge them. Jacob imagines the equivalent of preserving an archive but forbidding anyone to consult it or to interpret it.

Remembering the past nonetheless challenges Jacob's reluctance to critique half-recollected ideals. It forces him, for instance, to reconsider his resurgent longing for Doc as he unwillingly recalls how Doc consistently disregarded him. For "almost twenty years," Jacob remained loyal to his ideal of Doc as a "partner," which distracted him from his present, curtailing his desire to seek out a new lover. While nostalgia permeates queer AIDS literature reinforcing melancholic reflections over lost ideals of romance and freedom, Jacob exhibits a particularly self-destructive melancholia, as what limited memories he does consider, including new recollections prompted by Satan, scarcely undo his intense devotion to a man who while alive had largely ignored him. Indeed, although Jacob's returning memories recontextualize even his new figuration of Doc from an auditor for his stories into someone who petulantly stays "silent," refusing to engage or to encourage him, Jacob insists futilely on renewing their intimacy (2016: 173). Jacob resists letting Doc go but he does reassess how this relationship failed him, as his recollections of Doc consistently discounting his feelings confront his romanticization of his ostensible "partner." Satan pushes

Jacob to recall how Doc repeatedly sought out other lovers and cruelly brought them to the apartment that they still shared rather than to a "bathhouse" or to any place that was not partly Jacob's (219). Their relationship struggled on, even prior to Doc's illness, as Doc withdrew emotionally and sexually from Jacob but declined to seek out a new apartment, while Jacob stayed with Doc until he died from an AIDS-related illness. While these new memories push Jacob to reevaluate his life with Doc, to see it in a more accurate, less romantic light, Jacob continues to talk to Doc until the end of the novel, distancing himself from Doc's hold over him but only ever just a little.

Substantially more validating, because much less romantically ambivalent, are Jacob's memories of his deceased friends. When Saint Blaise notes to Satan that Jacob kept his "group of friends together," Satan observes that Jacob suspects that these men "only tolerated" his presence and he orders Blaise to "[e]nlighten" Jacob regarding his value to the group, to remind him that his friends really loved him (Alameddine 2016: 243). As if forcing one part of Jacob's mind to influence another, Satan challenges Jacob's insecurity by telling Blaise to recall Jacob's importance to his dead friends despite the pain that consciously missing them will cause him. The pain, Satan insists, stems from the pleasure of remembering the good he has lost and recalling this pleasure in the present will be worth the pain. Satan's interview with Blaise thus encourages Jacob to move past his insecure apathy toward an understanding that for his friends, at least, he was not an alienated or exiled figure but a central one. If for years Jacob has preferred to stare at empty spaces rather than at photographs, he will now recall and take pleasure from the help he gave his friends both before they got sick and while they were dying from AIDS-related illnesses.

Jacob's recollections of his friend Greg, in particular, illustrate the complex mental balancing of this self-affirming process. To add to this complexity of memory and valuation of self-worth through relationships, Alameddine describes how this particular friendship bridged erotic, social, and professional circumstances. When Jacob first met Greg, an affluent estate attorney, they had sex, which made Jacob feel attractive. When they subsequently became friends, Greg helped Jacob to get work as a typist at his law firm, indicating that Greg liked and trusted Jacob enough to associate with him professionally. In return, Jacob introduced Greg to Doc, helping to cement their group of friends. When Greg tested positive for HIV, Jacob remembers painfully and yet fondly how he spent time helping Greg prepare to die, helping him to clean his house and sort through his possessions. Greg, who "couldn't commit" to one lover, who remained romantically set apart, nonetheless let Jacob "into his heart" after getting "diagnosed" with HIV, choosing Jacob as one of his final close companions. Jacob recalls to the imaginary Doc how valuable this last bit of "time with him" was, "I loved him" (Alameddine 2016: 267). As Doc increasingly devalued and pushed Jacob away physically and emotionally, Jacob recalls that his connection with Greg expanded. Although these memories hurt, they allow Jacob to contradict his feeling of subsisting as a perpetual exile. They bolster his sense of his value in his past as well as in his present as they evidence his capacity to help and to be loved.

Equivalently, under Satan's influence Jacob recalls how his friend Lou lovingly designated him as the chief repository for his memory, giving Jacob a moral responsibility to celebrate and to lament the past. With Satan's prodding, Jacob remembers how Lou revealed his diagnosis of HIV to Jacob "first," and Jacob recollects how he sat with Lou and listened as Lou imparted to him the parts of his life, his curated "story," that he wanted Jacob to hold on to, telling Jacob afterward, "Remember me" (Alameddine 2016: 227–8). This request is an intensely intimate act as Lou feels that Jacob alone can be trusted to recall the most complete, non-prejudicial account of his virtues and thereby keep him alive in however attenuated a fashion. If for twenty years Jacob had neglected this charge, he fulfills it in the present as only he can, both because he remains alive and because he had the most respect for Lou. Lou had generally made their group of friends, largely "masculine" white-collar professionals, "uncomfortable," as he had been effeminately "pretty" and his overarching "ambition" had been to be an excellent hairdresser so as "to help others look better" and thus to feel good about themselves (243, 244). Of their group, Jacob alone considers this goal "laudable" and he misses Lou's unpretentious geniality and skill (244). Jacob experiences a bittersweet pleasure then in recollecting to Lou now decades after his death, "thou wast perfect in thy ways" (228). Jacob's use of a pseudo-biblical rhetoric, with his "thou"s and "thy"s and his evocation of eternity, works to exalt Lou's only seemingly simplistic desire to help others by improving their looks and thereby helping to increase their self-esteem and optimism. Jacob alone, of their friends, can fully take joy in Lou's life while more fully mourning his passing. As such, Alameddine suggests, he has a moral responsibility to eschew his own apathy to do so.

As his relationships with Greg and Lou illustrate, Jacob's value to his close friends was, at least in part, his ability to counter feelings of exile and loneliness by nurturing a community. Avoiding what Death imagines would have been Jacob's life in a Yemeni village, stuck with a child bride who "remained a virgin" as Jacob ignored her, spending his erotic energy "masturbating" in another room alone, Jacob moves to the United States for a better chance of finding romance and supportive environments (2016: 52). Still, even amid the greater sexual openness of the 1980s in San Francisco, he remains aware of his estrangement from mainstream America. Jacob observes to the dead Doc, "I wasn't American," though they "may have thought [he] was," a perhaps overly defensive statement. Pointedly, Jacob draws on a bitterly narrow, monolithic sense of Americanness, as his brown skin, his preference for wearing a "jellabiya," his religious mix of Islamic and Middle-Eastern Catholic beliefs, combined with his queerness during the rise of the AIDS epidemic, all heighten his difference from a WASPish heteronormative mainstream American culture (100). This very sense of difference, however, encourages him to pursue and to sustain a queer community, especially as his friends get sick. After learning of Lou's diagnosis, Jacob notes an initial reluctance to go to him, which would acknowledge the breaking up of their group and Jacob's own impending isolation. Walking the Castro, Jacob sees individuals "dead and alive," everyone "lost in loss," as sick gay men walked "exiled and stateless in our native city," a community of potential friends and lovers become "strangers" (228). Alameddine indicates here how gay men become three-times estranged when they get sick. First, they are alienated still further from mainstream society, including from their government as it withheld adequate national resources to care for its minority citizens and as officials considered containment camps.[6] Second, facets of the queer community itself too often avoid sick or even just infected gay men, as Jacob initially avoids Lou, unable to face this new tragedy.[7] Third, people such as Greg, Lou, and Jacob's other friends lose the steadying rhythms of their previous lives. Queer people with AIDS thus walk as "stateless ... strangers," now feeling as foreign to the United States as Jacob once felt. Jacob, however, using his previous feelings of isolation as inspiration, overcomes his fears and nurses his friends, echoing the work of myriad gay support groups and countless individuals who maintained queer social networks as people with HIV/AIDS fell under siege within their own cities and within their own local queer communities.

 Jacob's politicized language draws, of course, on the rhetoric surrounding HIV/AIDS, which so often worked to exclude queer Americans with the virus from full US citizenship. Descriptions of an "invading" virus, as Anthony Petro has argued, frequently positioned queer people with HIV/AIDS as themselves foreign infiltrators of national as well as social and religious institutions. Such language, Petro notes, resonated insidiously with older descriptions of "homosexuals as communists, bent on infiltrating America," hoping to corrupt American capitalism, patriarchy, and Christianity through covert agents

(2015: 28). This medical-political rhetoric served, as Jacqueline Foertsch has noted, as a faulty protection against multiple unstable borders in the twentieth century. "The depth of the hysteria generating postmodern plague," Foertsch argues, was "determined by the condition of the *barrier* perceived to separate healthy or contagious, patriot from traitor, straight from queer: the more difficult we feel this barrier is to locate, erect, or maintain, the more virulent the reaction against those suspected of belonging on the other side" (2001: 27). For conservative and even some liberal commentators, queer people with AIDS became a new facet of invasive outside agents or subversive fifth columnists who must be expelled or contained to preserve an ineffectively cordoned-off nationalistic ideal of health and superiority. Compounded then with the trauma of their "loss" of health, as Jacob notes, is the further curtailment of citizenship and community for queer people with HIV/AIDS. Alameddine uses this rhetorical context to parallel Jacob's experiences as a queer non-Protestant immigrant of color to the experiences of even white native-born Americans who become infected with HIV. The rights and privileges of citizenship, Alameddine reasserts, are more contingent and tenuous than most Americans want to believe. Recognizing this, Jacob quickly overcomes his own sense of horror and fear and goes to comfort Lou, as he will comfort his friends Greg, Pinto, Chris, and his one-time lover Doc.

Jacob then, like so many earlier queer angelic outlaws, bridges barriers by presenting a hybrid figure, holding multifaceted identities in tension: past and present, healthy and sick, vital and apathetic, American and Middle Eastern, lawbreaker and law firm employee, as well as a former-Muslim Catholic in a predominantly Protestant United States. A politically, socially, and spiritually Luciferian figure, during the early AIDS epidemic Jacob becomes an angel of mercy and also an angel of queer history, committed to remembering the marginalized friends he so lovingly nursed. These memories, after an interval, challenge his own apathy in his present. In his loneliness, they remind him of his responsibility to his friends and to a chronological community between the past and the present. For who save a queer survivor could understand the pleasure, the sorrow, and the necessity of sustaining this community across time? To support this notion, Jacob remembers Benjie, a gay HIV-positive Filipino tailor whom he describes once as a "fairy" and subsequently as an "angel" of kindness after Benjie carefully provides professional services for Greg so that Greg can wear his suit over a leather vest at his funeral, thereby exhibiting both his lawyer and his leatherman identities (2016: 268, 269). During the fittings, Benjie asks Greg to "tell the angels" that the tailor expects to die soon himself and that he hopes to join their angelic choir in style with "big wings" of his own (269). As Benjie helps Greg exhibit both his chief identities, so Benjie trusts that Greg in the future will help Benjie transition from an earthly angel into a heavenly one. Recalling Benjie reinforces for Jacob his own angelic responsibility to maintain communities across cultural, sexual, spiritual, and even chronological barriers and this helps to shed his apathy in his own present.

Leather Martyrologies: Anger, Insult, and Ecstasy

While Jacob's relationships with his friends prove valuably enduring, Alameddine resists idealizing them. To acknowledge the complexities of seeking belonging in marginalized groups, Alameddine shows how Jacob's search for a supportive community simultaneously risked a self-injurious masochism. Already subject to internalized degradations and repressions due to his frequent dislocations, as if by habit Jacob seeks refuge in S&M and leather subcultures as his early romance with Doc falters. These queer communities, however, offer only a problematic solace, as Jacob's personal engagement with S&M resonates with broader debates in the 1980s and 1990s regarding its liberational potential. While prominent critics such as Gayle Rubin linked sadomasochists to "religious heretics" and argued that such spiritually inflected "sexual outlaws" challenged repressive erotic hierarchies by seeking new "methods to maximize sensation and minimize danger," critics such as Leo Bersani countered that "S/M is nonetheless profoundly conservative in that its imagination of pleasure is almost entirely defined by the dominant culture" (Bersani 1995: 87; Rubin 2011: 135, 136, 118).[8] Alameddine offers a more extensively ambivalent perspective. While emphasizing that S&M can teach its acolytes new unconventional pleasures, he critiques how degradations that promise a spiritually erotic transcendence to the disenfranchised members of a hierarchical community too often reinforce a self-destructive abjection.

Increasingly under Satan's influence, Jacob reconsiders how repeated alienations can masochistically encourage one to seek out securely familiar, if intensely problematic, aggressive encounters. Jacob recalls, for instance, how Doc bringing a trick to their apartment one night caused him to flee temporarily their clean comfortable home, moving through the then "seedy," not yet gentrified South of Market leather neighborhood to the "Eagle," his first visit to an S&M bar (2016: 220). Feeling degraded by his lover and self-exiled to San Francisco's socioeconomic margins, Jacob hoped to find extreme physical manifestations of his psychic pain that might also signal his desirability, wanting a vicious touch that could purge his emotional anguish and offer visceral proof of his attractiveness. Here, Jacob first met Greg, who took him home and who through a moderate sadomasochistic encounter facilitated a sociable affirmation of Jacob's displacement into new erotic practices. Rather than humiliate Jacob, Greg "kissed" him before tying him up and whipping him. This sadomasochistic sex functioned not to abuse Jacob but to manifest his psychological pain physically so that it he could feel it somewhat subside. Simultaneously, this process established a new community, new ties that bound both literally and metaphorically. Greg whipped Jacob in a fashion that did not substantially injure him but that he felt "disinterred" him and reenergized his "soul," revitalizing him physically and spiritually (224–5). It served as an introduction to wanted but as yet unexplored sensations and a psychic or even spiritual release, the disinterring achieved when someone recognizes and claims one's buried or repressed psychic life. The intense sensations broke through inhibitions and fears to allow the emergence of hidden identities and previously blocked bridges to a new union. This union subsequently facilitates Jacob's and Greg's close friendship even if they did not become long-term lovers.

As a result, even after sex, Jacob finds with Greg a transcendence from his loneliness that persists in nonromantic love throughout their friendship and after Greg's death. Having been cast off by Doc, Jacob longed for someone who wanted him enough to fix him in place, even if only temporarily, almost to the degree that God fixes his angels and martyrs into place. God acquiesces to his martyrs being tortured so that they could prove their loyalty to a hierarchical divine rule, with this very process of physical, emotional, and psychic pain ecstatically evidencing a spiritual loyalty and transcendent unity with an existence greater than one's lonely, otherwise alienated self. Through his S&M encounter with Greg, Jacob achieved a more earthly physical and spiritual variation on such a commitment. After their first S&M session, Jacob remembers, Greg gave him "guidance and affection" and "like all saints" prior to him, Jacob "relished the ecstasy of martyrdom" (2016: 225). Rather than feel humiliated or degraded, Jacob felt desired, cared for, and mentored. He had sacrificed his dignity and some of his freedom for his and Greg's union through domination and submission. Even after the discovery of HIV/AIDS, and Jacob's implicit understanding of how he had been at risk, he cherishes his memories of his one night with Greg, then little more than an unknown trick.

Of course, when contextualized with racism, imperialism, and legal and sexual domination, this queer role-playing becomes deeply troubling. This is especially so as Jacob shades these S&M encounters with a spirituality that overshadows and thus colludes with racist and imperialistic religious forces, much liked the French Nuns in his Lebanese school who emphasized Western European martyrs over Middle Easter ones. Jacob's pleasure and ecstasy fit uneasily then with the implications of a white European lawyer, albeit a queer man from historically subjugated Catholic Ireland, whipping a poor Middle Eastern minor poet. To be sure, Jacob does not feel subjugated and this stresses the partial pleasures that he takes in this bad beatitude, in a queer erotic martyrdom or his Luciferian rejection of norms to find pleasure. For whatever one thinks of S&M, Jacob lives in a flawed world and some masochistic practices work for him as an erotic catharsis for his psychological and spiritual pain regardless of political moralities. After his night with Greg, he walked home in the morning self-determined and self-confident, he was "sizzling," feeling hot and attractive and in control of his desires, "[s]elf-tempted, self-depraved" (Alameddine 2016: 225). Bucking social constraints and even psychological dangers, Jacob rebelliously, dangerously, yet purposefully pursued new forms of belonging. Nonetheless, Alameddine uses the racial and religious dislocations spread throughout the novel to imply that Jacob's martyrdom colludes with repressive religious and political ideologies, even if at times he willfully refuses to recognize it.

Alameddine indicates, moreover, how sublime pleasures achieved through profane practices can shift from minor to traumatic collusions with self-destructive behaviors and beliefs. By depicting severer forms of S&M, Alameddine highlights the collusive risks of longing to be lashed into place to ensure a sense of belonging, almost no matter where. From a heretical perspective, Satan fought comparable bondage in God's firmament, but as Jacob fights Satan's calls to remember he likewise ignores Satan's rebellious paradigm. Jacob's consequent submissiveness invites injuries that outweigh any comfort in inclusion. When Doc brings another man home for sex, Jacob again flees his apartment to find a community that embraces his internalized spiritual and physical abjection. In a sex club, Jacob finds a man whom he associates with familiar Muslim and Christian religious and political repressions. The man wears "leather" like a "niqab," an almost full-face cover for women, and he has a "rope," reminiscent of the belt used by an "ascetic" nun who taught "French history" in Lebanon; subsequently, Jacob notes his own careful speech because many "leather masters" are "language Nazis" (2016: 124, 125). Amplifying Greg's sadism, Jacob equates this leather master with large-scale oppressions against public appreciations of bodily beauty, spiritual variations, and intellectual breadth, for example, appreciations of French and Middle Eastern history, as well as a linguistic diversity. If the scene begins with a watered-down version of oppression, as the phrase "language Nazis" obscures the Nazis' mass murders, the violence increases as the man whips Jacob, calling him "faggot" and "sand nigger" (128). The man merges verbal insults that recall Jacob's identity as a gay exile from his Muslim Yemeni roots, his Catholic Lebanese roots, a Caucasian heteronormative Protestant US culture, and even a queer American subculture that gains a perverse facade of power from imitating fascist brutalities. Outside the club such queer sadists hold scant authority, so inside they welcome masochists like Jacob, who troublingly invites this violent intimacy as proof that he could be welcomed because of his internalized abjection. Jacob thus colludes with a violent hierarchical power by embracing it despite its denying him any self-worth besides being the whipping boy for racist and homophobic brutalities. He risks his spiritual, psychological, and physical well-being for the chance that the transient communion he obtains through pain is worth re-entrenching his internalized self-loathing and others' prejudices.

Worse still, the community that Jacob finds in the S&M club proves too transient and superficial to maintain his erotic or romantic ideals. Pursuing his welcome as this leatherman's avenue to power, Jacob imagines, misguidedly, that he can claim some clout of his own. He pursues a queer variation of Hegel's Master/Slave Dialectic, but one that fails to synthesize. At the club, he feels that the "prey had trapped the predator" and although the man's riding crop is extremely "painful" he still feels that he has chosen this communal ritual (2016: 125, 128). Yet this choice was contingent upon his unwanted humiliation at home. To seek out in reaction a second humiliation so intense that it briefly drowns out the first remains a provisional, even paradoxical self-empowerment at best. For although Jacob exploits this leatherman for his own purposes, to overwhelm however briefly his thoughts of Doc, this power proves a pyrrhic one. Jacob hopes that if the leatherman can desire him because he despises him then perhaps Doc might follow suit, though he suspects that Doc will not. Jacob allows the leatherman to beat him until both orgasm after which Jacob finds that his mind and body are so discombobulated that he had forgotten how to "move" his limbs. Yet if unable or perhaps unwilling to move his body, Jacob's mind returns to Doc safe and secure in their "clean, well-lighted place" (130). Jacob's martyrdom thus remains incomplete. His bad beatitude of gaining a blessed sense of belonging, even if at the bottom of a hierarchy, remains partial because he ends the session not with loving companionship as with Greg or in even a temporary unity with the anonymous leatherman, but actively longing for Doc while knowing that Doc remains separate from him, in his own room in their allegedly shared apartment. Jacob's reference to their "clean, well-lighted place," moreover, implicitly connects his situation to Ernest Heming's story "A Clean, Well-Lighted Place" wherein Hemingway expounds his nihilistic theory of "*nada*" or nothingness in a world absent of even a tyrannical God, "Our *nada* who art in *nada*, *nada* be thy name" (Hemingway 2017: 347). Jacob's reference indicates his own sense of the failure of his masochistic pursuits. He seriously risks his body and mental health in the hopes of convincing himself that he might regain a romantic nothingness with Doc. Indeed, Jacob's balance of pain and hope remains lopsided as Doc never again seems to desire Jacob romantically though he will want Jacob's help at home when he gets sick from AIDS-related symptoms.

If Jacob's hope for passionate communion with others falls flat, so too does his desire to achieve any personal physical, psychological, and spiritual coherence through S&M. As the leatherman reaches a sadistic apex, Jacob's "tears" mingle with other bodily fluids, such as "snot," as he "turned human," ostensibly asserting his basic biological connection to humanity. This human commonality, however, subsists with scarcely any of Jacob's psychological, emotional, or even creative grace. What little poetic faculty Jacob retains offers hardly more than a compromised spirituality. When his beating exceeds his physical capacity for cathartic pain, Jacob hopes to access the spiritual connections obtained by ancient martyrs or even by Satan, whose respective narratives present pain as an instrument for communion with and communion apart from a tyrannical God.[9] Thinking along similar lines to these predecessors, Jacob nominally conceives of his torture as a means to transcend his physical and psychological loneliness. He imagines all fourteen Holy Helpers arriving to help him survive, with Saint Denis rejoicing, "beatification, here we come" (2016: 129). But Jacob consistently fails to maintain the focus necessary for a personal coherence, much less a transcendent beatification. His mind consistently undermines his physical pain, his attraction to the leatherman, and even his spiritual visions of the saints as he thinks back to Doc. Upon subsequent returns to the S&M club, Jacob even considers his beatings as akin to a "break" from more serious endeavors, his body engaging so many intellectually and spiritually empty, quasi-ludic rituals that lead less to a self-fulfillment or martyrdom than to an interlude from the transcendent bliss he wants with his ostensible partner (127). As such, despite Saint Denis's prediction, Jacob's beatification never quite arrives, as his body, mind, and heart pull him in different directions. In the end, this route to a beatitude proves bad less because it is profane than because it remains ineffective. Jacob's desire to be beaten results therefore in one of the most self-injurious and contradictory forms of a bad beatitude yet discussed. For Jacob engages willingly in self-destructive S&M rituals knowing that they will harm him while suspecting that they will fail to manifest the communion and transcendent ideals that he so desperately seeks.

Jacob's subsequent encounters with humiliation reduce him to such a base animalism that they inspire the deadening apathy with which he begins the novel. After AIDS destroyed his chosen community, despite his best nursing efforts, Jacob feels so worthless as to pursue Deke, a predominantly straight drug addict who he knows will never return his desire. If this connection offers comfort, it is in knowing that it will fail. Jacob buys drugs for, bathes the feet of, and occasionally fellates Deke, but save for when Deke beats Jacob for taking too much crack, Deke himself would not actively "touch" Jacob (2016: 69). Suffering self-punishment rather than penance, with its offer of saving grace, Jacob's masochism hits its nadir as he abandons even his sublime humanity to assume an animalistic and then bacterial abjection. When Deke leaves Jacob abruptly, Jacob looked for him, returned home, "howled, then left [his] kennel" and returned to his job in the "bowels" of the wealthy law firm. Feeling dog-like or like fecal bacteria, living in a "kennel" and working in the "infern[al]" commercial "bowels" of the US legal system, Jacob feels less like Satan still revolting in Hell than like metaphorical shit, shit not even moving healthily but impacted within a body (70, 68). Turning to psychiatric help, Jacob abandons seeking romance and establishes a relationship with a cat and a nurturing lesbian best friend, Odette. While this withdrawal from his self-destructive S&M patterns could be productive progress, it proves awful in simply a new way as Jacob's life stultifies, filled with routine meals and, save for Odette, "perfunctory" acquaintances (96). As opposed to this unthinkingly mechanical death-within-life even Jacob's masochism, when not taken so far so as to injure him seriously, was comparatively vital and beautiful even if it lacked the full seraphic rebelliousness that he had sought. Rather than his anxious passion to transcend religious, social, legal, and medical limitations or a search for an analogously outcast community, Jacob retreats to a calm, collected, yet defeated indifference to life.

Homonormative Horrors: The Sadomasochism of Queer America's Quiet Assimilationists

Albeit more exciting than a static mediocrity, Alameddine suggests that an extreme masochism risks creating only a partial, imperfect bad beatitude, a bad bad beatitude because it risks internalizing an individual's extreme degradation.

In these cases, any temporary pleasures of acute masochistic acts offer only willfully misleading consolations. In Jacob's case, his final masochistic encounters reveal only the smallest spark of the sacred in the profane and the profane in the sacred and they prove unable to initiate more than a burnt-out transcendence that fades into solitary miseries. His masochism offers little joyful connection to anyone, including a more spiritually humanized, beatific version of himself. Plummeting from Doc to anonymous sadists to Deke, the more degradation Jacob accepts the more he internalizes his worthlessness in ways that lead not to a communion with lovers much less to martyrs and angelic rebels but to new isolations. As such, Jacob's self-injurious masochism engages a particularly high level of collusion with homophobic and racist political, cultural, and religious patterns, all directly or indirectly imitated in a queer "Nazi aesthetic," such that his sought-out combinations of liberating and repressive forces disproportionately emphasize the latter (2016: 220). Unfortunately, as Jacob realizes, this small leather subculture he engages risks intensifying subtler yet broader-ranging sadomasochistic collusions pervasive within more homonormative or ostensibly mainstream gay American communities.

While Rechy, Nugent, and Ginsberg likewise critique sadomasochisms that imitate without effectively subverting racist, classist, and homophobic cultural practices, Alameddine considers such sadomasochistic appropriations after the advent of HIV/AIDS.[10] To emphasize this new context, Alameddine has Jacob consider the irony of gay men who play quite seriously with physical pain and degradation, albeit for consensual cathartic purposes, when their peers were dying horribly from AIDS-related causes in a still predominantly homophobic nation.[11] Extrapolating from this irony, Jacob raises the dilemma that for gay men to actively degrade any underprivileged minority risks colluding too extensively with the cruelest factions of American intolerance, which exacerbates the personal pains caused by impersonal biological tragedies. In such cases, queer individuals have failed to learn any humane lesson from the AIDS epidemic while reinforcing national intolerances that risk backfiring on their own community, particularly on queer people of color, despite any assimilationist successes. Alameddine positions such considerations as a sign of Jacob's critical maturation, for following his apathetic malaise, he moves beyond his rejection of too self-injurious degradations to highlight and to attack subtler self-destructive homonormative assimilations into a racist, classist, and ableist American culture.

Jacob's most thoughtful censure of queer egotistic cruelties comes through his short story about two affluent homonormative white partners who exude vicious imperialist values. In many ways, in fact, this story evokes Hiram Pérez's observation that "[t]he modern gay male subject remains inscribed in the nation's imperialist project in ways that require significant analytical disentangling" (2015: 3). Jacob performs such a theoretical disentangling by imagining how a gay male employer could advance capitalistic excesses and a white privilege that align with one of his conservative, homophobic employee's own avaricious and racist values. Having moved to New York City from Indiana, a state with strong support for conservative, often homophobic politics, the employee and his wife attend a party at the queer couple's condo and happily learn that some big city "gays" and "liberals" live according to principles almost more repressive and conservative than their own (2016: 230). Reflecting on his boss's home, the employee observes that someone had shipped a "Victorian mansion," presumably Victorian architectural features and furniture from the UK, and set it up within "a New York penthouse," undoubtedly at great expense (231). This Victorian excess, built upon a distantly violent financial exploitation of non-European nations, becomes modernized and Americanized in New York. At the party, British colonialism merges with past and present American racism as the narrator notices that the gay couple has specifically "black" servers carrying around appetizers (232). The narrator realizes that despite his hosts' sexual liberalism, they use their wealth, education, and technology to re-entrench themselves into a traditional, conservatively cosmopolitan ruling class, one that continues to place economic and racial minorities into subservient positions. A liberal embrace of same-sex desire, he realizes, does not intrinsically signal financial and social radicalism or even a distaste for extending, fairly explicitly, the exploitative practices of white Anglo-American plantation-owning classes.

This racism moves into sadism when the hosts flaunt a caged Arab man as a sign of their dominating power. Treating the man as a pet, the hosts explain that one of them is "allergic to cats" and the other thinks "dogs" create excessive "work," implying that they leave the man in his cage as they would not even a dog. Constraining the man's physicality, the hosts likewise try to constrain his spirituality as they give him a Quran to keep him "distracted" but only after they have made it "safe" by taking out any passages that they consider "naughty," presumably verses that might reinforce anti-homosexual or anti-capitalist ideologies (2016: 233). Despite their hint of camp by using the word "naughty," the gay couple quite seriously considers it necessary to subjugate this man. The couple implies that in controlling him they protect themselves, their guests, and the man himself, who might otherwise embrace a rabidly anti-gay and anti-American religiosity. As these Muslim religious beliefs pose a supposed threat, never fully contextualized in light of Western imperialism, the couple pointedly reframes them as animalistic and self-destructive, and thus in need of their intervention.¹² Conflating what they see as the Arab man's bestiality and his spirituality, the hosts placed in the cage two sandboxes, one for use as a "litter box" and one for "[c]leaning" so that the man can pray after following a minimum of ritual ablutions (237, 236). Early in his captivity, the man once mistook the boxes and, having used the toilet box for cleaning he became exceptionally "distressed" such that he would have committed suicide save that his hosts refused to let him (237). This mistake indicates that if processes for achieving purification and desecration, sanctity and profanity, can at times be almost indiscernible, if ultimately clear, the immediate life-and-death consequences of purity and impurity can be externally imposed. The Arab man's brief desire to end his life becomes irrelevant as his nominal owners thwart him as a sign of their dominance over their own alleged property and over foreign ideologies.

Indeed, these men so dominate this foreign representative that they can train him to impersonate Western caricatures of exceedingly religious, wealthy, and violent Arabs, thereby shifting disquieting stereotypes into entertainments seemingly safe for Western elites. The hosts note, for instance, that although Muslims are traditionally supposed to pray "five times" in a twenty-four-hour period, they permit what they call this man's prayer "trick" solely when they are treating visitors (2016: 237). In this context, the man's prayer becomes as much a secular performance as an act of devotion, a parlor trick commanded less by God than by sadistic humans. Analogously, the couple has taught the caged man to perform what they call "Rich Arab tricks," which have him call for a Mercedes Benz or a Rolls-Royce in an "accented English," presumably an upper-class British accent, and declare that he wants to "buy some real estate" and "girls" (236, 235). These "tricks" mock Arab men who enact linguistic and commercial reverse colonialisms, feats that make Westerners nervous. They lampoon foreigners able to afford European luxury vehicles and property beyond the reach of many Westerners, while the "trick" of an Arab man seeking to purchase "girls" censures a commercialized eroticism that Western culture generally decries despite flagrantly sustaining. As an additional racist insult, this "trick" also implies that any white women interested in Arab men must primarily want money. Finally, to appear to control Arab violence, the gay men also display the "al-Qaeda trick," during which the man shouts "exterminate all the brutes" (236). These parodies of Arab individuals' greed stretch to militaristic levels as the man mimics a fanatical Muslim terrorism that uncomfortably resembles the violence of Western imperialism. While the hosts blithely ignore this similarity, Alameddine signals it by having this Arab man echo Kurtz in Joseph Conrad's *Heart of Darkness*, who in his report for the "International Society for the

Suppression of Savage Customs" exclaims "Exterminate all the brutes!" (2003: 125). As this man remains in his fancy cage however, his displays of Muslim fanaticism, wealth, and power remain an impotent entertainment. These displays represent foreign desires expressed yet unfulfilled, and fully controlled by the gay couple's preferred versions of secularism and capitalism.

Jacob's satire emphasizes the hypocritical nature of the couple's cruelty as they treat the Arab man comparably, though not equivalently, to how anxious heterosexuals treated same-sex desiring and gender nonconforming individuals in previous decades, imprisoning, hospitalizing, and deriding these minorities to bolster their own self-images. Rather than reenvisioning or dismantling social hierarchies, these men now use them to their advantage. To distract from their own only recent social acceptability, these men degrade those people still marginalized in the United States and they do so with an ostentatiousness that implies how their new power has in fact outpaced that of many heterosexuals. This Arab man, the narrator's boss explains, was "caught in the wild," was "tamed," apparently by a professional human-tamer, a not precisely pretty thought, and then the gay men "had to train him" upon receipt and this effort makes the "difference" in the quality of their captive. Obviously impressed, the narrator notes, "I had to admit that I agreed" as this "thing" behind bars "looked like the real deal" (2016: 235). By being able to pay to have this man "caught" and "tamed" and then being able to "train" this "thing" themselves, nominally stripping him of his humanity, the gay couple signals their ability to discipline "real" natural forces in ways that their heterosexual guests cannot. The homophobic narrator's own reluctance to acknowledge this ability, "I had to admit," caves in front of the couple's overwhelming signs of power. Similarly, when a guest with "a humongous pendant diamond" announces that her family too has a captive Arab woman, she is forced to confess that her captive is just a "poet from Albuquerque" (234). In addition to money, this bejeweled woman has the cultural capital of her traditional family, including progeny, but she concedes that she does not have the gay couple's resources. Rather than a formidable foreign enemy, the woman's family can only dominate a fellow citizen with already minor influence, being first a woman, second an Arab American, and third a poet, poets having less political efficacy in twenty-first-century America than almost anyone. In dominating the Arab man then, the gay hosts reaffirm their substantial forms of traditional power, namely wealth and social control, in front of—and, more implicitly, over—their guests.

Jacob's satirical apex comes, however, when he indicates that provincial American conservatives can actually learn new extremes of racism and capitalism from supposedly liberal, urban, white, gay men, whose progressivism scarcely extends past their penises. Having seen the hosts' caged man, the narrator's wife desires her "own Arab," albeit a "less expensive" one, as she realizes that such slaveholding offers a way to symbolize the social and financial prowess to which she aspires (2016: 238). To clarify her intentions, and Jacob's satire of a regressive liberalism, the narrator's wife announces obsequiously her willingness to "learn from you people," i.e., "gays" and "liberals," indicating both her flattery of their power and her welcomed discovery of revitalized methods of oppression from supposedly progressive individuals (232, 230). The wife matches, moreover, her husband's admiration for the deceptively conservative socioeconomic clout of the gay hosts, who convince him that so long as everyone has entertainment, lovely food, and someone in common to dehumanize, conservatives and moderate liberals can temporarily get along: later that evening, the employee reflects that there exists "no discernible difference between the liberals and my people" (238). As such, even if he has to accept publicly a same-sex relationship, the husband determines that he will continue to work for his gay boss, sensing that he can learn how to make still more money from such an expert proponent of a vicious American capitalism.

Yet, in critiquing this homonormative couple's sadistically conservative liberalism, Jacob also highlights their intrinsic, albeit subtle, masochism. The partners' limited, self-serving liberalism has sacrificed another man's humanity and thus their own human empathy in order to affirm their dominant role within an immoral American elite. By repressing others to win admiration from those who tolerate them primarily for their wealth and power, these men subsist eagerly in a milieu and among guests that accept them *despite* their sexuality. Same-sex desire manifests as a problem that must be overcome in a tacitly hostile environment, one where liberalism can easily veer into conservatism. The employee notes "no discernible difference" between gay liberals and straight conservatives, so long as everyone has good food and a common enemy. This superficial similarity remains a precarious détente because these men embrace the fundamental violence of modern socioeconomic hierarchies. The gay men perversely take pleasure then in bolstering a society in which should the current common enemy disappear, the straight community might very well return to re-marginalizing queer communities, even homonormative gay men. The power of these gay men is one that intrinsically leaves them on the edge of a normative American society.

Finally, this satire indicates Jacob's now conscious rejection of the intensities of his own earlier masochism, his submission to the constraints and the lashes, real and metaphorical, of a predominantly Western white gay community. Under Satan's influence, Jacob's reviving memories emphasize how despite his queer community's erotic liberalism, his lovers had no problem devaluing his Middle Eastern identity. Doc, for instance, disliked Jacob's "jellabiya," preferring him to wear "tight jeans," because Jacob was "in America" and he ought to want to fit in with American styles (2016: 100). Jacob's subsequent conception of his home as a "kennel" when he was with Deke echoes the "cage" of the captive Arab man. The caged Arab man and the caged Arab-American poet are Jacob's self-satire of his pursuit of men whose sense of American-ness excluded all but their own cultural codes, such as those pertaining to dress and appropriate professions. In this vein, Jacob's story rebukes his masochism as an internalized shame, one that his younger self brought explicitly to the fore so that his lovers/abusers could expiate it and shape him into a more palatable form, a submissive Arab American, much as the gay couple "trained" the Arab man. Analogously, the gay men turning the Arab man's Muslim prayers into a "trick" echoes, albeit hyperbolically, Doc's eagerness to mock Jacob's spiritual faith. Noting the similarity between the "cross" flanked by stag's "antlers" that serves as the symbol of St. Eustace and the logo of the liqueur Jägermeister, Doc would refer to the latter as "Saint Mustache" when taking shots of the alcohol. Doc turned Jacob's faith into an aggressive drinking game, with Doc becoming a Hunt Master or Jägermeister with Jacob's dignity as his prey (25). This story clarifies then that while Jacob's initial interest in S&M may have been due to his psychological and physical penchant for intense sensations, in practice his S&M encounters represented self-injurious attempts to bring himself into and to punish himself for remaining outside of cultural American norms.

 If Jacob's revolt against a collusive masochism in his early erotic relationships succeeds, Alameddine indicates the difficulties of achieving similar results against professional middle-class economics. Unable to earn a living through his poetry, Jacob has worked "for decades" as a word processor for a law firm (2016: 247). Greg got Jacob the job, but after his death Jacob has had very "little" association with the firm's attorneys and thereby retained some freedom from the pressures to confirm to a middle-class professional culture, such as those signaled by Greg's concern for how to combine his leather and lawyer identities at his funeral (8). Still, Jacob increasingly regrets the ethical and financial dilemmas of working for an affluent firm that proudly boasts that "JUSTICE," supposedly sightless and impartial, "SEES IT OUR WAY 90% OF THE TIME," implying a financial influence over justice (68). Much like Louis Ironson, an intellectual word processor for a circuit court in Kushner's *Angels*, Jacob remains a mere scribe, a private-sector word processor for money for an exploitative legal system. In this system Jacob's words, like Louis's, have little power to protect any minority communities through legal institutions. More personally, he can barely help himself as he continues to sell his dependable, submissive labor to a firm that denies him "health insurance" and pays him just enough to keep him going (247). Jacob takes some pleasure in the job because of its minimal demands, and because it connects him indirectly to Greg, but his willful refusal to seek better employment leaves him minimal or no legal, medical, and financial professional benefits. As such, Jacob masochistically colludes, however indirectly and tangentially, with the social forces that reflect, if more broadly and in less rarefied elements, the deeply classist traits of the gay couple from his short story. Not until Satan forces a reevaluation of his life, does Jacob begin to use his long employment experience to refresh his anger against his society, including the law firm, and begin to rekindle his relative independence by slowly renewing his interest in writing. This writing turns his masochism into a minor activism, but he never signals that he will seek new work. Revolting too much against financial stability, even a limited one, proves a difficult if not impossible task with his age, his education, and his renewing interest in having time to write.

Queer Outcasts from Queer Communities: Jacob among the Cherubs

Alameddine suggests, however, that a poor, middle-aged, queer immigrant's refusal to reject a small-scale financial stability need not dull critiques of more privileged individuals' accommodations to traditionally queer-phobic mainstream moderations. While renewing his interest in writing social satires, Jacob comes to resent younger queer authors' assimilation into a gentrified aesthetic elite. He detests how such assimilationists disregard prior queer rebels and their own critical independence for the insufficient return of a superficial and thus stultifying welcome into US public life. Jacob's frustration comes to the fore when in a restaurant two young men see him as someone to impress, but in their anxiety over their own status, they physically and psychologically jar him. Jacob despises the "rude" authors' unintended battery, a faint echo of his S&M experiences, as they get his attention first by grabbing his "wrist" and then by calling him "Jake." The young men assume a familiarity that insults by its very ignorance, both through their unwanted touch and through their disregarding Jacob's self-chosen American name, already altered from Ya'qub, which dislocates him further, albeit unintentionally, from his Middle Eastern identity. These young men mean well but they make no real effort to engage Jacob. Having lightly assaulted him physically, they continue to bombard him verbally as they laud one's recent interview on NPR and, when Jacob starts to leave, Joan Didion's latest book. While the young men's one-party conversation indicates a flattering desire to interest Jacob it nonetheless substantiates his perception of them as "nouveau-bland" writers interested primarily in "white gay boys" who want to "live homo-happily ever after," but who offer little else of substance (2016: 30). In addition to his understandable anger over white middle-class dominance regarding national queer visibility, Jacob reveals intense jealousy here, as he himself has never been on NPR and he has failed to "live homo-happily ever after."[13] But if this failure stems partly from his racial, religious, sexual, and cultural alienation in the Middle East and then in the United States, it also stems from his proud rejection of a white-ish blandness that mutes any rebellion against larger sociopolitical and spiritual oppressions.

Jacob's frustration boils over into protest when he perceives the younger writers aligning themselves with assimilationist values, highlighting heterosexual familial losses instead of queer losses due to AIDS. By focusing on Didion's familial losses, these young writers ignore the heartbreaks facilitated by mainstream US society's continuing hesitancy to support queer communities. Amid an awed paean to Didion, who one of the young writers observes experienced "her husband" die and then soon afterward their "daughter," Jacob counters that he had experienced the tragedy of having "six friends die" within half a year, one of whom was his "partner" (2016: 31, 32). If unaware of how he too idealizes heteronormative or at least homonormative romance, as indicated through his reference to his "partner"-ship with Doc, whose withdrawal from Jacob stopped only because of his illness, Jacob nonetheless fumes at the young men's focus on heterosexual as opposed to queer suffering. If extreme, Jacob's fury remains justified by the young men's "elision of queer history" in favor of a more narrowly focused heterosexual memoirist (32). This elision strikes Jacob as an enormous betrayal of his generation's public challenge to received religious, legal, and medical sanctities. "We refused everything," Jacob hyperbolically claims, "rejected their heavens and their hells," and he indicts these young men and their circles for being grateful for any space that the mainstream establishment offers them at all, be it a small queer-themed bookshelf or marriage. For a tiny slice at inclusion and an acceptance of traditional marriage vows, these men gain only subservient pleasures doled out by antiquated normative institutions, which they continue to believe are preeminent. These writers parallel the weaker, more cowardly cherubs who remain in heaven fearing a conventional idea of the horrors of hell while greater angels brazenly rebel to forge their own paths, rejecting their spiritual father and his sadistic feudalism.

Equally enraging, for Jacob, is how when these young men do reference the early HIV/AIDS crisis, they do so largely through art that achieved mainstream critical success. These men, Jacob suspects, appreciate primarily the major awards won by AIDS-related film, drama, and literature and only secondarily the emotional, psychological, and physical horrors of the epidemic or the bravery of the queer community that fought homophobic government officials. One of the men, for instance, tries to calm Jacob by saying that he appreciates Jacob's pain because he had seen the popular film remake of "*Rent*," though he thinks that it would have been better to have seen the live "musical," which, he notes, had won accolades from the Pulitzer and Tony organizations, and he asks Jacob if he had seen "*Angels in America*," which had likewise moved from stage to television screen via HBO in 2003 (2016: 34). The young man's interest seems to be principally in the popular cultural capital of celebrated AIDS art, preferring to watch Larson and read Didion rather than David Feinberg or Melvin Dixon, thereby colluding treacherously with cultural gatekeepers of a non-radical albeit leftish middle-class intelligentsia. Meanwhile, Jacob accuses, all the "AIDS books" not widely admired by award committees or a liberal literati are now "out of print" (33). Rebelling against such queer collusions with repressive bourgeois standards, Jacob imagines himself becoming an avenging queer angel and taking a "butter knife" to smear the young men's "cherubic faces" with butter (34). Unwilling to resort to actual violence, he simply yells and imagines a minor assault with the least threatening of all knives. Jacob wants to disrupt the young men's neatly packaged queer history but he also refuses to play into what he imagines to be the other diners' visions of him as a deranged "Arab faggot terrorist" (33). Thanks to Satan, Jacob revitalizes his rebelliousness but he resists the normative modes of political or religious fundamentalist violence, be it Christian, Muslim, or Jewish.

Alameddine realizes, however, that sustaining a rebellious energy after years of lethargy can be difficult. Feeling old, with his own writing and attractions largely overlooked by others, Jacob waffles between being a fiery and a fading Luciferian figure, variously reenvisioning present and future satisfactions and lamenting past defeats.[14] After his outburst at the young men, Jacob feels deflated, as if he himself had become a Miltonic angelic rebel "hurled headlong flaming from th'ethereal sky," away from his ideals of queer community, of his own limited literary prowess, and of his own more vigorous youth. Intensifying this breakdown, Jacob adds his self-identification with Lucifer to one with Walter Benjamin's more disillusioned and defeatist "Angel of History." Mistaking the nametag of a mustachioed man as reading Walter Benjamin instead of "Walter Bartender," Jacob announces to him, "I am your angel of history" (2016: 35). While even Milton's Lucifer planned defiantly for the future, encouraging his followers and empowering Eve with knowledge, Benjamin's angel looks perpetually backward, seeing history's horrific destruction without foresight regarding the fruits that demolition might bring. Assuming the role of Benjamin's angel, Jacob temporarily abandons himself to fate, an angelic outlaw in abeyance. He becomes a beaten, colluding angel with little or no agency. Jacob's future measure of success then must be to keep from deflating his rage and relapsing into apathy. As Satan increases Jacob's active recovery of his memories, allowing him to reinterpret his past, Jacob must balance this historical weight with Satan's ideal of an evolving, more independent, less repressive present and future. If, unlike Satan, Jacob has neither the charisma nor the energy to sway large portions of his community, his previous poetic output providing a small influence at best, he can enact a personal late-middle-age rebellion. He can refuse to let his rekindled personal rage fade into impotence and, following Satan's urging, he can appreciate how his memories can enrich his present life.

Conclusion: Ambivalent Angelic Outlaws

Satan's role in the novel then, whether he be a facet of Jacob's psyche or an independent angelic agent, is to recall Jacob to the fullness of his present through his memories of the past. As the novel moves toward its conclusion, Alameddine details how Jacob wrestles continually, psychologically and spiritually, with the fallen archangel to avoid the potency of his memories' influence on his current life. Alameddine uses Jacob's uncertain rebelliousness in part to indicate the difficulty of overcoming apathy and in part to suggest that, for some rebels, individual pleasures prove more difficult than socially minded ones. Jacob more easily accepts the pleasures within the pains of his responsibility to remember his friends and the social morality of rejecting the most self-destructive forms of sadomasochism, but Satan struggles to convince him to resume more personal spiritual, erotic, and poetic joys. Tired and set in his ways, Jacob often resists Satan and relapses into enervating half-memories of exile, alienation, betrayal, pain, and death such that he lives a sort of death-in-life. Satan in turn propels Jacob to embrace present joys, such as writing poetry and a reignited interest in sex, in part by the exciting memories of past dangerous sexual experiences, memories that become traumatizing, consoling, and revitalizing. Such a balance would enrich Jacob's current existence and turn him more optimistically toward the future. Indeed, as Jacob accepts Satan's rebellious approach to complex memories, he achieves a healthier if still imperfect merger of his past and his present.

If the novel can be said to have a happy conclusion then, it stems from Jacob's qualified willingness to follow Satan's guidance. Leaving the psychiatric clinic he had visited to block Satan's voice, Jacob insists that he can "ignore" his supposed adversary but he refuses to do so completely (2016: 290). Discarding the Ativan prescribed to him, he follows Satan's suggestion and calls on the sainted Fourteen Holy Helpers. These symbols of subversive histories and a non-Western spirituality work with Death, a symbol of a strategic forgetfulness, and with Satan to reinvigorate Jacob. As if finally allowing divisions of Jacob's spirituality, psyche, emotions, and body to coalesce, the Holy Helpers take out Jacob's "heart," then "clean," "warm," and "kissed" it, before returning it to his chest. This process clears away some of the patina of Jacob's pain and self-loathing so that he can reconsider anew the joys of his taboo spiritual, emotional, and sexual pleasures. Heading home, for instance, he stops when one of the Holy Helpers directs his attention to a "worshipful blow job" being given and received in an alley. Jacob admires the men and tells them "[t]hank you," expressing appreciation for what he views as a semi-public sacrament or an artful rite (292). Jacob's appreciation of this spiritually endorsed fellatio offers the first indication since Deke that Jacob might be taking a renewed interest in sex.

Infused now with a healthier spiritual eroticism, Jacob offers his own spontaneous outlaw art by composing short verses on public structures. If vandalism from a legal perspective, from an aesthetic one Jacob builds on his present recollected pleasures of faith, of blow jobs, and of Milton and uses his improvised art to change a dreary, increasingly corporatized San Francisco into a living page or even a makeshift urban Eden. On a "bus stop" he writes "*Tempt me, Satan*," thereby publicizing his personal rebellion against an oppressive mainstream American Christianity to inspire downtrodden public-transportation passengers who might pass his message along. On a "No Parking sign" he writes, "*I still walk*," as he shakes off his aesthetic apathy, refocusing on progress in the present and into the future (2016: 293). Memories of what he and his friends have lost heighten the important sweetness of his enjoying his life. These poems signal Jacob's acceptance of his responsibilities to his friends and his renewed desire for outlaw pleasures and excitements. Sights, sounds, ideas, and rhythms still excite him and tempt him to appreciate the world in which he moves. Even simple phrases become monumental art as he writes on spaces on his way home, phrases equivalent to "Chris lived here," which document where friends resided or worked (293, 294). Jacob uses this memorializing art to reclaim his friends' and his own place in this gentrified neighborhood. Jacob's revolt becomes more successful as he brings his personal joys and pain into public spaces.

Still, while Jacob revitalizes his personal interests in sex, poetry, and reclaimed space, he detrimentally preserves an ideal of Doc that allows for only a painfully ambiguous or ambivalent optimism at the novel's end. By this point, Jacob has recalled how Doc's cruelty incited his masochism and how he kept faith with an unfaithful lover, thereby remaining romantically alone for decades, and yet even so Jacob continues to all but deify Doc in his memory. Returning to his apartment in the novel's final paragraph, Jacob repeats his Miltonic phrase about being "hurled headlong flaming from th' ethereal sky" and he remembers how he tried to touch Doc as the man lay dying only for Doc to reject him, echoing the famous Latin phrase "*Noli me tangere.*" Doc echoes Jesus's reputed words to Mary Magdalene following his resurrection, but rather than a faithful disciple like the Magdalene, Jacob understands that he must now be Jacob wrestling, psychologically and spiritually, with God's Angel, as well as be both Judas and Satan as they betray their God. Jacob fulfills these latter roles by at last reconceptualizing myriad deaths with Doc. He recalls here both Doc's death due to AIDS, not to be resurrected, and the death of any valorization of their relationship, as Doc had verbally hurled Jacob away from any last romantic ideal. This de-idealizing stems from Doc's use of "*Noli me tangere*," which evokes first his reluctance to be physically intimate with Jacob, "do not touch me," secondly his request "do not hold me back" from dying to remain with you, and finally, perhaps as a generous last gesture toward Jacob's future, "do not hold on to me," advising Jacob not to cleave to a false ideal of a dead partner.[15] Struggling to let go rather than just to repress Doc as he had before, Jacob writes on his door, "[T]his is where I betrayed you, shadow that hell unto me," and he goes into his building and the story ends (2016: 294). Jacob's sense of his betrayal of Doc is, of course, his acknowledgment of his own affairs and his recent reassessments of Doc's cruelties, which together acknowledge failures on all sides. Still, despite Jacob's coming to terms with Doc's final request not to obsess over him and the end of their romance, Jacob cannot help but place Doc in a Christ-like position and himself in the traditional role of the sinner/betrayer resigned to shadows of hell.

Rather than a celebratory bad beatitude however, a Luciferian rejection of the degradation wrapped up with a troubled relationship, Jacob's guilt over supposedly having "betrayed" Doc vitiates any psychological or emotional achievement. As such, if Jacob's rebellion signals a healthy new beginning for him, it also signals a new "hell," a freedom that Jacob simultaneously wants and resists. Echoing John Donne's elegy "His Parting from Her," wherein Donne's speaker laments his loneliness, "Shadow that hell unto me, which alone / I am to suffer when my love is gone," Jacob declares his suffering independence from Doc (2001: 71). This hell need not, however, be an entirely dire one. For Jacob also echoes Satan's recent observation to him, "I am your shadow," and thereby claims the primacy of his own actions (2016: 289). Satan's individualism or even "hell" shadows the decisions that Jacob himself makes as he rebels for his own good against his self-injurious faith in a Christ-like Doc. If Jacob rebels with extreme reluctance and an extreme sense of guilt, this is because, as Alameddine suggests, rebelling against corruptive long-held ideals of love remains difficult.

One must endure a redemptive hell then to stay safe from a torturously detrimental heaven. As such, Alameddine's ending represents only an ambiguous optimism, at best. More than any author discussed in this study, I think, Alameddine pushes the uncertain successes of angelic outlaws and bad beatitudes almost to a breaking point. Are the traumas worth the validations and ecstasies one gains through them or would it be better to avoid such traumas, such degradations, to the extent that one can, an avoidance that itself would be rare for most queer individuals, particularly those from previous generations. To consider the importance of this ambiguous or even ambivalent optimism, I want to return to it in my brief, and I hope slightly more optimistic, concluding remarks.

Conclusion: Angelic Anxieties and Outlaw Expectations

Ambiguous optimisms, of course, as the previous chapters illustrate, run rife through literature presenting bad beatitudes. Rechy's *City of Night* ends with the suggestion that the narrator might eventually accept the sex-sharing that he longs for without curtailing himself with monogamy; but, he might just as easily suffer long stretches of chaos and nihilism broken only by pitifully brief orgasms enabled by dirty semi-public spaces. Nugent's ending to "Uranus in Cancer" offers the optimism of a relatively happy relationship between Jesus and Angel; but, this optimism seems inherently curbed, from one perspective because the novel itself was never published and from another because of the violence that Nugent weaves throughout, from the boys in Angel's childhood who chase the "*pato*" to the "rape" rhetoric that Nugent uses to describe Jesus's intimacy with Angel. With slightly less violence, Ginsberg consistently imagines how repressive institutional representatives can easily co-opt angelic tropes of earthly and spiritual rebellions so as to promote aggression and rapacious mechanical commercialisms, while lazier or misguided would-be angelic rebels unintentionally collude with imperialistic immoralities. These writers celebrate the ability of queer angelic outlaws to find solace and even a communal transcendence in America, one queer community made out of many queer individuals. But, since such moments so often remain contingent upon alienated spaces, taboo desires, and behaviors generally considered dirty, immoral, criminal, and sinful by previously and in some places still all too normative medical, social, legal, and religious authorities, they are never easy, wholly joyful, or entirely successful. As these writers evidence then, an ambiguous optimism, although rarely an outright ambivalence, remains baked into the early post–Second World War literature of bad beatitudes.

Understandably, this ambiguous angelic optimism persisted within AIDS-era literature. Hemphill recounts how despite the risk of a "lethal leak" in a condom, black queer outlaws will still be loving, with a spiritual eroticism, "fallen angels" (2000: 169, 176). Refusing to abandon safer sex despite its dangers, Hemphill's Luciferian falling angels offer a valuable bad beatitude that rebels against the institutionalized racism, homophobia, and classism surrounding the AIDS epidemic in the United States. Similarly, if less viscerally, in Gurganus's *Plays Well with Others*, Hartley Mims rejoices in a vision of heaven that includes his dead friends, who while they lived were hard-drinking, drug-taking, highly sexed artists. Hartley imagines God functioning more like a low-octane Satan than like Milton's staid tyrant as He makes angels out of humans whose "virtue," when alive, ran "alongside a scofflaw's hatred for paying parking tickets" (1999: Appendix 1). Writers such as Hemphill and Gurganus acknowledge a queer melancholia in AIDS literature that dampened any too optimistic spiritual ecstasies, but they continue to validate a spirituality, though never a dogmatically religiosity, within queer life and death. Whether referencing fallen rebel angels such as Lucifer or an unconventional rebelliously Luciferian God, one misinterpreted by misanthropically prudish bigots, these spiritual figures provide largely hopeful if at times less than ideal moral models for angelic queer outlaws in fiction.

Alameddine's presentation of God and Satan is much more ambivalent. In Jacob's world, God is a largely absent figure who allows war, terror, and HIV/AIDS to wreak havoc. As such, in his stories, Jacob imagines that God has become so distanced from human concerns that He allowed George Bush and Dick Cheney to co-opt "Azrael," His angel of death, whom they embody in a warplane equipped with "Hellfire" missiles sent to Pakistan (2016: 164, 165).[1] Due to this divine indifference, Jacob listens when Satan argues that it is an allegedly benign or peaceful "God who's sick" rather than Jacob (289). By working with Jacob's beloved Holy Helpers, Satan and not God proves beneficial to this disinclined disciple. Yet while Satan revitalizes some good individuals, such as Jacob, he just as eagerly facilitates the unwarranted deaths of others. Noting how in Jacob's country of birth, people could get killed simply for unconscious human reactions to a natural environment, such as "blinking" if something gets blown into their face, Satan announces early in the novel that when visiting this part of the world, he would swirl up "sandstorms" just because he felt like it, essentially gambling with people's lives (22). God's absence, his refusal to stop sickness or men like Bush and Cheney, remains heartless and cruel, but Satan's casual approach to death and destruction counteracts the virtue of his rebellious independence from sexual, racist, and narrowly nationalistic repressions. While queer AIDS-era writers such as Hemphill and Gurganus, among others, likewise resisted simplistically assigning peace, love, and kindness to one source and violence, hatred, and evil to another, Alameddine imagines divine figures who are more indifferent and almost entirely arbitrary when it comes to influencing humans. Alameddine therefore forces Jacob to confront a complex, multifaceted, and horrifically ambivalent spiritual vision. Using Satan as a spiritual model, Alameddine indicates, will help Jacob but this will remain a problematic and dangerous strategy, one never to be quite trusted.

Equally as fraught as this complex spirituality is Jacob's ambivalent sense of his own American-ness, of his own place within US culture. Jacob thinks of himself as a natural, an inveterate, even an irredeemable "immigrant," but after settling in the United States as a young man, he adopted an American identity that retains its hold on him despite his subsequent denial of it (Alameddine 2016: 15). Although Jacob reflects to the dead Doc that he had never been "American" despite any potential appearance or mindset, Jacob has in fact been weaving his own version of an "American" identity, just as immigrants and marginalized queer individuals have been for centuries (100). While Alameddine never identifies Jacob's legal citizenship status, Jacob has clear claims to being geographically, socially, and culturally an American regardless of any legal status. Jacob has lived and worked in the United States longer than anywhere else, paying taxes and socializing within a queer American culture. During the height of the AIDS epidemic in the 1980s he considers queer men with AIDS to be "exiled and stateless in our native city," and his self-declared "native city" is San Francisco, a progressive, urban, cosmopolitan manifestation of the United States (228). More personally, the apartment he has lived in for decades has clearly become an essential part of his identity, as has his small but active role in San Francisco's literary scene. As such, in his poem "*My New Sana'a*," a reference to the traditional if no longer actual Yemeni capital, Jacob weaves in his San Francisco address, including his "zip code," thereby claiming San Francisco as his own capital, if with only a quasi-official, never quite certain status (99).[2] Highlighting the multifaceted nature of any home and of any nationality, Jacob acknowledges his having merged his Middle-Eastern experiences with his newer American culture. Much like the Fourteen Holy Helpers, whom the Catholic Church downgraded to the fringes of the faith yet to whom Sœur Salwa taught Catholic Arab children to pray, Jacob maintains an uneasy presence in a multidimensional American life. Alameddine suggests then that contrary to Jacob's middle-aged acceptance of more mainstream definitions of a white Protestant America, he has in fact attained his own Arab Catholic queer American identity.

As such, Jacob presents a valuable but uncomfortable inclusion into the queer bad beatitudes of American literature. Perhaps most uncomfortable about Jacob is his reluctance to move beyond an idealized lover who left him feeling so worthless that he sought pleasure through degradations and intense beatings, that he sought punishments that went well beyond a careful and caring S&M. The angelic queer outlaws I have examined in previous chapters find solace, joy, and new identities through marginalized spaces, relationships, and communities that tolerate or even facilitate taboo genders and sexualities. They likewise take advantage of or even make spaces in a queerphobic America that allow for them to create new identities, new relationships, and new healthier modes of existing in time. If being in America is, at times, akin to being in an S&M relationship, it is a relationship that allows for give and take and change, hopefully for the better. One has to admit though that this relationship can change and be oneself an active force for this change. Jacob, despite his rational and spiritual self-awareness, longs for his oppressors and fights his sense of his own expansive American culture. As such, for readers who might have fantasized about hooking up with homophobic hunks or pining to make a constricted life with men who humiliate them, Jacob's desire for "beatification" through degradation may hit unnervingly close to home. Jacob, much more so than the previous angelic outlaws I have discussed, has internalized a conservative vision of US identities, including queer ones, which exclude him, even as he represents a queer immigrant who strives for his own safe space, however minor, in American culture. To achieve this, Jacob takes part, albeit out of necessity, in an avariciously capitalistic legal system that he detests and in which he must struggle to maintain what independence he can while avoiding the racist, homophobic, and classist imperialistic tendencies of mainstream America, including an egotistic homonormative American neo-liberalism. Outside of his employment, Jacob retreats to a perfunctory life of loneliness and apathy, even as he simultaneously longs to continue his contributions to queer literary traditions that blend American and Middle Eastern tropes, while resisting a commercialized blandness. Despite his shyness, loneliness, and struggles with conservative ideologies, Jacob has become part of a queer American culture though he rebels against its penchants for self-absorption, assimilation, and gentrification, much as he rebelled against the repressively religious and cultural elements of his Middle Eastern heritage, with its diverse Muslim and Catholic influences. At his basic level then, Jacob represents the hard, unhappy compromises one has to make in a complex and wounded queer life in order to seek joy.

Conclusion

I want to end this study thinking then of Jacob, whose reluctant bad beatitudes foreground the anxieties and, at times, the traumas risked by all angelic outlaws. As society evolves, as legal, medical, and even many reformed spiritual institutions continue to come to their senses, as gay bars include brighter lights and windows, and as Americans of all backgrounds across the country continue to come out as gay, as trans, and as asexual, society will no doubt continue to revise its notions of the sacred and the profane. Queer individuals then, not just gay men, but queer individuals of all varieties, will hopefully move beyond the difficult hybridity of establishing the sacred in the profane and the profane in the sacred. At the same time, however, the establishment of any too sure or any too unambivalent sense of what counts as sacred or profane or moral or immoral or good or bad or ugly or beautiful would inevitably present its own problems and tyrannies, new forms of homonormativity, which would then themselves have to be rebelled against. As such, while it seems worth hoping that someday bad beatitudes might be a rich, beautiful, and yet troubling trope of the past, it seems more likely that they will remain a sign of cultural, aesthetic, and erotic strengths, a challenge to any too violently rigid morality. If this latter is the case, then I hope to keep finding queer angelic outlaws in writing, painting, and film.

Notes

Introduction

1. In addition to literature, diversely queer angelic outlaws maintain a presence in a variety of American art forms, including films such as Kenneth Anger's vaguely queer *Lucifer Rising* (shown as a work in progress as early as 1974), which came on the heels of his more overtly homoerotic *Scorpio Rising* (1963), and in visual depictions such as George Platt Lynes's photographic stills from George Balanchine's ballet *Orpheus and Eurydice* (1936). These particular aesthetic histories have still to be written.
2. An additional relevant reference here is the slang designation "angel with a dirty face," which Gershon Legman in 1941 linked to the film *Angels with Dirty Faces* (1938) about gangster kids in New York (1157). The connection between the film and the phrase seems tangential at best, indirectly connecting undervalued children or affable mostly harmless parodies of juvenile gangsters with undervalued same-sex desiring men.
3. For the critical tradition regarding same-sex desire among Milton's angels, see Woods (1998: 114), Karma deGruy (2012: 117–21), and Stephen Guy-Bray (2018: 140). For the critical tradition regarding Blake and queer desire, see Helen Bruder and Tristanne Connolly (2010: 1–3), as well as Christopher Hobson who discusses Blake's engagement with homoeroticism and Milton (2000: xi, 130, et passim).
4. See, for instance, Hobson (2000: 135–40).
5. See Chauncey (1989: 295), Rechy's descriptions of cops "lovingly" patting down hustlers legs in *City* (2013: 150), Daniels's intriguing discussion of undercover cops in queer circumstances in *Black Angel* (21–4), and Steve Burns's identity crises toward the end of *Cruising*.
6. See von Hoffman (1988: 148, 215–16, 222, 418).
7. See, for instance, Theoharis and Cox (1988: 107–10, 209–12; see also 288–92, 331–2).
8. Such subversions could be as subtle as burying complaints against queer individuals in an already overfull government "in-box" or as forthright as a direct protest to a superior officer that a division would "lose some of the best people" if an investigation was launched into gay men and women within its ranks; see David Johnson (2004: 169).

9 Of course, many individuals had to navigate between competing loyalties; see for instance Nan Boyd's discussion with Del Martin and Phyllis Lyon regarding the debates over wearing pants in lesbian meetings in the 1950s and 1960s; see Boyd (2003: 153–4, 156, and 180). See also D'Emilio's discussion of the Mattachine Society's debates over and then rejection of its founders' radical political associations in favor of a vocal loyalty to the American government, to its laws, and to a conservative politics of respectability; D'Emilio (1983: 84–5).
10 See Feinberg (1993: 135–6) and Lorde (1982: 224).
11 See for instance Carpenter (1912: 32–3), Ellis (1915: v–vi, 27–8), and Gerber (1975: 291).
12 The first half of William Eskridge's book *Gay Law* and the volume's appendices provide an invaluable broad introduction to the laws that affected same-sex sexuality and gender nonconformities in the United States and in individual American states.
13 See Simon (1968: *c.* 27 minutes, 40 seconds into the film).
14 Cruising in movie theaters, for instance, often gets described as a new frontier of sorts for queer Americans, even American immigrants, to conquer within their own land, a form of reverse queer colonialism. In *Numbers* (1967), Johnny Rio, that "angel of dark sex" cruising in a theater balcony, conceives of this space "as though it were a foreign country that must be conquered" (Rechy 2007: 16, 74), and in Tennessee Williams's short story "Rio Joy" (written 1941, published 1954) the older "angel" Pablo Gonzales cruises the "earthly heaven" of an old cinema's upper galleries (1985: 103–4, 107). The river of the theater's name provides a boundary, like the Rio Grande, between the "great expanse of arid country" of celibacy and a pleasurable oasis in which one must hide from hunters, such as the ushers who chase away allegedly deviant men seeking company (105). David Savran notes that the theater is "an enigmatic, if slightly queer, site of resistance," one that takes place in the realm of cowboy pictures and violence (1992: 78). Part of Williams's resistant strategy in this story, to borrow Savran's apt term, is his angelic bad beatitudes, which present Pablo, already an international boundary-crosser, as likewise bridging sacred and profane pleasures.
15 For discussions of the productive nature of queer shame or abjection in relation to queer studies, see Sedgwick (2003: 62–4), Scott (2010: 17–18), and Pérez (2015: 10, 12, 97–9).

Chapter 1

1 The figure of the "fairy" remained what George Chauncey has called "the primary image of the 'invert' in popular and elite discourse" up until at least mid-century and the effeminate queer man thus "stood at the center of the cultural system by which male-male sexual relations were interpreted" (1994: 47).

2. Charles Casillo noted that in college Rechy wrote a relatively Byronic "paper 'proving' that John Milton was on the side of the rebel angels and had succeeded in justifying the ways of man to God" (2002: 57).
3. I emphasize Rechy's relationship to a Hispanic or more precisely Mexican American Catholic tradition here because it so deeply informs his conception of angelic outlaws and bad beatitudes. María DeGuzmán has recently pointed readers to the "ways in which almost every work of his deals in one way or another with the effects of colonialism, socioeconomic and ethno-racial inequalities, and minoritization (active disempowerment foisted upon a particular group by a hegemonic group)" (2019: xiii). Indeed, these qualities identified so carefully by DeGuzmán likewise apply to his Hispanic American Catholic conception of queer angelic outlaws.
4. For local and state laws against cross-dressing, see Eskridge (1999: 27–8, 338–40).
5. Miss Destiny may even force God to cede her some space through dance, as the phrase "shake the beads" was slang for "to dance" in the post–Second World War era; see Rodgers (1972: 29).
6. For social and legal repressions along these lines, see Katz (1976: 129–34) and D'Emilio (1983: 17–18, 45–52).
7. See, for instance, Johnson (2004: 1–2; 98, 151–2).
8. See Bersani (1995: 94–5, 164).
9. The narrator here thus foreshadows what Ben Gove notes becomes a repeated quandary for Rechy's hustling and cruising protagonists, namely a "disavowing rejection of intimacy or reciprocity—whether in monogamous or promiscuous sex—even as they sometimes yearn for that interconnection" (2000: 43).

Chapter 2

1. I use the term "queer" here because Nugent, whom this chapter deals with most extensively, uses "queer" to refer to same-sex desires as well as tendencies toward pansexual desires without a firm binary divide between homo- and heterosexualities (2008: 113). While I acknowledge differences between the racial and religious communities of the writers in this study, I also want to emphasize seeing them all as a part of our queer American culture.
2. See Du Bois's "The Talented Tenth" (1986: 842); for Cullen's reading of Carpenter, see Molesworth (2012: 55).
3. Michael Miller has noted that as "adamant as Locke was on the subject of propaganda … he agreed with Du Bois about the 'decadent strain' that he saw emerging in younger New Negro writers," a trait both men disliked (2008: 31). In opposition to decadence, Locke preferred, as James Kelley has shown, an African inspired "primitivism" (1997: 507).

4 For his discussion of specifically queer interzones, see Mumford (1997: 78–80, 85–6).
5 The hounds can also function as a metaphor for beastly men, as in Cullen's "Black Christ" when Jim refers to the "two-limbed dogs" that hunt him (2013: 177).
6 D. Dean Shackleford has argued that in "some of his greatest poems," Cullen "contrasts paganism with Christianity, recognizing his own 'pagan' inclinations, which he cannot quite overcome despite his commitment to a Christian worldview," though as Cullen grew older he grew "ready to embrace a Christ who was 'black' and reject the images of white religion," which became reminiscent of black individuals' "bondage" to white individuals (1992: 382). Drawing on this critical tradition, Kelley has rightly noted the "hybrid" version of "paganism and Christianity" in Cullen's poem "Heritage," a hybridity that equally applies to "Shroud" (1997: 511); Powers has noted that in "Cullen's work 'paganism' stands primarily as a marker for erotic desire," a desire that was "primarily gay" or same-sex oriented (2000: 664).
7 Trudier Harris has noted how trees often evoke "the paradoxical nature of the southern landscape—as a source of death and a source of beauty" in African American literature as white men used otherwise beautiful trees as torture instruments for lynching (2009: 11).
8 See Gary Holcomb's fine discussion of McKay's critical inversions of the term "nigger heaven" and "nigger hell" in *Home to Harlem* within Harlem's queer contexts (2007: 109). Holcomb points out that McKay responds as much to casual racist theater terms as to Carl Van Vechten's prior novel *Nigger Heaven* (1926).
9 Chauncey has noted "the ascendancy of *gay* as the preeminent term (for gay men among gay men) in the 1940s" (1994: 14).
10 See Woods (1993: 136) and Schwarz (2003: 75).
11 Drafts of the nearly complete manuscript reside at Yale's Beinecke Library in the James Weldon Johnson Collection. With the exception of scenes from "Lunatique," which I cite from Wirth's published excerpt in *Gay Rebel* so that readers can follow references with greater ease, I quote from the first extant ribbon copy, which is the most complete draft. Nugent reworked several portions over time but the changes were small. I cite portions that remained almost entirely consistent from draft to draft. Wirth notes that "a handwritten version [of 'Lunatique'] appears in one of Nugent's early notebooks from the twenties" (2002: 248); the Beinecke dates the ribbon copies of "Uranus" from *c.* 1955 to *c.* 1965, and references in later portions of the novel bring its events from the Second World War up to Dr. Martin Luther King Jr.'s early career.
12 This is not a negative assessment of Wirth's editorial interventions; it's simply a reflection that time and the economics of book production require difficult cuts.
13 See, for instance, Chauncey (1994: 15–16) and Garber (1989: 320).

14 Exploring the roughly contemporary Newport Naval Training Station incident in 1919 to 1920, Chauncey has noted that even adults consciously engaged in articulating sexualities had difficulty agreeing on terms to define "the relationship between homosexual behavior and identity in the cultural construction of sexuality. Even when witnesses agreed that two men had engaged in homosexual relations with each other, they disagreed about whether both men or only the one playing the 'woman's part' should be labelled as 'queer'" (1989: 295).
15 Bérubé has detailed how many men and women in the US armed forces found new freedoms and queer communities even as the military and government offered an evolving series of horrific punishments when they caught queer men and women serving their country; see Bérubé's chapter "The Gang's All Here" for the former and "The Fight for Reform" for the latter.
16 For a discussion of such exploitations, see, for instance, Blackmon (2008: 376–9).
17 Citing German news sources, Stefan Kühl reports that in the 1930s, "Nazi propagandists reacted to American criticism by arguing that ethnic minorities in the United States were treated in a similar way as were Jews in Germany," particularly black individuals (1994: 98–9).
18 For definitions of "trade" roughly contemporary to "Uranus," see Chauncey (1989: 303).
19 The nickname "rat" need not necessarily imply an insult. Russell Cheney enjoyed the nickname "[r]at" and his partner F. O. Matthiessen used the nickname affectionately for Cheney throughout the 1920s, 1930s, 1940s; see Matthiessen and Cheney's *Rat & the Devil* (1988).
20 I focus on the ostensibly encompassing term "queer" here but similar dilemmas attend to the racial "exclusions" that often attend the term "gay," as so clearly analyzed by Darieck Scott (1994: 301).
21 For discussion of the racial tensions inherent in mid-century multiracial queer encounters, particularly in the South, see D'Emilio (1983: 24–7, 31–2) and Howard (1999: 105, 253).
22 See Holland (2000: 104) and Weise, Carbado, and McBride (2011: xiv-xvii).
23 See Bost (2019: 4, 8, 21); Martin Duberman has likewise linked Hemphill's work to a "second Harlem Renaissance, 'second' in relation to time, not quality, and this time around, moreover, centrally, *overtly* gay" (2014: 32). Black angelic characters in the works of this new renaissance also resonate, of course, with the spiritual if not quite angelic elements found throughout the work of James Baldwin and Randall Kenan.

Chapter 3

1 See Morgan (2006: 4–6, 18).
2 For Ginsberg's sense of his Jewish connections, see Schumacher (1992: 11–12). Morgan notes that the Ginsberg family followed closely Hitler's rise in Germany

and Ginsberg suspected that his college dormitory maid at Columbia rarely cleaned his room because she was "probably Anti-Semitic" (2006: 62). In comparison, Langston Hughes was the only African American permitted to live in a dormitory at Columbia, and with an obscene reluctance on the university's part; see Berry (1995: 28) and Rampersad (2002: 52).

3   For Ginsberg's initial consideration of his same-sex desires as a mental illness, see Morgan (2006: 120–1); for Ginsberg's less than successful attempts to date women, see Morgan (2006: 124–5, 1334, 142, and 182–4). Even by 1958, Ginsberg had still not quite come to terms with his homosexuality, which he once referred to as a "[m]ental cancer"; see Morgan (2006: 273).

4   For Ginsberg's erotic and visionary reading of Blake, see Morgan (2006: 103).

5   For Ginsberg's prepublication familiarity with *On the Road*, see Morgan (2006: 133 and 143).

6   Hassan Melehy suggests that Kerouac "sneaks in a little French-Canadianness" into Sal's character as his "last name isn't Paradiso but Paradise—Englishized while at the same time approaching the French Paradis, a common name in Québec, also regularly occurring in the Franco-American areas of New England, where many have anglicized it as Paradise" (2017: 63).

7   Kerouac generally approached queerness with a defensive violence in his writing, though in helping to promote his friend, Ginsberg once somewhat hyperbolically described Kerouac as "mellow in the sense of infinitely tolerant" and notes that he and Kerouac occasionally ended up "sleeping together" (2003: 305, 306).

8   Ginsberg states that it was Malcolm Cowley who eliminated a short more specific same-sex encounter in *On the Road* but that "Jack consented to that," having little problem it seems with eliding any overtly fulfilled same-sex encounters from the novel (2001: 305).

9   For Ginsberg's work with early versions of *Naked Lunch*, see Morgan (2006: 185 and 237).

10 Burroughs noted of these scenes in 1960, "Certain passages in the book that have been called pornographic were written as a tract against Capital Punishment …. These sections are intended to reveal capital punishment as the obscene, barbaric and disgusting anachronism that it is" (2007: 205). While this might be true, these scenes are, by means of their very imagery, also about Burroughs's sense of the connection of violence to same-sex desire. His claim regarding capital punishment might then in addition link this violence to excessive state responses to certain minor crimes, such as consensual queer sex.

11 For these connotations of "ice," see Green (2005: 760).

12 See, for instance, Ginsberg's Fall 1947 letter to Neal (1977: 26–30).

13 For Cassady's distance from Ginsberg in Denver, see Schumacher (1992: 82).

14 For Cassady's and Ginsberg's vows to each other, see Schumacher (1992: 83).

15 *Howl* was also angelic in its sense of heralding what Ginsberg hoped would be a socioeconomically liberating as well as a specifically pro-queer message, contexts he

himself promoted. He advertised his famed first performance of the unfinished *Howl* in Berkeley, for instance, by printing up a hundred postcards announcing the event as a "[r]emarkable collection of angels all gathered at once in the same spot. Wine, music, dancing girls, serious poetry, free satori" (qtd. in Schumacher 1992: 214).

16 Finbow suggests that Ginsberg's Moloch has Milton's tyrannical, child-sacrificing devil as an influence (2012: 58).

17 In his study of bikers in queer culture and cinema, Juan Suárez has argued that the "physicality of the biker contrasted with the effeminacy, frailty, and neuroticism attributed to homosexuals both in popular representations and medical and psychological discourses" (1996: 158). Ginsberg's portrayal of mutually exchanged blow jobs, "who blew and were blown," is notable considering how performing oral sex was so often seen as challenging one's masculinity and thus prohibited such reciprocations; see for instance Nugent's portrayal of oral sex in "Uranus in Cancer," discussed in Chapter 2, wherein the more conventionally masculine men usually receive fellatio from the more effeminate Angel. Ginsberg considered eliding this mutuality but retained it to continue his connection of mutual, shared exchanges and unconventional forms of sexuality and gender; see Ginsberg (2006: 15).

18 Ginsberg observed once that he had been thinking of Hart Crane here, who spent time in Cuba and took erotic interest in a variety of sailors from European and Hispanic backgrounds; see Ginsberg (2001: 313) and Mariani (1999: e.g., 238, 297–8).

19 Noting the importance of Buddhism to Ginsberg's poetics, Tony Trigilio has observed that "from Ginsberg's first readings in Buddhism in the mid-1950s through his early incorporations of Buddhist terminology in *Howl and Other Poems* and *Kaddish and Other Poems* … his Buddhist practice was autodidactic and, as such, was eccentric and erratic" (2007: xii). Ginsberg's use of Jewish and other religious tropes was, of course, it should be noted, equally eccentric.

20 For the symbiotic relationship in the United States between corporate capitalism and Christianity in the middle of the twentieth century, see Kruse (2015: xiv–xv) and Herzog (2011: 149–52, 158–63).

21 Bill Morgan reports that Ginsberg was expelled from Columbia briefly for trying to get his landlady to clean his room by writing "Fuck the Jews" and "Butler [Columbia's president] has no balls!" on his dirty windows and accompanying these messages with finger-drawn images of a "skull and crossbones and a penis," in addition to having allowed Jack Kerouac, who had been banned from campus, to spend one night in his bed (2006: 62, 63).

22 Gershon Legman has identified "bananas" as a slang term for homosexuals in 1941 (1156).

23 For a brief overview of United Fruit's commercial and imperialist experiences in Latin America in the 1950s, see Bucheli (2005: 58–61, 104).

24 Ginsberg might also be riffing on "pork" or "pork chops" having various sexual connotations, for which see Green (2005: 1123). Given Ginsberg's interest in metaphorical food for thought in this poem, it's also worth noting that Ginsberg might have been thinking here, if only indirectly, of Hart Crane's description in *The Bridge* (1930) of Whitman and his verse as "*Panis Angelicus*" or angel bread (2006: 59).
25 For concerns of water sources being tainted with LSD and police responses, see Kusch (2004: 47, 51, 133).

Chapter 4

1 Watney lamented of certain religious oriented critics in 1987, "Aids takes us back to the pre-modern world, with disease restored to its ancient theological status as punishment" (1997: 126), while more recently Petro has examined "how religious leaders, organizations, and activists constructed AIDS as a *moral* epidemic" in the 1980s and 1990s (2015: 2). Many creative writers who consider HIV/AIDS, however, focus on queer moral virtues or failings that they associate with reactions to the virus but that do not link intrinsically to it.
2 Other examples of angels in queer 1980s art can be found in Steven Arnold's book of photography *Epiphanies* (1987), Deni Ponty's 1980s sketches and painting published in *Intimate Angel* (1990), and Isaac Julien's film *Looking for Langston* (1989), with Hemphill contributing to the latter, as well as Assotto Saint's *Stations*, a book of poems (1989).
3 For viciously exclusionary interpretations of US laws and immigration practices until circa 1990, see Eskridge (1999: 132–4).
4 While Alameddine at times connects Satan to Islam's Iblis, an added cosmopolitan influence, I want to focus on how his rebellious archangel evokes Miltonic (and indirectly Blakean) predecessors, in large part because these evocations resonate with the literature analyzed in previous chapters and because Alameddine alludes so frequently to Milton's *Paradise Lost*. Certainly, there is more work to be done on Alameddine's references to Iblis and to Islamic influences in the novel and in American queer culture more generally.
5 Alameddine indicates the importance of selective recollections by opening his novel with one epigram from Marc Augé emphasizing the importance of forgetting for survival and for loyalty, and one from Milan Kundera suggesting that memory can fight power and oppression, if not depression.
6 For fears in the 1980s regarding quarantine camps and mandatory, non-anonymous testing, see Bull (1987: 3) and "Poll Indicates" (1985: A24).
7 In 1987 Watney considered accounts of people with AIDS who had been "abandoned … by gay friends and lovers" and pointed out that such rhetorical emphases tended to distract from more widespread "rejection on the part of

governments, hospitals, welfare organisations, as well as the mass media" (1997: 123). See also Phil Zwickler's and David Wojnarowicz's short film "Fear of Disclosure," which recounts the isolation felt by gay men who were rejected by potential sex partners after reporting that they had HIV. On the other hand, queer individuals and queer-led organizations, from Gay Men's Health Crisis to ACT UP groups, were of course central in helping queer individuals with HIV/AIDS; see, for instance, Philip Kayal's *Bearing Witness*, at first tentatively titled "*Angels at War* … to acknowledge those who responded" to the epidemic "in a way that gave their work a deeper meaning" as they cared for people with AIDS (1993: ix, xv). For discussion of black volunteer support groups for HIV/AIDS, see Mumford (2016: 172–3) and Duberman (2014: 139–40).

8   See also, for instance, Geoffrey Mains's description of the "common spirituality" in the S&M leather scene in his *Urban Aboriginals*, originally published in 1984, as well as Patrick Moore's subsequent discussion of 1970s S&M leather scenes as from one perspective offering "spiritual transcendence" and from another "cliques and cruelty" (Mains 2002: 146; Moore 2004: 49). Fiction too emphasizes both the almost sacred pedagogical power of S&M, such as Corley's *Black Angel* (1968) and works by Samuel Steward, who, Steven Ruszczycky argues, depicted fantasy cops, prominent figures in the BDSM community, as able to "lead their erotic charges [submissive men] out of identities into potentially new forms of relation" through their presumptive power (2014: 234). John Rechy likewise acknowledged the erotic power, as well as the violent conservatism, of S&M in books such as *Rushes* (1979) and *The Sexual Outlaw* (1977).

9   Caroline Walker Bynum has indicated how for several medieval martyrs, extreme physical intensities seemed to connect them to Jesus and his martyrdom and to a larger spiritual community; see Bynum (1987: 245–52). Jeremy Carrette, meanwhile, has pointed to recent myriad explorations of "the apparent links between the history of religious suffering, particularly in Christianity, and asceticism and the practices of contemporary S&M," links that exist, as Carrette recalls, in a capitalist world economy (2005: 12).

10 In *City* Rechy's narrator, for instance, quickly leaves the sadist Neil, loathing his mix of masochistic and sadistic tendencies, such as wanting his testicles stomped and his wearing absurdly a "Nazi uniform" to "Exterminate" his "affectionate" cat, pathetically covering his fear of love with vicious displays of petty power (2013: 326, 301). In *Rushes*, *The Sexual Outlaw*, and *The Coming of the Night*, Rechy further explores the eroticism and the hypocritical, cruel contexts of S&M. At stake is not a rejection of abject settings and taboo eroticisms in-and-of-themselves but of too extreme, too self-injurious engagements with them. Similarly, in "Uranus in Cancer" Nugent explores how domination and submission can work in same-sex relationships as Angel and Jesus veer toward sadomasochistic sex, while pointedly resisting too self-destructive extremes. These lovers uncover their own powers

and vulnerabilities through aggression but they resist intentionally degrading and injuring each other and they reaffirm their mutual love. Like Rechy, Nugent critiques racist, misogynistic, and self-hating queer individuals through Aldo's hypocritical denigrations of Riccie/Angel, whom he secretly desires. Ginsberg imagines the eroticism of S&M in "Please Master" (1968) but overwhelmingly his poetry laments the false consolations of considering violence as a sacred righteousness. Ginsberg's "saintly motorcyclists" in *Howl*, after all, cause "joy" rather than hardcore lacerations and low self-esteem.

11   Dean points out that with the advent of pre-exposure prophylaxis or PrEP, the fatal implications of risky sex, including more aggressive forms of sex, have changed although not disappeared; see Dean (2009: 1–2). It is noteworthy then that most of Jacob's risky erotic adventures took place in the 1980s or 1990s prior to the advent of PrEP in the United States in 2012, for which see Roehr (2012: e4879).

12   The homonormative couple thus echoes the incursion of Western ideas on sexuality, eroticism, and romance into parts of the Arab world in the nineteenth century, which disrupted, to some degree, potential evolutions of traditional Arab and Islamic tolerations of limited forms of same-sex intergenerational romantic expression; see, for instance, El-Rouayheb (2005: 153–9).

13   For the anger of people of color, particularly African American same-sex desiring individuals, regarding the predominance of white middle-class men in post-Stonewall national gay movements, see Hemphill (2000: 42, 44–5); Duberman (2014: 16–17, 75–6, 80–2, 139–40, 191–920); and Mumford (2016: 172–3).

14   See, for instance, Milton's lines, "Thrice he [Satan] assayed and thrice, in spite of scorn, / Tears such as angels weep burst forth," which characterize Satan's intermittent sadness and frustration at his fall before he rallies and praises the other fallen angels (2005: 1.21).

15   For diverse understandings of and the difficulties of interpreting the phrase "noli me tangere," see Nancy (2009: 15–16) and Bieringer (2006: 17–19).

Conclusion

1   For Azrael as the "angel of death" in Judeo-Christian and Islamic religions, see Davidson (1967: 26, 64).

2   In 2015, a year before *The Angel of History*'s publication, Aden was declared the "temporary capital" of Yemen and Sana'a an "occupied capital" by then President Abd-Rabbu Mansour Hadi; see "Situation tense" (2015: np). San Francisco works as a similarly ambiguous capital for Jacob.

References

Primary Works

Alameddine, Rabih (2016), *The Angel of History*, New York: Atlantic Monthly Press.
Blake, William (1988), *William Blake* [poems], ed. Michael Mason, Oxford: Oxford University Press.
Burroughs, William (2007), *Naked Lunch: The Restored Text*, eds. James. Grauerholz and Barry Miles, New York: Grove.
Cheney, Russell and F. O. Matthiessen (1988), *Rat & the Devil: Journal Letters of F.O. Matthiessen and Russell Cheney*, ed. Louis Hyde, New York: Alyson Publications.
Conrad, Joseph (2003), *The Heart of Darkness*, New York: Broadview.
Crane, Hart (2006), *Complete Poems and Selected Letters*, New York: Library of America.
Cullen, Countée (2013), *Collected Poems*, ed. Major Jackson, New York: Library of America.
Daniels, Gordon (1972), *Black Angel*, San Diego: Greenleaf.
Donne, John (2001), *The Complete Poetry and Selected Prose of John Donne*, ed. Charles M. Coffin, New York: The Modern Library.
Du Bois, W. E. B. (1961), *The Souls of Black Folk*, New York: Fawcett.
Du Bois, W. E. B. (1986), "The Talented Tenth," in Nathan Huggins (ed), *Writings*, 842–61, New York: Library of America.
Ellis, Havelock (1915), *Studies in the Psychology of Sex: Sexual Inversion*, Philadelphia: F. A Davis.
Feinberg, Leslie (1993), *Stone Butch Blues*, Ithaca: Firebrand Books.
Feinberg, Leslie (1996), *Transgender Warriors: Making History from Joan of Arc to Dennis Rodman*, Boston: Beacon Press.
Ford, Charles and Parker Tyler (1989), *The Young and Evil*, London: Gay Men's Press.
Ginsberg, Allen (2001), *Spontaneous Mind: Selected Interviews 1958–1996*, ed. David Carter, New York: Perennial.
Ginsberg, Allen (2006), *Howl: Original Draft Facsimile, Transcript, and Variant Versions*, ed. Barry Miles, New York: Harper Perennial.
Ginsberg, Allen (2007), *Collected Poems: 1947–1997*, New York: HarperCollins.
Ginsberg, Allen (2017), *First Thought: Conversations with Allen Ginsberg*, ed. Michael Schumacher, Minneapolis: University of Minnesota Press.
Ginsberg, Allen (2017), *The Best Minds of My Generation: A Literary History of the Beats*, ed. Bill Morgan, New York: Grove Press.

Ginsberg, Allen (2019), "Public Heart: An Interview with Allen Ginsberg," with Jim Moore, in David Stephen Calonne (ed), *Conversations with Allen Ginsberg*, 165–9, Jackson, MS: University of Mississippi Press.

Ginsberg, Allen and Neal Cassady (1977), *As Ever: The Collected Correspondence of Allen Ginsberg and Neal Cassady*, ed. Barry Gifford, Berkeley: Creative Arts Book Co.

Gurganus, Allan (1999), *Plays Well with Others*, New York: Vintage.

Hemingway, Ernest (2017), *The Short Stories of Ernest Hemingway*, New York: Scribner.

Hemphill, Essex (2000), *Ceremonies: Prose and Poetry*, San Francisco: Cleis Press.

Hughes, Langston (1993), *The Big Sea*, New York: Hill and Wang.

Hughes, Langston (1995), *The Collected Poems of Langston Hughes*, ed. Arnold Rampersad, New York: Vintage.

Hughes, Langston (1997), *The Short Stories of Langston Hughes*, New York: Farrar, Straus and Giroux.

Kerouac, Jack (2003), *On the Road*, New York: Penguin.

Kushner, Tony (2014), *Angels in America: A Gay Fantasia on National Themes*, New York: Theatre Communications Group.

Locke, Alain (2012), *The Works of Alain Locke*, ed. Charles Molesworth, Oxford: Oxford University Press.

Lorde, Audre (1982), *Zami: A New Spelling of My Name*, Berkeley: Crossing Press.

McCourt, James (1993), *Time Remaining*, New York: Alfred Knopf.

Milton, John (2005), *Paradise Lost*, New York: W. W. Norton.

Nugent, Richard Bruce (2002), *Gay Rebel of the Harlem Renaissance: Selections from the Work of Richard Bruce Nugent*, ed. Thomas Wirth, Durham, NC: Duke University Press.

Nugent, Richard Bruce (2008), *Gentleman Jigger*, ed. Thomas Wirth, Philadelphia: Da Capo.

Nugent, Richard Bruce (*c*. 1955–65), "Uranus in Cancer," Bruce Nugent Papers: JWJ MSS 92 Series III. Long works of fiction, novels Box 42. Folders 1 and 2. James Weldon Johnson Memorial Collection, Beinecke Library, Yale University, New Haven, Connecticut.

von Praunheim, Rosa (1991), *Silence=Death*, New York, NY: First Run Features Home Video.

Rechy, John (1989), *The Sexual Outlaw: A Documentary*, New York: Grove.

Rechy, John (2003), "Interview with John Rechy," with Ramón García, *Chasqui*, 32 (1): 39–46.

Rechy, John (2004), *Beneath the Skin: Collected Essays*, New York: Carroll and Graf.

Rechy, John (2007), *Numbers*, New York: Grove.

Rechy, John (2013), *City of Night*, New York: Grove.

Russell, Bill and Janet Hood (1996), *Elegies for Angels, Punks, and Raging Queens*, New York: Samuel French.

Simon, Frank, dir. (1968), *The Queen*, New York: Evergreen Film, distributed by Grove Press.

Thurman, Wallace (1979), *Infants of the Spring*, Carbondale, IL: Southern Illinois University Press.
Whitman, Walt (2010), *Song of Myself, and Other Poems*, Berkeley: Counterpoint Press.
Williams, Tennessee (1985), *Collected Stories*, New York: New Directions.

Secondary Works

Adams, Stephen (1980), *The Homosexual as Hero in Contemporary Fiction*, Totowa, NJ: Barnes & Noble Books.
Arnold, Kevin (2011), "'Male and Male and Male': John Rechy and the Scene of Representation," *Arizona Quarterly*, 67 (1): 115–34.
Avi-Ram, Amitai (1990), "The Unreadable Black Body: 'Conventional' Poetic Form in the Harlem Renaissance," *Genders*, 7: 32–45.
Bailey, Marlon (2013), *Butch Queens Up in Pumps: Gender, Performance, and Ballroom Culture in Detroit*, Ann Arbor: The University of Michigan Press.
Bauer, J. E. (2015), "On the Transgressiveness of Ambiguity: Richard Bruce Nugent and the Flow of Sexuality and Race," *Journal of Homosexuality*, 62 (8): 1021–57.
Beavers, Herman (1995), *Wrestling Angels into Song: The Fictions of Ernest J. Gaines and James Alan McPherson*, Philadelphia: University of Pennsylvania Press.
Beemyn, Genny (2014), *A Gay Capital: A History of Queer Life in Washington*, New York: Routledge.
Benjamin, Walter (1968), *Illuminations*, ed. Hannah Arendt, trans. Harry Zohn, New York: Schocken Books.
Bergman, David (1991), *Gaiety Transfigured: Gay Self-Representation in American Literature*, Madison: University of Wisconsin Press.
Berry, Faith (1995), *Langston Hughes, Before and After Harlem*, New York: Wings Books.
Bersani, Leo (1995), *Homos*, Cambridge, MA: Harvard University Press.
Bérubé, Allan (2010), *Coming Out Under Fire: The History of Gay Men and Women in World War II*, Chapel Hill: University of North Carolina Press.
Bieringer, Reimund (2006), "*Noli Me Tangere* and the New Testament: An Exegetical Approach," in Barbara Baert, Reimund Bieringer, Karlijn Demasure, Sabine Van Den Eynde (eds), *Noli Me Tangere: Mary Magdalene: One Person; Many Images*, 13–27, Leuven: Peeters Publishers.
Blackmon, Douglas (2008), *Slavery by Another Name: The Re-Enslavement of Black Americans from the Civil War to World War II*, New York: Doubleday.
Boone, Joseph (1998), *Libidinal Currents: Sexuality and the Shaping of Modernism*, Chicago: University of Chicago Press.
Bost, Darius (2019), *Evidence of Being: The Black Gay Cultural Renaissance and the Politics of Violence*, Chicago: University of Chicago Press.
Bowlby, Rachel (2002), *Carried Away: The Invention of Modern Shopping*, New York: Columbia University Press.

Boyd, Nan (2003), *Wide-Open Town: A History of Queer San Francisco to 1965*, Berkeley: University of California Press.
Brim, Matt (2014), *James Baldwin and the Queer Imagination*, Ann Arbor: University of Michigan Press.
Bruce-Novoa, Juan (1979), "In Search of the Honest Outlaw," *Minority Voices*, 3 (1): 37–45.
Bruce-Novoa, Juan (1986), "Homosexuality and the Chicano Novel," *Confluencia*, 2 (1): 69–77.
Bruder, Helen and Tristanne Connolly (2010), "Introduction: 'What Is Now Proved Was Once, Only Imagin'd,'" in Helen Bruder and Tristanne Connolly (eds), *Queer Blake*, 1–20, New York: Palgrave Macmillan.
Bucheli, Marcelo (2005), *Bananas and Business: The United Fruit Company in Columbia, 1899–2000*, New York: New York University Press.
Bull, Chris (1987), "The Testing/Quarantine Mania Sweeps U.S," *Gay Community News*, Boston, June 21–27: 3.
Bynum, Caroline Walker (1987), *Holy Feast and Holy Fast: The Religious Significance of Food to Medieval Women*, Berkeley: University of California Press.
Carbado, Devon W., Dwight A. McBride and Donald Weise, eds (2011), *Black Like Us: A Century of Lesbian, Gay and Bisexual African American Fiction*, Berkeley: Cleis Press.
Carpenter, Edward (1912), *The Intermediate Sex: A Study of Some Transitional Types of Men and Women*, New York: Mitchell Kennerley.
Carrette, Jeremy (2005), "Intense Exchange: Sadomasochism, Theology and the Politics of Late Capitalism," *Theology & Sexuality*, 11 (2): 11–30.
Casillo, Charles (2002), *Outlaw: The Lives and Careers of John Rechy*, Los Angeles: Advocate Books.
Chauncey, George (1989), "Christian Brotherhood or Sexual Perversion? Homosexual Identities and the Construction of Sexual Boundaries in the World War One Era," in Martin Duberman, Martha Vicinus, George Chauncey (eds), *Hidden from History: Reclaiming the Gay and Lesbian Past*, 294–317, New York: New American Library.
Chauncey, George (1994), *Gay New York: Gender, Urban Culture and the Making of the Gay Male World, 1890–1940*, New York: Basic.
Christian, Karen (1992), "Will the 'Real Chicano' Please Stand Up? The Challenge of John Rechy and Sheila Ortiz Taylor to Chicano Essentialism," *Americas Review*, 20 (2): 89–104.
Cobb, Michael (2000), "Insolent Racing, Rough Narrative: The Harlem Renaissance's Impolite Queers," *Callaloo*, 23 (1): 328–51.
Coviello, Peter (2019), *Make Yourselves Gods: Mormons and the Unfinished Business of American Secularism*, Chicago: University of Chicago Press.
Damon, Maria (1993), *The Dark End of the Street: Margins in American Vanguard Poetry*, Minneapolis: University of Minnesota Press.
Damon, Maria (2015), "Beat Poetry: HeavenHell USA, 1946–1965," in Walter Kalaidjian (ed), *The Cambridge Companion to Modern American Poetry*, 167–79, Cambridge: Cambridge University Press.

Davidson, Gustav (1967), *A Dictionary of Angels including the Fallen Angels*, New York: The Free Press.

D'Emilio, John (1983), *Sexual Politics, Sexual Communities: The Making of a Homosexual Minority in the United States, 1940–1970*, Chicago: University of Chicago Press.

Dean, Tim (2009), *Unlimited Intimacy: Reflections on the Subculture of Barebacking*, Chicago: University of Chicago Press.

DeGruy, Karma (2012), "Desiring Angles: The Angelic Body in 'Paradise Lost'," *Criticism*, 54 (1): 117–49.

DeGuzmán, María (2014), "Swedenborgian Sentimentalism in John Rechy's *City of Night*," in Ashley Reed, Jennifer Larson and Jennifer Williamson (eds), *The Sentimental Mode: Essays in Literature, Film and Television*, 121–33, Jefferson, NC: MacFarland & Comp. Inc.

DeGuzmán, María (2019), *Understanding John Rechy*, Columbia, SC: University of South Carolina Press.

Delany, Samuel R. (1999), *Times Square Red, Times Square Blue*, New York: New York University Press.

Duberman, Martin (2014), *Hold Tightly Gently: Michael Callen, Essex Hemphill, and the Battlefield of AIDS*, New York: The New Press.

Duncan, Robert (1944), "The Homosexual in Society," *Politics*, 1 (7): 209–11.

Edelman, Lee (2004), *No Future: Queer Theory and the Death Drive*, Durham, NC: Duke University Press.

El-Rouayheb, Khaled (2005), *Before Homosexuality in the Arab-Islamic World, 1500–1800*, Chicago: University of Chicago Press.

Eskridge, William (1999), *Gaylaw: Challenging the Apartheid of the Closet*, Cambridge, MA: Harvard University Press.

Ferguson, Roderick (2019), *One-Dimensional Queer*, Cambridge, UK: Polity.

Finbow, Steve (2012), *Allen Ginsberg*, London: Reaktion Books.

Foertsch, Jacqueline (2001), *Enemies Within: The Cold War and the AIDS Crisis in Literature, Film, and Culture*, Urbana, IL: University of Illinois Press.

Freeman, Elizabeth (2010), *Time Binds: Queer Temporalities, Queer Histories*, Durham, NC: Duke University Press.

Freeman, Elizabeth (2019), *Beside You in Time: Sense Methods and Queer Sociabilities in the American 19th Century*, Durham, NC: Duke University Press.

Garber, Eric (1989), "A Spectacle in Color: The Lesbian and Gay Subculture of Jazz Age Harlem," in Martin Duberman, Martha Vicinus, George Chauncey (eds), *Hidden from History: Reclaiming the Gay and Lesbian Past*, 318–31, New York: New American Library.

Gates Jr., Henry Louis (1993), "Black Man's Burden," in Michael Warner (ed), *Fear of a Queer Planet*, 230–8, Minneapolis: University of Minnesota Press.

Gerber, Henry [Parisex] (1975 [1932]), "In Defense of Homosexuality," in Jonathan N. Katz (ed), *A Homosexual Emancipation Miscellany, c. 1835–1952*, 286–97, Arno Press.

Gerstner, David (2011), *Queer Pollen: White Seduction, Black Male Homosexuality, and the Cinematic*, Urbana, IL: University of Illinois Press.
Gove, Ben (2000), *Cruising Culture: Promiscuity, Desire and American Gay Literature*, Edinburgh: Edinburgh University Press.
Green, Jonathon (2005), *Cassell's Dictionary of Slang*, 2nd edn, London: Weidenfeld and Nicolson.
Guy-Bray, Stephen (2018), "'Fellowships of Joy': Angelic Union in *Paradise Lost*," in D. L. Orvis (ed), *Queer Milton*, 139–51, Cham, Switzerland: Palgrave Macmillan.
Halberstam, J. (1998), *Female Masculinities*, Durham, NC: Duke University Press.
Halberstam, J. (2005), *In a Queer Time and Place: Transgender Bodies, Subcultural Lives*, New York: New York University Press.
Harris, Trudier (2009), *The Scary Mason-Dixon Line: African Americans Writers and the South*, Baton Rouge, La: Louisiana State University Press.
Heise, Thomas (2011), *Urban Underworlds: A Geography of Twentieth-Century American Literature and Culture*, New Brunswick, NJ: Rutgers University Press.
Herring, Scott (2010), *Another Country: Queer Anti-Urbanism*, New York: New York University Press.
Herzog, Jonathan (2011), *The Spiritual-Industrial Complex: America's Religious Battle against Communism in the Early Cold War*, Oxford: Oxford University Press.
Hobson, Christopher (2000), *Blake and Homosexuality*, New York: Palgrave Macmillan.
Hoffman, Stanton (1964), "The Cities of Night: John Rechy's 'City of Night' and the American Literature of Homosexuality," *Chicago Review*, 17 (2/3): 195–206.
Holcomb, Gary (2003), "Diaspora Cruises: Queer Black Proletarianism in Claude McKay's *A Long Way from Home*," *Modern Fiction Studies*, 49 (4): 714–45.
Holcomb, Gary (2007), *Claude McKay, Code Name Sasha: Queer Black Marxism and the Harlem Renaissance*, Gainesville, FL: University of Florida Press.
Holland, Sharon (2000), *Raising the Dead: Readings of Death and (Black) Subjectivity*, Durham, NC: Duke University Press.
Howard, John (1999), *Men Like That: A Southern Queer History*, Chicago: University of Chicago Press.
Hurley, Natasha (2018), *Circulating Queerness: Before the Gay and Lesbian Novel*, Minneapolis: University of Minnesota Press.
Hyde, Lewis (1984), "Introduction," in Lewis Hyde (ed), *On the Poetry of Allen Ginsberg*, 1–8, Ann Arbor: The University of Michigan Press.
Johnson, David K. (2004), *The Lavender Scare: The Cold War Persecution of Gays and Lesbians in the Federal Government*, Chicago: University of Chicago Press.
Johnson, E. Patrick (2005), "'Quare' Studies, or (Almost) Everything I Know About Queer Studies I Learned from My Grandmother," in E. Patrick Johnson and Mae G. Henderson (eds), *Black Queer Studies: A Critical Anthology*, 124–57, Durham, NC: Duke University Press.
Johnson, Toby (1993), "Facing the Edge: AIDS as a Source of Spiritual Wisdom," in Judith Laurence Pastore (ed), *Confronting AIDS through Literature: The Responsibilities of Representation*, 124–41, Urbana, IL: University of Illinois Press.

Johnston, Allan (2005), "Consumption, Addiction, Vision, Energy: Political Economies and Utopian Visions in the Writings of the Beat Generation," *College Literature*, 32 (2): 103–26.
Kayal, Philip M. (1993), *Bearing Witness: Gay Men's Health Crisis and the Politics of AIDS*, Boulder: Westview Press.
Katz, Jonathan (1976), *Gay American History: Lesbians and Gay Men in the U.S.A*, New York: Thomas Y. Crowell Company.
Kearful, Frank (2013), "Alimentary Poetics: Robert Lowell and Allen Ginsberg," *Partial Answers*, 11 (1): 87–108.
Kelley, James (1997), "Blossoming in Strange Forms: Male Homosexuality and the Harlem Renaissance," *Soundings*, 80 (4): 498–517.
Kühl, Stefan (1994), *The Nazi Connection: Eugenics, American Racism, and German National Socialism*, New York: Oxford University Press.
Kruger, Steven F. (2013), *AIDS Narratives: Gender and Sexuality, Fiction and Science*, New York: Routledge.
Kruse, Kevin (2015), *One Nation under God: How Corporate America Invented Christian America*, New York: Basic.
Kusch, Frank (2004), *Battleground Chicago: The Police and the 1968 Democratic National Convention*, Westport, CT: Praeger.
Lee, Ben (June 2004), "Howl and Other Poems: Is There Old Left in These New Beats?" *American Literature*, 76 (2): 367–89.
Legman, Gershon (1941), "The Language of Homosexuality: An American Glossary," in G. W. Henry (ed), *Sex Variants: A Study of Homosexual Patterns*, 2nd vol., 1149–1179, New York: Harper Brothers.
Levine, Martin (1998), *Gay Macho: The Life and Death of the Homosexual Clone*, ed. Michael Kimmel, New York: New York University Press.
Love, Heather (2007), *Feeling Backward: Loss and the Politics of Queer History*, Cambridge, MA: Harvard University Press.
Mains, Geoff (2002), *Urban Aboriginals: A Celebration of Leathersexuality*, Los Angeles: Daedalus Publishing.
Mariani, Paul (1999), *The Broken Tower: The Life of Hart Crane*, New York: W. W. Norton.
McClure, John (2007), *Partial Faiths: Postsecular Fiction in the Age of Pynchon and Morrison*, Athens, GA: UGA Press.
McCune, Jeffrey (2014), *Sexual Discretion: Black Masculinity and the Politics of Passing*, Chicago: The University of Chicago Press.
Melehy, Hassan (2017), *Kerouac: Language, Poetics, and Territory*, London: Bloomsbury.
Merrill, Thomas (1988), *Allen Ginsberg*, New York: Twayne.
Miller, Michael (2008), "Activism in the Harlem Renaissance," *Gay and Lesbian Review*, 15 (1): 30–3.
Miller, Monica (2009), *Slaves to Fashion: Black Dandyism and the Styling of Black Diasporic Identity*, Durham, NC: Duke University Press.

Molesworth, Charles (2012), *And Bid Him Sing: A Biography of Countée Cullen*, Chicago: The University of Chicago Press.

Monteiro, George (2006), "Peaches and Penumbras: Ginsberg's 'Supermarket in California,'" *Notes on Contemporary Literature*, 36 (2): n.p. Academic OneFile, accessed September 25, 2018.

Moon, Jennifer (2006), "Cruising John Rechy's City of Night: Queer Subjectivity, Intimacy, and Counterpublicity," *disClosure: A Journal of Social Theory*, 15 (10): 42–59.

Moore, Marlon Rachquel (2014), *In the Life and In the Spirit: Homoerotic Spirituality in African American Literature*, Albany: SUNY Press.

Moore, Patrick (2004), *Beyond Shame: Reclaiming the Abandoned History of Radical Gay Sexuality*, Boston: Beacon Press.

Morgan, Bill (2006), *I Celebrate Myself: The Somewhat Private Life of Allen Ginsberg*, New York: Viking.

Mount, Douglas (1972), "Forward," in Bruce Rodgers (ed), *The Queens' Vernacular: A Gay Lexicon*, San Francisco: Straight Arrow Books.

Mumford, Kevin (1997), *Interzones: Black/White Sex Districts in Chicago and New York in the Early Twentieth Century*, New York: Columbia University Press.

Mumford, Kevin (2016), *Not Straight, Not White: Black Gay Men from the March on Washington to the AIDS Crisis*, Chapel Hill, NC: UNC Press.

Muñoz, José Esteban (2009), *Cruising Utopia: The Then and There of Queer Futurity*, New York: New York University Press.

Nancy, Jean-Luc (2009), *Noli Me Tangere: On the Raising of the Body*, New York: Fordham University Press.

Pearl, Monica (2013), *AIDS Literature and Gay Identity: A Literature of Loss*, New York: Routledge.

Pérez, Hiram (2015), *A Taste for Brown Bodies: Gay Modernity and Cosmopolitan Desire*, New York: New York University Press.

Pérez-Torres, Rafael (1994), "The Ambiguous Outlaw: John Rechy and Complicitous Homotextuality," in Peter F. Murphy (ed), *Fictions of Masculinity: Crossing Cultures, Crossing Sexualities*, 204–25, New York: New York University Press.

Petro, Anthony (2015), *After the Wrath of God: AIDS, Sexuality, and American Religion*, Oxford: Oxford University Press.

"Poll Indicates Majority Favor Quarantine for AIDS Victims" (1985), *New York Times*, December 20: A24.

Powers, Peter (2000), "'The Singing Man Who Must Be Reckoned With': Private Desire and Public Responsibility in the Poetry of Countée Cullen," *African American Review*, 34 (4): 661–78.

Rampersad, Arnold (2002), *The Life of Langston Hughes*, 2 vols, Oxford: Oxford University Press.

Reid-Pharr, Robert (2001), *Black Gay Man: Essays*, New York: New York University Press.

Reimonenq, Alden (1993), "Countee Cullen's Uranian 'Soul Windows,'" *Journal of Homosexuality*, 26 (2/3): 143–65.

Reimonenq, Alden (1995), "The Harlem Renaissance," in Claude Summers (ed), *Gay and Lesbian Literary Heritage*, 358–61, New York: Henry Holt and Company.

Rodgers, Bruce (1972), *The Queens' Vernacular: A Gay Lexicon*, San Francisco: Straight Arrow Books.

Roehr, Bob (2012), "FDA Approves First Drug to Prevent HIV Infection," *BMJ*, July 17: e4879.

Rubin, Gayle (2011), *Deviations: A Gayle Rubin Reader*, Durham, NC: Duke University Press.

Ruszczycky, Steven (2014), "The Law of Pornography: John Rechy and Samuel Steward," *Genre*, 47 (2): 231–53.

Satterfield, Ben (1982), "John Rechy's Tormented World," *Southwest Review*, 67 (1): 78–85.

Savran, David (1992), *Communists, Cowboys, and Queers: The Politics of Masculinity in the Work of Arthur Miller and Tennessee Williams*, Minneapolis: University of Minnesota Press.

Schumacher, Michael (1992), *Dharma Lion: A Critical Biography of Allen Ginsberg*, New York: St Martin's Press.

Schwarz, A. B. Christa (2003), *Gay Voices of the Harlem Renaissance*, Bloomington: Indiana University Press.

Scott, Darieck (1994), "Jungle Fever? Black Gay Identity Politics, White Dick, and the Utopian Bedroom," *GLQ*, 1 (3): 299–321.

Scott, Darieck (2010), *Extravagant Abjection: Blackness, Power, and Sexuality in the African American Literary Imagination*, New York: New York University Press.

Sedgwick, Eve Kosofksy (2003), *Touching Feeling: Affect, Pedagogy, Performativity*, Durham, NC: Duke University Press.

See, Sam (2009), "'Spectacles in Color': The Primitive Drag of Langston Hughes," *PMLA*, 124 (3): 798–816.

Shackleford, Dean D. (1992), "The Poetry of Countee Cullen," in Frank N. Magill (ed), *Masterpieces of African American Literature*, 382–6, New York: HarperCollins.

Shilts, Randy (1987), *And the Band Played On: Politics, People, and the AIDS Epidemic*, New York: St. Martin's Press.

Sinfield, Alan (2012), *On Sexuality and Power*, New York: Columbia University Press.

"Situation Tense in South as Yemen Crisis Deepens" (2015), *Yemen Post*, Proquest, March 11, accessed December 12, 2019.

Snediker, Michael (2009), *Queer Optimism: Lyric Personhood and Other Felicitous Persuasions*, Minneapolis: University of Minnesota.

Somerville, Siobhan (2000), *Queering the Color Line: Race and the Invention of Homosexuality in American Culture*, Durham, NC: Duke University Press.

Sontag, Susan (1989), *AIDS and Its Metaphors*, New York: Farrar, Strauss, Giroux.

St. Clair, Cody (2017), "A Dilettante unto Death: Richard Bruce Nugent's Dilettante Aesthetic and Unambitious Failure," *African American Review*, 50 (3): 273–89.

Suárez, Juan (1996), *Bike Boys, Drag Queens, and Superstars: Avant-Garde, Mass Culture, and Gay Identities in the 1960s Underground Cinema*, Bloomington, IN: IU Press.

Tatum, Charles (1979), "The Sexual Underworld of John Rechy," *Minority Voices*, 3 (1): 47–52.

Theoharis, Athan G. and John Stuart Cox (1988), *The Boss: J. Edgar Hoover and the Great American Inquisition*, Philadelphia: Temple University Press.

Trigilio, Tony (2007), *Allen Ginsberg's Buddhist Poetics*, Carbondale, IL: Southern Illinois University Press.

Tytell, John (1991), *Naked Angels: Kerouac, Ginsberg, Burroughs*, New York: Grove Press.

Vogel, Shane (2006), "Closing Time: Langston Hughes and the Queer Poetics of Harlem Life," *Criticism*, 48 (3): 397–425.

Von Hoffman, Nicholas (1988), *Citizen Cohn*, New York: Doubleday.

Watney, Simon (1997), *Policing Desire: Pornography, AIDS, and the Media*, 3rd edn, London: Cassell.

Wehr, Hans (1979), *A Dictionary of Modern Written Arabic*, 4th edn, ed. J. Milton Cowan, Wiesbaden: Otto Harrassowitz.

Wirth, Thomas (1985), "Richard Bruce Nugent," *African American Review*, 19 (1): 16–17.

Wirth, Thomas (2002), "Introduction," in Thomas Wirth (ed), *Gay Rebel of the Harlem Renaissance: Selections from the Work of Richard Bruce Nugent*, 1–61, Durham, NC: Duke University Press.

Woods, Gregory (1993), "Gay Re-Readings of the Harlem Renaissance Poets," *Journal of Homosexuality*, 26 (2/3): 127–42.

Woods, Gregory (1998), *A History of Gay Literature: The Male Tradition*, New Haven: Yale University Press.

Zamora, Carlos (1979), "Odysseus in John Rechy's *City of Night*: The Epistemological Journey," *Minority Voices*, 3 (1): 53–62.

Index

Note: Locators followed by "n." indicate endnotes.

Adams, Stephen 48
African American/black culture
　"anti-homophobic resistance" 5
　black gay cultural renaissance (Bost) 102
　blackness, conceptions 79, 81
　identity 22, 93
　literary traditions 16, 68
　queer angels, genealogy 102–3
　racism suffered by 105, 193 n.13
　sexual discretion 86
Alameddine, Rabih 8, 14, 16, 28, 63, 103, 146, 177
　Angel of History (*see Angel of History* (Alameddine))
ambiguous optimism 176–7, 179
"angel" as queer slang 6–7, 12–13
　vs. iron angel 20
angelic inspirations 3–21
angelic outlaws 18, 23, 180, 182
　ambivalent 174–7
　bad beatitudes of 29–33, 144
　in *City of Night* 33–47
　fairies and 57–62
　literary works/imagery 3–4, 7–8, 13, 15, 20–1, 28, 102, 143, 145–6, 148, 184 n.1, 191 n.2 (*see also* specific literary works)
　as model for action 47–57
Angel of History (Alameddine) 3, 15, 24, 144, 146–7, 150
　"American" identity, Jacob 181
　anger, insult, and ecstasy 159–64
　beatification, Jacob's desire 163, 182
　Benjie 158–9
　cherubs, Jacob among 171–4
　depressing forgetfulness, Jacob 152–3
　Didion's familial losses 172
　Doc, reimagined version of 154–8, 162–3, 170, 176–7
　experiences, Jacob's 158, 171, 175, 181
　Greg and Jacob 155–6, 158, 160–1, 170–1
　Holy Helpers 152–3, 163, 175, 180–1
　"invading" virus 157
　Lou's diagnosis (HIV) 156–7
　recollections, Jacob 154–5, 176, 180, 191 n.5
　sadomasochism (S&M) 159–61, 164–71, 182
　Satan's guidance/rebellious approach 151–5, 159, 161, 170, 173, 175, 180–1, 191 n.4
　social life, Jacob's loss 150–1
Angel Stuartti, love life (*Uranus in Cancer*, Nugent) 79–102
antihomosexuality, feelings of 34
anti-relationality (Bersani) 19
Arbian's suicide, Paul, (*Infants of the Spring*) 84, 92–3
Arnold, Kevin 59
Arnold, Steven 1–2, 20
　Epiphanies 191 n.2
　Heal-a-zation, photograph 1, 3–4
Augé, Marc 191 n.5
Avi-Ram, Amitai 71

bad beatitudes 2–3, 11–12, 21, 25, 28, 67, 79, 113, 143, 179, 182–3
　aesthetic perspective 4–5
　American 15–16, 67, 108
　of angelic outlaws 17–18, 29–33, 63, 144, 177, 186 n.3
　embodiment 20
　HIV/AIDS tropes 24, 143–4, 147, 150 (*see also Angel of History* (Alameddine))
　profanities/sanctities 2, 5–6, 12–13, 18–19, 109
Bailey, Marlon 28, 54
Baraka, Amiri, *The System of Dante's Hell* 102

Index

Barnes, Djuna 91
Bauer, J. E. 93
Beam, Joseph
   Brother to Brother 79
   In the Life 79
Beavers, Herman 71
Benjamin, Walter 18, 174
   "angel of history" 27, 174
Bergman, David 13
Berry, Faith 77
Bersani, Leo 18–19, 49, 159
Bérubé, Allan 88, 188 n.15
bikers in queer culture 127, 190 n.17
black culture. *See* African American/black culture
Blaise, Saint 155
Blake, William 8, 11, 17, 21, 28, 106, 122
   America: A Prophecy 118
   engravings 8
   The Garden of Love 116, 118, 128
   literary tradition 28, 80
   The Marriage of Heaven and Hell 8, 15, 106, 118
   Songs of Experience 106
   Songs of Innocence 106
   visionary model to American transcendentalism 108
Boone, Joseph 81, 87, 100
Bost, Darius 102
Botticelli, *Birth of Venus* 3
Bowlby, Rachel 134
Brass, Perry
   Angel Lust 3
   King of Angels 3
Brim, Matt 100
Brown, Foreman, *Better Angel* 3
Bruce-Novoa, Juan 60, 62
Burrill, Mary (Mamie) 20
Burroughs, William 107, 120, 128
   Naked Lunch 109–12
   violent homoeroticism 113, 126, 189 n.10
Bynum, Caroline Walker 192 n.9

Callen, Mike 12–13
Carpenter, Edward 12
   Ioläus 66
Carrette, Jeremy 192 n.9
Cassady, Neal 106, 109, 112–14, 120–1, 123–4

Chauncey, George 17, 82, 185 n.1, 187 n.9, 188 n.14
Christian, Karen 49
Christianity 129
   paganism and 65, 71, 187 n.6
   religious suffering 192 n.9
circulations of themes, queer 17
City of Night (Rechy) 9, 14–15, 21–2, 28–33, 49, 133, 179, 192 n.10
   angelic outlaw-ship, Professor/Robbie 44–5
   Chuck 51–3
   fat man's egotism 46–7
   Jeremy 59–62
   Jocko/Kathy, relationship 56–7, 59
   Kathy, "realness" and 54–5
   Larry 43
   Miss Destiny, fear of inertia 35–7, 51–2, 141
   the myth of Icarus 44–5
   narrator, hustling career 14, 22, 31–9, 42, 44–5, 47–54, 57–62
   Pete 58
   Professor's outlaw morality 38–43
   recollections of angels 34
   Robbie 41–2
   Skipper, tragedy 45–7, 51–2
   virgins and dolls 33–4
Cobb, Michael 93
Cohn, Roy (fictional character, *Angels in America*) 10–11
"common spirituality" 192 n.8
Connelly, Marc, *The Green Pastures* 74
Conrad, Joseph, *Heart of Darkness* 167
Corley, Carl, *Black Angel* 3, 192 n.8
Coviello, Peter 5–6
Cowley, Malcolm 189 n.8
Crane, Hart, *The Bridge* 191 n.24
cross-dressing 2, 10, 22, 36–7
Cruising 9
Cullen, Countée 8, 16, 22, 28, 65–7, 75, 78, 80, 99, 102, 118–19, 187 n.6
   The Black Christ 70, 112
   Heritage 187 n.6
   More than a Fool's Song 72–3
   race and sex, Miltonic critiques of 68–73
   She of the Dancing Feet Sings 72
   The Shroud of Color 68, 70

Damon, Maria 106, 135
Daniels, Gordon, *Black Angel* 3, 9, 102, 184 n.5
Dean, Tim 145, 193 n.11
"decadent Orientalist" 79
DeGuzmán, María 38, 186 n.3. *See also* Swedenborgian sentimentalism (DeGuzmán)
Delany, Samuel 94
divine salvation 32–3, 63
Donne, John 177
  His Parting from Her 177
  Holy Sonnet 14, "Batter My Heart" 101
"doubly marginalized position" 31–2
Duberman, Martin 12–13, 188 n.23
Du Bois, W. E. B. 65, 78, 92, 186 n.3
  art-as-propaganda approach 66
  The Souls of Black Folk 65
Duncan, Robert 12

earthangel 38
Edelman, Lee 19
effeminacy 3, 7, 20, 31, 38, 55–6, 58, 60, 81–2, 86, 92, 101, 109, 128, 190 n.17
Ellis, Havelock 12
entrapping angel 35–6
eroticized angels 108–12
Eskridge, William, *Gay Law* 185 n.12
evil angel, Miss Destiny's vision 36, 38, 45, 52, 141
Exposition (*Uranus in Cancer*, Nugent) 79–80, 90

"fairy," figure of 28, 127, 185 n.1
"fallen" angel 4, 7, 13, 72, 180
Federoff, Alex, *The Side of the Angels* 3, 10–11
Feinberg, Leslie 11
  Transgender Warriors 21
femininity. *See* effeminacy
Ferguson, Roderick 16, 92
Foertsch, Jacqueline 21, 158
Ford, Charles 6
Freeman, Elizabeth 5–6, 15

Garber, Eric 82
Gates, Henry Louis, Jr. 66
gay liberation 13, 18
gay sensibility 31
gender queerness. *See* queerness, gender

Gerber, Henry 12
Gerstner, David 79
Ginsberg, Allen 8, 16, 28, 63, 103, 105, 179, 188–9 n.2, 190 n.21
  America 134–8
  American Angel machine 140–1
  Car Crash 124
  Collected Poems 124
  early life 105–6
  family's marginalized position 106
  Going to Chicago 107, 139
  Grandma Earth's Song 142
  The Green Automobile 121–4, 129
  Howl and Other Poems 10, 14–15, 23, 27, 105, 121, 125–9, 131, 139, 189–90 n.15, 190 n.19, 193 n.10
  Hymn 117–19
  importance of Buddhism 107–8, 190 n.19
  Kaddish and Other Poems 23, 190 n.19
  Love Letter 113–14, 121
  Please Master 193 n.10
  Psalm II 115–17, 119, 121
  queer beat angels 113–20
  queer socioeconomic critiques 23, 142
  Rain-wet 124
  Research 142
  September on Jessore Road 140–1
  Song 125
  Sphincter 142
  A Supermarket in California 131–4, 137
  The Terms in Which I Think of Reality 119–20
  Thoughts Sitting Breathing 107, 139
  Two Sonnets 114–16
  Violence 138–9
Gove, Ben 186 n.9
Grimké, Angelina Weld 20
"Guardian Angel" 38, 42
Gurganus, Allan 146
  Plays Well with Others 144, 149–50, 180

Halberstam, Jack 14, 28
Harlem Renaissance 66, 82, 93, 188 n.23
Harris, Trudier 187 n.7
Heal-a-zation (Arnold) 1, 3–4
Heise, Thomas 40, 48
Hemingway, Ernest, *A Clean, Well-Lighted Place* 163
Hemphill, Essex 101, 146, 150–1, 179–80, 188 n.23, 191 n.2

Brother to Brother 79
Conditions 102, 143, 148
Now We Think: Now we think / as we fuck 149
Herring, Scott 28
Hispanic sensibility 31
HIV/AIDS, trauma 18, 24, 28, 142–3, 192 n.7
   AIDS-inspired apathy 152–9
   angelic outlaw tropes 143–4 (*see also Angel of History* (Alameddine))
   anger, insult, and ecstasy 159–64
   homonormative horrors 164–71
   memories in angelic literature 147–51
   queer losses 172
Hoffman, Stanton 29
Holcomb, Gary 66
Holleran, Andrew 99
holy global consumerisms 131–7
homoeroticism/homonormativity 72, 109, 117, 138
   forms of 183
   hybrid interzones 67
   Western ideas 193 n.12
homosexual rights 12
Hood, Janet, *Elegies for Angels, Punks, and Screaming Queens* 3, 144
Hoover, J. Edgar 10
Howard, John 10, 28
Hughes, Langston 8, 22, 28, 65–7, 78, 99, 189 n.2
   The Big Sea 73–4, 76–8
   black stereotypes, portrayal 73
   The Little Virgin 75–6
   The Trouble with Angels 74–5, 78
   The Weary Blues 73
humanity/human behavior 4, 25, 39, 43, 68–9, 108, 118, 120, 125, 163–4
   divinity and 28, 69, 99, 106, 115, 131
   HIV/AIDS 142
   rejects God 40
Hurley, Natasha 17
Hurston, Zora Neale 78
hybrid queer angels 80, 107–8
Hyde, Lewis 138

identity expression 2, 41
immigrants, queer 147, 151, 158, 171, 181–2, 185 n.14
industrialism, angelic appropriations of 120–31
interzones 67, 82, 84
iron angel 7, 20

Jesus's intimacy with Angel (*Uranus in Cancer*, Nugent) 98–102, 179
Johnson, David 9–10, 14
Johnson, E. Patrick 100
Johnson, Toby 145
Johnston, Allan 131
Jones, LeRoi, *The System of Dante's Hell* 102
Julien, Isaac
   The Attendant 102
   Looking for Langston 79, 102, 191 n.2

Kaufman, Bob 135
Kearful, Frank 132
Kelley, James 186 n.3, 187 n.6
Kerouac, Jack 106–7, 113, 120, 124, 126, 189 n.6, 189 n.7, 190 n.21
   On the Road 108–9, 189 n.8
King, Martin Luther, Jr. (early career) 98–9, 187 n.11
Kruger, Steven 144
Kundera, Milan 191 n.5
Kushner, Tony, *Angels in America* 3, 5, 11, 20, 27, 144, 170

Larson, Jonathan, *Rent* 144, 173
Lavender Scare 9–10, 100, 107, 121
Lee, Ben 127
Legman, Gershon, *Angels with Dirty Faces* 184 n.2
Letters into Limbo (*Uranus in Cancer*, Nugent) 79, 90–6
Levine, Martin 28
Leyland, Winston, *Angels of the Lyre* 3
Liu, Timothy, *Vox Angelica* 144
Locke, Alain 65–6, 78, 92, 186 n.3
Lorca, Federico García 132
Lorde, Audre 11
   For Each of You 20
   Movement Song 20
   Zami 11
Love, Heather 17
Lucifer's Fall/rebellion 8, 29–30, 41, 44, 68–70, 118, 148–9, 180
Lunatique (*Uranus in Cancer*, Nugent) 79–91, 93, 97, 187 n.11

machines and industry, distrust of
  (Thoreau) 108
Mains, Geoffrey, *Urban Aboriginals* 192 n.8
masculinity 3, 8–9, 20, 31, 53, 59, 75, 77, 80, 82, 86–7, 109, 128, 143, 190 n.17
McClure, John, *Partial Faiths* 5
McCourt, James 146, 150
  Time Remaining 144, 149
McCune, Jeffrey 86
McKay, Claude 74–5, 99
  Home to Harlem 66, 187 n.8
Melehy, Hassan 189 n.6
Merrill, Thomas 107
Miller, Michael 186 n.3
Miller, Monica 93
Milton, John 8, 11, 17, 21, 52, 112, 119, 122, 174–5, 180, 184 n.3, 186 n.2
  critiques of race and sex, Cullen's 68–73
  literary tradition 28, 80
  Paradise Lost 10, 15, 37, 69, 113, 115, 191 n.4
Mizer, Bob 127
Monteiro, George 133
Moon, Jennifer 48
Moore, Marlon Rachquel 4–6
Moore, Patrick 192 n.8
morality and immorality 6–7, 15, 21–3, 30–1, 40, 43, 74, 94, 105–6, 112, 121, 129–30, 161, 174, 179, 183
Morgan, Bill 107, 188 n.2, 190 n.21
mortal danger, theme (Woods) 144
Mount, Douglas 12
Mumford, Kevin 5–6, 17, 67, 82. *See also* interzones
Muñoz, José Esteban 19

Naked Lunch (Burroughs) 109
  Burglar, valorous fall 111–12
  Johnny 110
  Mark 110–11
Niles, Blair, *Strange Brother* 17
nonconformist genders. *See* same-sex sex/desire
Nugent, Richard Bruce 8, 16, 28, 63, 65–6, 103, 105–6, 108–9, 111, 113, 119, 142, 165, 179, 186 n.1, 187 n.11
  angelic dreams 78–90
  bourgeois aesthetics 79
  Gay Rebel of the Harlem Renaissance 79, 187 n.11
  Geisha Man 99
  Gentleman Jigger 79
  Porgy 78
  queer prismatic modernism 90–7
  queer world-vision 100
  Smoke, Lilies and Jade 81, 99–100, 102
  spiritualized angelic rhetoric 22–3, 66–7
  Uranus in Cancer (*see* Uranus in Cancer (Nugent))

Orlovsky, Peter 124

Pearl, Monica 148
Pérez, Hiram 16–17, 165
Pérez-Torres, Rafael 31
Perry, Edward 73
Petro, Anthony 157, 191 n.1
Picano, Felice 99
Pickett, James Carroll, *Queen of Angels* 3, 144
pink angel/Mike relationship (*The Little Virgin*, Hughes) 75–8
Pitt, Hannah (fictional character, *Angels in America*) 20–1
Pitt, Joe (fictional character, *Angels in America*) 11
poetic perceptions (*Uranus in Cancer*, Nugent) 85–6
Ponty, Deni, *Intimate Angel* 191 n.2
von Praunheim, Rosa, *Silence=Death* 142
pre-exposure prophylaxis (PrEP) 193 n.11

"queer," defining 100, 186 n.1, 188 n.14, 188 n.20
queer communities 5, 11–12, 24, 159, 169, 188 n.15
  critiques of 28–9
  HIV/AIDS 147, 149, 157
  queer outcasts from 171–4
queer critique 6, 78
queer historiography 6
queer hypersociability 5
queer men 4, 17, 20, 82, 86, 111, 128
  angelic characterizations 7
  depictions 13, 19
  as "fallen" angels 7
  HIV/AIDS 181 (*see also* HIV/AIDS, trauma)

queer movements 16
  and mechanics 120–31
queerness, gender 5, 7, 33, 77, 82, 85, 110, 137
  angelic humanism 72
  as collectivity 19
  "death drive" 19
  with defensive violence 189 n.7
  denigrations of 41, 92, 97, 193 n.10
  and political radicalism 9
  race and 19
queer oppression 1, 50, 105, 135, 162, 169
queer optimism 18, 24, 61, 156
queer outlaws 129
  American citizenships and 14
  angelic (*see* angelic outlaws)
  as attractive rebels 4
queer shame/abjection 17–18, 146, 150, 185 n.15
queer theory 6
queer time and space 14–15, 146

race and sexuality 66, 68–73, 79, 88, 148
Rampersad, Arnold 73
Ransom, Llewellyn 68
reactionary angels 137–41
"realness" 54, 98
rebels, "angels" as 41, 58, 70, 105, 121, 139, 165, 179
Rechy, John 8, 16, 23, 63, 66, 105–6, 108, 110–11, 113, 119, 135, 142, 151, 165
  beatas 30
  City of Night (*see City of Night* (Rechy))
  The Coming of the Night 192 n.10
  critiques of queer communities 28–9, 138
  Hispanic Catholic tradition 22, 30, 34, 65, 113, 186 n.3
  hustling and cruising protagonists 186 n.9
  Outlaw Sensibility 28–33
  Rushes 192 n.8, 192 n.10
  The Sexual Outlaw 192 n.8, 192 n.10
Red Scare 9–10, 107, 121
Reid-Pharr, Robert 16, 101
Reimonenq, Alden 66, 68
religious suffering 192 n.9
Rich, Adrienne
  Gabriel 20
  Lucifer in the Train 20
  This Beast; This Angel 20

Rio, Johnny, *Numbers* 185 n.14
Rodgers, Bruce, *The Queens' Vernacular* 7
Rubin, Gayle 21, 159
Russell, Bill, *Elegies for Angels, Punks, and Screaming Queens* 3, 144
Ruszczycky, Steven 29, 192 n.8

"*sacra/mentality*" 5
sadomasochism (S&M) 110, 159–61, 164–71, 182, 192 n.8, 192 n.10
Saint, Assotto
  Stations 102, 143, 191 n.2
  Wishing for Wings 102, 143
Salwa, Sœur 153, 181
same-sex sex/desire 2, 11, 15, 20, 28, 65–6, 72, 100, 186 n.1
  as anti-American 10
  couple's cruelty 168
  criminalization 113
  depiction of 82, 84, 97, 109–10, 113, 121
  hustling 48, 53
  laws affected 185 n.12
  mistreatment 10, 168
  multi-edged 50
  multiracial 67, 100
  spiritual evolution 125
  violence and 83, 89, 189 n.10
Satterfield, Ben 33
Savran, David 185 n.14
Schumacher, Michael 121
Schwarz, A. B. Christa 66–7, 73, 75, 99
Scott, Darieck 17, 19, 101, 188 n.20
Sedgwick, Eve Kosofsky 17
self-shattering (Bersani) 19
Selvon, Sam 91
Shilts, Randy, *And the Band Played On* 147–8
Simon, Frank, *The Queen* 14
sin and salvation 72–3
Sinfield, Alan 54
Sing a Dream (*Uranus in Cancer*, Nugent) 97–102
Snediker, Michael 18
sociability 5–6, 89, 93, 128
Somerville, Siobhan 79
Sontag, Susan 145
spirituality/spiritualization 4, 24, 115, 125, 180
  aesthetic uses of 5
  common 192 n.8

Jacob (*Angel of History*, Alameddine) 181
   physicality and 14, 118
   and safety 146
   same-sex eroticism 6
   secularity and 65, 145
   of sex amid sickness 145
"spiritual transcendence" 192 n.8
St. Clair, Cody 78
Steward, Samuel 192 n.8
Suárez, Juan 190 n.17
Swedenborgian sentimentalism (DeGuzmán) 38

Tatum, Charles 49
Thurman, Wallace 78
   Infants of the Spring 17, 84, 92–3
Tinney, James 5
Tolson, Clyde 10
Tom of Finland 127
Trigilio, Tony 138, 190 n.19
troubled angels 73–8
Tyler, Parker 6
Tytell, John 126
   Naked Angels: Kerouac, Ginsberg, Burroughs 107–8

Uranus in Cancer (Nugent) 14–15, 79, 87, 179, 187 n.11, 190 n.17, 192–3 n.10
   effeminacy/same-sex desires 82
   Exposition 79–80, 90
   heterosexuality as quasi-demeaning model 87
   Letters into Limbo 90–6
   Lunatique 79–90, 93, 97
   Sing a Dream 97–102

Veracity, equity/equality 69–70
Vogel, Shane 73

Watney, Simon 191 n.1, 191 n.7
Whitman, Walt 119–20, 132–4, 136–7
   egalitarian gusto 108
   Panis Angelicus 191 n.24
   Song of Myself 119
Williams, Tennessee, *Rio Joy* 185 n.14
Wirth, Thomas 79–80, 99, 187 n.11. *See also* Nugent, Richard Bruce, *Gay Rebel of the Harlem Renaissance*
Woods, Gregory 66, 144

Zamora, Carlos 32, 44, 49

www.ingramcontent.com/pod-product-compliance
Lightning Source LLC
Chambersburg PA
CBHW062226300426
44115CB00012BA/2238